D1551364

The World of Women
in the Ancient and Classical Near East

The World of Women
in the Ancient and Classical Near East

Edited by

Beth Alpert Nakhai

Cambridge Scholars Publishing

The World of Women in the Ancient and Classical Near East, Edited by Beth Alpert Nakhai

This book first published 2008

Cambridge Scholars Publishing

12 Back Chapman Street, Newcastle upon Tyne, NE6 2XX, UK

British Library Cataloguing in Publication Data
A catalogue record for this book is available from the British Library

ISBN (10): 1-4438-0030-9, ISBN (13): 978-1-4438-0030-3

TABLE OF CONTENTS

List of Abbreviations vii

Introduction ix
Beth Alpert Nakhai

Map xix

Chapter One 1
*Dark Men, Light Women: Origins of Color as Gender Indicator
in Ancient Egypt*
Mary Ann Eaverly

Chapter Two 13
*A Taste of Women's Sociality: Cooking as Cooperative Labor
in Iron Age Syro-Palestine*
Aubrey Baadsgaard

Chapter Three 45
*Baking and Brewing Beer in the Israelite Household: A Study
of Women's Cooking Technology*
Jennie R. Ebeling and Michael M. Homan

Chapter Four 63
*Bringing Home the Artifacts: A Social Interpretation of Loom Weights
in Context*
Deborah Cassuto

Chapter Five 79
Infant Mortality and Women's Religion in the Biblical Periods
Elizabeth Ann R. Willett

Chapter Six 99
*Mut'a Marriage in the Roman Near East: The Evidence from Palmyra,
Syria*
Cynthia Finlayson

Chapter Seven.. 139
A Restless Silence: Women in the Byzantine Archaeological Record
Marica Cassis

Chapter Eight.. 155
Fe(male) Potters as the Personification of Individuals, Places,
and Things as Known from Ethnoarchaeological Studies
Gloria London

Chapter Nine... 181
"Working Egyptians of the World Unite!": How Edith Nesbit Used Near
Eastern Archaeology and Children's Literature to Argue for Social
Change
Kevin McGeough and Elizabeth Galway

Contributors... 203

Index.. 207

LIST OF ABBREVIATIONS

AAR	American Academy of Religion
AASOR	Annual of the American Schools of Oriental Research
ABD	*Anchor Bible Dictionary.* D. N. Freedman, ed. 6 vols. New York: Doubleday, 1992.
ADAJ	*Annual of the Department of Antiquities of Jordan*
AEL	*Ancient Egyptian Literature: A Book of Readings.* M. Lichtheim. 3 vols. Berkeley: University of California Press, 1971-1980.
ANET	*The Ancient Near East: Supplementary Texts and Pictures Relating to the Old Testament.* J. B. Pritchard, ed. Princeton: Princeton University Press, 1969.
ArSt	Arabian Studies
ASOR	*American Schools of Oriental Research*
AuOr	*Aula orientalis*
BA	*Biblical Archaeologist*
BAR	*Biblical Archaeology Review*
BASOR	*Bulletin of the American Schools of Oriental Research*
CAD	*The Assyrian Dictionary of the Oriental Institute of the University of Chicago.* A. L. Oppenheim, E. Reiner, and R. D. Biggs, eds. Chicago: Oriental Institute, 1956-.
CBQ	*Catholic Biblical Quarterly*
CIS	*Corpus inscriptionum semiticarum,* Paris: French Academy of Sciences, 1926-1975.
CSHB	*Corpus scriptorum historiae byzantinae.* M. Pindar and T. Buttner-Wobst, eds. Bonn: n.p., 1841-1897.
DOP	*Dumbarton Oaks Papers*
ErIsr	*Eretz-Israel*
HSM	Harvard Semitic Monographs
HSS	Harvard Semitic Studies
IEJ	*Israel Exploration Journal*
JA	*Journal asiatique*
JAOS	*Journal of the American Oriental Society*
JARCE	*Journal of the American Research Center in Egypt*
JBL	*Journal of Biblical Literature*
JEA	*Journal of Egyptian Archaeology*

JNES	*Journal of Near Eastern Studies*
JRS	*Journal of Roman Studies*
JRAS	*Journal of the Royal Asiatic Society*
JSOTSup	Journal for the Study of the Old Testament: Supplement Series
JSS	*Journal of Semitic Studies*
KTU	*Die keilalphabetischen Texte aus Ugarit*, M. Deitrich, O. Loretz, and J. Sanmartin, eds. AOAT 24/1. Neukirchen-Vluyn, 1976, 2nd enlarged ed. of *KTU: The Cuneiform Alphabetic Texts from Ugarit, Ras Ibn Hani, and Other Places.* M. Deitrich, O. Loretz, and J. Sanmartín, eds. Münster, 1995.
LASBF	*Liber annuus Studii biblici franciscani*
MAMA	*Monumenta Asiae Minoris Antiqua*
NEA	*Near Eastern Archaeology*
NEAEHL	*The New Encyclopedia of Archaeological Excavations in the Holy Land.* E. Stern, ed. Vols 1-4. Jerusalem: Israel Exploration Society and Carta, 1993. *The New Encyclopedia of Archaeological Excavations in the Holy Land.* E. Stern, ed. Vol. 5. Jerusalem: Israel Exploration Society and Carta, 2008.
OEAE	*The Oxford Encyclopedia of Ancient* Egypt. D. B. Redford, ed., 3 vols. Oxford: Oxford University Press, 2001.
OEANE	*The Oxford Encyclopedia of Archaeology in the Near East.* E. M. Meyers, ed. New York: Oxford University Press, 1997.
PEQ	*Palestine Exploration Quarterly*
RA	*Revue d'assyriologique et d'archéologie orientale*
RB	*Revue biblique*
RDAC	*Report of the Department of Antiquities, Cyprus*
SBL	Society for Biblical Literature
TA	*Tel Aviv*
VT	*Vetus Testamentum*
YOS	Yale Oriental Series, Texts
ZDMG	*Zeitschrift der deutschen morgenländischen Gesellschaft*

INTRODUCTION

THE WORLD OF WOMEN IN THE ANCIENT AND CLASSICAL NEAR EAST

BETH ALPERT NAKHAI

Perhaps a decade ago, curious about the extent to which papers on women in the ancient Near East had been presented at the annual meeting of the American Schools of Oriental Research, I looked into program books dating from the early 1970's to the late 1990's. What I discovered astounded me: many more papers had been devoted to pigs than to women.[1] Furthermore, finding papers that discussed real women rather than goddesses was virtually impossible. To remedy that egregious lapse, I introduced a program unit entitled *World of Women: Gender and Archaeology* into ASOR's annual meeting. The first session took place in 2000 and after a few years, women finally outnumbered pigs as a topic worthy of professional consideration.

Some informally gathered information provides a backdrop for the articles in this volume and substantiates the vital importance of the *World of Women: Gender and Archaeology* to ASOR, and of this volume to the field of Near Eastern archaeology. Between the early 1970's and the late 1990's, almost every paper in which one could use the pronoun "she" was about a goddess (most often Asherah). A few papers, primarily from the last years of the twentieth century, looked at women and religion (mostly figurines but also domestic cult), women in South Arabia and Roman Palestine, sexuality and gender roles, royalty and wet nursing, hunting and ethnography. Still, there was hardly a year in which more than one of these topics was presented and unfortunately, the papers presented in the *World of Women: Gender and Archaeology* notwithstanding, the situation has hardly changed since its 2000 inauguration.

---

[1] The focus on pigs relates to their potential as an ethnic marker for Israelites, Philistines and other Iron Age ethnic groups.

It might seem surprising to find so little attention paid to reconstructing women's lives in the ancient and classical Near East, but there are several reasons for this. For one, archaeology in this region has been dominated by biblically based research and both the Hebrew Bible and the New Testament are incontrovertibly androcentric documents. Furthermore, in response to the rich textual record for all historic periods across ancient western Asia, questions of history (conceptualized as kings and battles), religion (conceptualized as priesthoods and temples) and the lives of the elite (conceptualized as kings, palaces and luxury goods) have provided the foci for archaeological research. What this means is that domestic quarters, daily tasks, private life, personal religion and the like have found little traction among Near Eastern archaeologists. Indeed, even when these topics have been explored, women have rarely populated either the ancient places or the modern discussions.[2] Similarly, the subsistence economy, in which women played such an integral role, has been considered the near exclusive purview of ancient men. A further complicating factor is the paucity of academic positions in Near Eastern archaeology. Many archaeologists secure employment by affirming their willingness to teach courses in biblical studies. The introduction of a gender component to teaching or research is not required and indeed, many fear that any move away from the academic mainstream might lead to professional marginalization.

To contextualize this, consider the following. Women's studies courses and programs were introduced in colleges and universities throughout the United States and internationally beginning in the late 1960's and early 1970's. M. Conkey and J. Spector published their groundbreaking article, "Archaeology and the Study of Gender," in 1984.[3] Beginning with the early 1970's, between 5 and 11 percent of the program units at the annual meetings of the American Academy of Religion/Society of Biblical

[2] For a discussion about why this is so, see B. A. Nakhai, "Daily Life in the Ancient Near East: New Thoughts on an Old Topic," *Religious Studies Review: A Quarterly Review of Publications in the Field of Religion and Related Disciplines* 31/3-4 (2005) 147-53.
[3] M. W. Conkey and J. D. Spector, "Archaeology and the Study of Gender," in *Advances in Archaeological Method and Theory*, vol. 7 (ed. M. Schiffer; New York: Academic Press, 1984), 1-38. For further discussion, see B. A. Nakhai, "Gender and Archaeology in Israelite Religion," *Compass Religion* 1/5 (2007): 512-28 and references therein. See also M. C. Root, "Introduction: Women of the Field, Defining the Gendered Experience," pp. 1-33 in *Breaking Ground: Pioneering Women Archaeologists* (eds. G. M. Cohen and M. S. Joukowsky; Ann Arbor, Mich.: University of Michigan, 2006), 2-4, on the discomfort professional women may feel about investigating topics pertaining to women.

Literature (each with 4-5 papers) have been devoted to some aspect of the study of women. Given the interests of the AAR/SBL, their focus was on religion to the exclusion of other areas of life but this does not obviate the fact that both these societies have been much more aware of the "gender revolution" of the past four decades than has ASOR. This fact is even more compelling when one realizes that many members of ASOR are also members of SBL. Therefore, they receive the AAR/SBL annual meeting program and can read about program units devoted to the study of women and religion. In addition, the ASOR and AAR/SBL annual meetings were coterminous until 1997, and since then have met back-to-back or even overlapped.[4] Many ASOR members also attend SBL sessions.

Accentuating the positive, the work by the authors represented in this volume, and many of the articles and books to which they refer, indicate a growing attention to the field. Some scholars devote themselves primarily to gender-based research while others look at gender less systematically, but either way they contribute to our knowledge of the lives of women in antiquity. Archaeology, text studies and ethnographic comparanda are all tools employed in this endeavor, and the articles in this volume utilize a skillful blending of these and other resources. They are culled from the twenty-nine papers presented in the *World of Women: Gender and Archaeology* between 2000 and 2007.[5] They represent a broad geographic and chronological range, investigating Egypt and western Asia from the Predynastic to the Byzantine periods, and England in the Victorian era.

The Papers

In *Dark Men, Light Women: Origins of Color as Gender Indicator in Ancient Egypt* (Ch. 1), Mary Ann Eaverly discusses the use of color as a gender indicator in Pre- and Early Dynastic Egypt, where men were depicted as dark or reddish brown and women as white or yellow. Earlier scholars understood this to be a "realistic" reflection of men's outdoor and women's indoor lives. Eaverly's paper positions the color convention as a key component within an ideology promulgated as Egypt adopted a dynastic political structure; this ideology promoted the importance of the

---

[4] J. D. Seger, "Part Two: The New ASOR 1975-2000," pp. 34-77 in *An ASOR Mosaic: A Centennial History of the American Schools of Oriental Research, 1900-2000* (ed. J. D. Seger; Boston: ASOR, 2001), 68.
[5] By the time the invitation to publish this volume was made by Cambridge Scholars Publishing, a number of *World of Women: Gender and Archaeology* presentations had already been published. Most of these publications are listed at the end of this introduction.

pharaoh, and thus of male power. While Pre-Dynastic tombs show equality of offerings, Dynastic period tombs reveal imbalance. Even as the color convention similarly indicates imbalance, there is also complementarity. Yellow and red are colors understood to complete each other, as gender roles were part of a series of dualisms that permeated Egyptian thought. This insight impacts our understanding of gender roles not only in Egypt but also in the other Mediterranean civilizations that adopted Egyptian color conventions (Crete, Greece and Rome), and those (such as Mesopotamia) that did not.

A Taste of Women's Sociality: Cooking as Cooperative Labor in Iron Age Syro-Palestine (Ch. 2) is Aubrey Baadsgaard's study of social constructions of gender, focusing on domestic activities in the Iron Age. Moving beyond idealized notions of domestic practice based upon the assumption of a patriarchal social structure, Baadsgaard examines the material remains of cooking as made evident by ovens, together with associated features and utensils. She shows that cooking was a domestic activity organized according to women's personal preferences; it was carried out along with other domestic tasks in ways that allowed women to develop and sustain informal social networks among multiple households. The variation in the material record undercuts traditional views of cooking and other domestic activities as static, repetitive tasks restricted to fixed spaces. Instead, it indicates that cooking was a social activity occurring on a larger domestic stage, on which factors relating to family life, gender roles, and women's responsibility for the well-being of family members came together, and social relationships among households were negotiated and formed.

According to Jennie R. Ebeling and Michael M. Homan, women in antiquity played a large, though often overlooked, role in the production and consumption of alcoholic beverages fermented from malted cereals. Baking and Brewing in the Israelite Household: A Study of Women's Cooking Technology (Ch. 3) first highlights written and artistic records that reference women and beer in the ancient Near East and Egypt, in order to demonstrate the fundamental association between them. It then turns to Syro-Palestine, as it inspects the written and material record by exploring evidence for beer production and consumption. Ebeling and Homan examine evidence such as ceramic vessels, ground stone tools and fermentation stoppers, which are commonly overlooked by excavators or misidentified during excavation. Next, they investigate gender and domestic space, in order to reconstruct women's daily lives as they relate to beer production and consumption. Finally, they consider the cultic dimensions of women and beer, and conclude by reflecting upon the socioeconomic impact of women's involvement with beer production at the household level.

In *Bringing Home the Artifacts: A Social Interpretation of Loom Weights in Context* (Ch. 4), Deborah Cassuto examines the traditional association between women and the crafts of spinning and weaving, which is known from contemporary traditional communities (as attested by cross-cultural studies) and ancient Near Eastern societies (as attested by historical texts and by iconographical references that use the spindle whorl and weaving loom to depict feminine attributes). Loom weights, which are remnants of vertical warp-weighted looms, have been found in numerous excavations of Iron Age II sites throughout the Land of Israel. By focusing on the contexts in which these loom weights are found and on the artifacts associated with them, Cassuto engenders the Iron Age house. She investigates the association between weaving and food preparation activities, both of which were carried out in the same activity areas. After reconstructing patterns of behavior, Cassuto interprets them in light of ethnographic data and archaeological parallels, and highlights the role of the Iron II woman at the center of all household activities.

Elizabeth A. R. Willett's study of *Infant Mortality and Women's Religion in the Biblical Periods* (Ch. 5) shows that the well-justified fear of infant mortality resulted in mythologies of child-stealing goddesses and in family religious practices designed to combat them. Willett demonstrates that the household was the locus of women's religious activities. Aramaic incantations from Nippur designed to protect children from child-stealing demons affirm women's leadership in protective household rituals, since women frequently procured the incantations, which required the name of the mother of the household but not that of her husband. Passages in the Hebrew Bible show women performing religio-magical activities in their homes and mention family support for some of these rituals. In some Israelite houses, ritual lamps, incense altars, female figurines and amulets used to deflect evil forces are found alongside the remains of food preparation and textile production; significantly, no specifically male accoutrements accompany these votive objects. Domestic shrines from elsewhere in the ancient Near East, at which residents offered food and incense to personal deities, provide parallels that help interpret the cultic finds from Israelite houses.

In *Kinship and Marriage in Early Arabia* (1903), William Robertson Smith introduced the discussion of *mut'a* or temporary contract marriage in Arab tribal contexts. Cynthia Finlayson's *Mut'a Marriage in the Roman Near East: The Evidence from Palmyra, Syria* (Ch. 6) explores *mut'a* marriage through a study of Palmyrene funerary portraits, which comprise

the largest collection of community portraits and genealogies known from
the late Roman Near East. She presents the findings of a five season, on-
site study of women's portraits, emphasizing the evidence for *mut'a*
marriage and its manifestations among the Arab/Aramaean tribes of late
Roman Palmyra. She demonstrates that there were multiple forms of *mut'a*
marriage, including a matriarchal form that allowed upper class women to
initiate unions with designated males; the offspring of those unions built
up the clans of the women rather than those of her male partners, affording
women influence and the ability to be the progenitors of their own
subclans and tribes. This evidence provides a link in the evolution of
mut'a marriage and highlights its importance in understanding the socio-
political roles of women in the ancient Near East.

There are comparatively few studies of women in the Byzantine Near
East. In *A Restless Silence: Women in the Byzantine Archaeological
Record* (Ch. 7), Marica Cassis demonstrates that the archaeological record
is increasingly important as a source for evidence about the lives of
women in this period, and as a tool for assessing their social status.
Archaeological data are especially important since there are few texts from
antiquity either written by women, or written by men about women. The
predominance of men among Byzantine authors, and the andocentric
nature of modern scholarship, have created a falsely masculine perspective.
Cassis utilizes the advances made possible by gendered archaeology to
illuminate the many active roles women played in the Byzantine world. In
both Christian and Jewish communities, women were variously
participants, religious donors, residents of monastic communities and even
holy figures. Archaeological evidence, particularly from the site of Çadır
Höyük in Turkey, illustrates the roles women may have fulfilled within a
previously uninvestigated venue, secular rural residential communities.

In *Fe(male) Potters as the Personification of Individuals, Places, and
Things as Known from Ethnoarchaeological Studies* (Ch. 8), Gloria
London uses pottery, the most common artifact found on archaeological
excavations, to investigate the roles of women in the ancient economy.
Pottery production is a high-risk low-return seasonal industry, which can
best be understood through the reconstruction of its manufacturing
techniques. London's ethnoarchaeological work with contemporary female
pot-making communities in Cyprus and the Philippines highlights
elements of this industry. She shows the ways in which teaching is an
essential element; how female potters may seasonally involve their entire
families in the work of pottery production; and, how women mark their
pots to highlight self-expression in an industry ruled by convention. Her
ethnoarchaeological research explains the paucity of pot-making locations

on excavation sites by revealing that much pot-making is home-based, taking place in multi-purpose domestic spaces, and seasonal, so that areas used for pot-making at one time of year, at other times bear no evidence of the industry.

Edith Nesbit was a British author and activist who used Near Eastern scholarship to comment on social conditions in Edwardian England. In *"Working Egyptians of the World Unite!": How Edith Nesbit Used Near Eastern Archaeology and Children's Literature to Argue for Social Change* (Ch. 9), Kevin McGeough and Elizabeth Galway contend that Nesbit sought to inspire social change and cultivate national sensibilities in her 1906 *The Story of the Amulet*. This book, which provided British children with an entertaining fantasy story and an educational account of ancient civilizations, is dedicated to E. A. Wallis Budge of the British Museum, whose influence is evident in the book's use of Edwardian scholarship about the Near East. McGeough and Galway examine the ways in which the study of the Near East provided a framework for understanding contested issues in Edwardian society, including concepts of progress and decline, problems of empire, conceptions of race, and the evaluation of gender roles. Nesbit's understanding of Near Eastern history, though more sophisticated than that of many popular writers, reflects many assumptions about the Near East, some of which remain unquestioned in current scholarship and public outreach.

Final Notes

The articles in *The World of Women in the Ancient and Classical Near East* make an important contribution toward combating modern scholarship's marginalization of women in antiquity. They prove beyond all doubt that women's roles in the home and in the workplace were essential for the survival of the family and the community. This is true even when (or, perhaps, especially when) the workplace was the home. Locating women within the domestic sphere no longer diminishes appreciation of their extensive responsibilities and accomplishments. To the contrary, their domestic contributions are proven to be essential components of human survival; it is only in recent times that this fact has been questioned.[6] In addition, women's contributions are evident elsewhere throughout society, in royal, religious, and funerary contexts,

---

[6] See Nakhai, "Gender and Archaeology in Israelite Religion," for a discussion of the impact biases in modern scholarship have on the reconstruction of women's roles in antiquity.

highlighting the fact that the traditional scholarly reliance upon dichotomization and compartmentalization must be resisted, and new paradigms developed and adopted. This book takes important steps in that direction.

The World of Women in the Ancient and Classical Near East would not be possible without the support of a number of people, and I would like to acknowledge and thank them. In the American Schools of Oriental Research, they include Rudolph Dornemann, who as Executive Director gave me access to 30 years of ASOR/SBL Annual Meeting programs; Douglas Clark, who as head of ASOR's Program Committee encouraged me to introduce the World of Women: Gender and Archaeology into the Annual Meeting; Carol Meyers and Susan Ackerman, whose keynote addresses in the first year of the session set the highest of standards; and, the many presenters who have contributed to its on-going success. Thanks, too, to my editors at Cambridge Scholars Publishing, Dr. Andy Nercessian, Carol Koulikourdi, and especially Amanda Millar, without whose diligence this book would never have been published. I am grateful to Cynthia Finlayson for the cover image, and to Nuala Coyle of Cambridge Scholars Publishing for the eye-catching cover design. My thanks to Gary Christopherson, Director of the Center for Applied Spatial Analysis at The University of Arizona, who generously produced our map. Thanks, too, to Jeanne Davenport and to financial support from the Arizona Center for Judaic Studies at The University of Arizona for the index. I am grateful for the friendship and support of Jeanne Davenport and Martha Castleberry at the Arizona Center for Judaic Studies. Two dear friends, Jennie Ebeling at the University of Evansville, and J. Edward Wright, Chair of the Arizona Center for Judaic Studies, provide me with invaluable collegial support. My husband Farzad and our daughter Mandana Lily bring great joy to my life. The memory of my grandmother, Rea Cohen Racoosin, is always with me. I dedicate this book to my mother, Esther Racoosin Alpert, and to my late father, Seymour Alpert, M.D., with much love.

Papers Presented in ASOR's *World of Women: Gender and Archaeology* and Published in Other Venues

Susan Ackerman, "Digging up Deborah: Recent Hebrew Bible Scholarship on Gender and the Contribution of Archaeology," *NEA* 66/4 (2003): 172-84.

Celia J. Bergoffen, "Plank Figures as Cradleboards," in *Proceedings of the Conference Finds and Results from the Swedish Cyprus Expedition: A Gender Perspective," March 31–April 2, 2006.* Medelhavsmuseet: Focus on the Mediterranean 5 (2009).

Joan Branham, "Women as Objects of Sacrifice? An Early Christian 'Chancel of the Virgins'," in *La cuisine et l'autel: Les sacrifices en questions dans les sociétés de la Méditerranée ancienne* (eds. S. Georgoudi, R. Koch Piettre and F. Schmidt; Turnhout: Brepols, 2006), 371-86.

Norma Dever, "They Also Dug! Archaeologists' Wives and Their Stories," *NEA* 67/3 (2004): 162-73.

Nili Fox, "Gender Transformation and Transgression: Contextualizing the Prohibition of Cross-Dressing in Deut 22:5," pp. 49-71 in *Mishneh Todah: Studies in Deuteronomy and Its Cultural Environment in Honor of Jeffrey H. Tigay* (eds. N. Fox, D. Gilad-Glatt, and M. Williams; Winona Lake, Ind.: Eisenbrauns, 2009).

Jack D. M. Green, "Anklets and the Construction of Gender and Age in the Late Bronze and Early Iron Age Southern Levant," in *Archaeology and Women: Ancient & Modern Issues* (eds. S. Hamilton, R. D. Whitehouse, and K. I. Wright; Walnut Creek, Calif.: Left Coast Press, 2007), 283-311.

Gloria A. London, "Women Potters and Craft Specialization in a Pre-Market Cypriot Economy," in *Engendering Aphrodite: Women and Society in Ancient Cyprus* (ASOR Archaeological Reports Series 7, CAARI Monographs 3; eds. D. Bolger and N. Serwint; Boston: ASOR, 2002), 265-80.

Carol Meyers, "Engendering Syro-Palestinian Archaeology: Reasons and Resources," *NEA* 66/4 (2003) 185-97.[7]

Jane D. Peterson, "Gender and Early Farming Societies," in *Handbook of Gender in Archaeology* (ed. S. M. Nelson; Lanham, Md.: AltaMira Press, 2006), 537-70.

---

[7] While this paper was not delivered in the *World of Women: Gender and Archaeology*, its publication was an outcome of Meyers' 2000 keynote address.

Susan Pollock, "The Royal Cemetery of Ur: Ritual, Tradition, and the Creation of Subjects," in *Representations of Political Power: Case Histories from Times of Change and Dissolving Order in the Ancient Near East* (eds. M. Heinz and M. Feldman; Winona Lake, Ind.: Eisenbrauns, 2007), 89-110.

Joe D. Seger, "Queen or Crone? Gendered Archaeology in an LB Tomb at Gezer," in *The Archaeology of Difference: Gender, Ethnicity, Class and the "Other" in Antiquity, Studies in Honor of Eric M. Meyers*, AASOR 60/61 (eds. D. R. Edwards and C. T. McCollough; Boston: ASOR, 2007), 85-93.

Jurgen Zangenberg, "The 'Final Farewell.' A Necessary Paradigm Shift in the Interpretation of the Qumran Cemetery," *Qumran Chronicle* 8 (1999): 213-18.

Jurgen Zangenberg, "Bones of Contention. 'New' Bones from Qumran Help Settle Old Questions (and Raise New Ones). Remarks on Two Recent Conferences," *Qumran Chronicle* 9 (2000): 51-76.

MAP

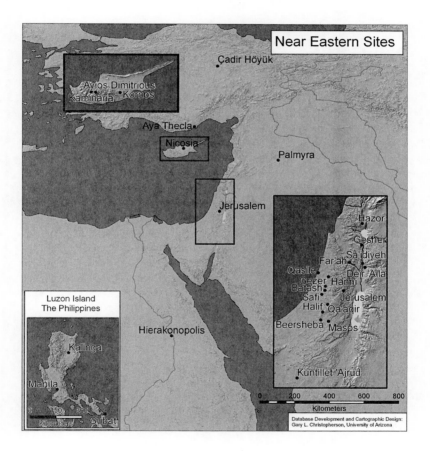

Near Eastern Sites

Çadir Höyük

Ayios Dimitrious
Kaminaria   Kornos

Aya Thecla

Nicosia

Palmyra

Jerusalem

Hazor

Gesher

Sa'idiyeh
Far'ah
Qasile   Deir 'Alla
Gezer Hanni
Batash
Safi   Jerusalem
Halif Qa'aqir

Beersheba Masos

Kuntillet 'Ajrud

Hierakonopolis

Luzon Island
The Philippines

Kalinga

Manila

Cubat

0   200   400   600   800
Kilometers

0   150   300
Kilometers

Database Development and Cartographic Design:
Gary L. Christopherson, University of Arizona

CHAPTER ONE

DARK MEN, LIGHT WOMEN: ORIGINS OF COLOR AS GENDER INDICATOR IN ANCIENT EGYPT

MARY ANN EAVERLY

Throughout the millennia of Dynastic rule, Egyptian art adheres to a series of formulae that regulate representation. For example, figures in relief sculpture are shown in profile view, while freestanding statues are posed frontally. Sculptors use canons to establish proportional relationships between the various parts of the human body. Scale is manipulated to emphasize importance: Pharaoh is always shown much larger than his enemies; tomb owners are larger than the servants they supervise. All of these features give Egyptian art its remarkable feeling of permanency. Scholars have long recognized that this "unchanging" quality of Egyptian art reflects and in turn helps to construct a worldview based on *maat*—the concept of a carefully balanced cosmos with pharaoh serving as guarantor. As Gryzmiski notes, pharaoh was "...the key element of the society, not because of the political power of his office but because of his centrality to Egyptian ideology and religion. Without a king there would be no society to speak of, no state, no order; there would only be chaos."[1] Tombs—the source of the best-preserved Egyptian art—were designed as microcosms of the established order. Funerary art provided the visual manifestation of this phenomenon, serving as a site which "...associated earthly life processes of birth, maturation, parenthood and

---

[1] K. Gryzmski, "Royal Statuary," pp. 51-56 in *Egyptian Art in the Age of the Pyramids* (eds. D. Arnold and C. Ziegler; New York: Metropolitan Museum of Art, 1999), 51.

death with cosmic cycles and enduring time,"[2] thus formalizing the relationships between individuals and classes of individuals within society. As Wilkinson notes, "The formation of the Egyptian state at the end of the fourth millennium BC crystallized social distinctions in a particularly marked way, placing the king at the apex of the pyramid."[3] This system was designed not only to exalt the pharaoh but also to promote the vision of an unchanging and right social order that his rule guaranteed.[4] Many indicators suggest that the change to pharaonic rule was supported by a deliberately controlled artistic program. Among these is the fact that artistic production is placed under the control of the state and artists are trained in the canonical style. Cult statues, temple decorations for the gods, and images to house the spirits of the deceased throughout the afterlife were used as vehicles to convey pharaoh's message.[5] Even access to the materials used (hard stone, wood, precious metals, etc.) was under the king's control.[6] While scholars have studied intensely the Roman use of art in the service of the state, other than for the Amarna period, scholars have generally not recognized "pharaonic agency" in the creation of Egyptian art. That Augustus, the first Roman emperor, could manipulate art to legitimize his rule is a scholarly given.[7] It seems no less likely that the earliest unifiers of Egypt would have done the same thing. Rice points to a "powerful, united and supremely well-focused elite" as the catalyst for such a deliberate iconographical program.[8] An important component of this artistic program was the articulation of the status and role of women within society.

Analyses by Robins have revealed artistic devices that prioritize male over female.[9] For example, in group statues men are shown standing on the right or dominant side, women on the left. Men are shown striding (implying the capacity for action), while women stand with their feet

---

[2] J. Lustig, "Kinship, Gender and Age in Middle Kingdom Tomb Scenes and Texts," pp. 43-66 in *Anthropology and Egyptology, A Developing Dialogue* (ed. J. Lustig; Sheffield: Sheffield Academic Press, 1997), 63.
[3] M. Rice, *Egypt's Making: The Origins of Ancient Egypt 5000-2000 B. C.* (London: Routledge, 2003), 72.
[4] K. Michalowski, *Art of Ancient Egypt* (New York: Harry N. Abrams, n.d.) 191.
[5] A. Kozloff, "Sculpture: an Overview," pp. 218-28 in *OEAE* 3, 218.
[6] Ibid.
[7] See, for example, P. Zanker, *The Power of Images in the Age of Augustus* (Ann Arbor, Mich.: University of Michigan Press, 1988).
[8] Rice, *Egypt's Making*, 72.
[9] G. Robins, "Some Principles of Compositional Dominance and Gender Hierarchy in Egyptian Art," *JARCE* 31 (1994): 33-40.

together. These compositional devices reflect the dominant role of men in Egyptian society. While women in Egypt had greater legal rights than women of the ancient Classical world (they could, for example, own property) the bureaucracy of government was entirely male and the role of pharaoh was gendered male, even in the rare cases when a woman occupied the throne.

Egyptian sculpture and painting also distinguish male from female through color—men are painted dark brown /red and women white/yellow (Fig. 1-1). Traditionally, scholars have attributed this feature to a difference in lifestyle, i.e., a natural difference of skin tone between men, whose lives are conducted outside, and women, who remain secluded within the house. Yet, because of the many formulae regulating Egyptian art, the question of an artistic choice based on "natural" considerations remains problematic. It is more instructive to ask how such a distinction functions in the ideology promulgated by the Egyptian world-view of *maat* and the consequent role of pharaoh as guarantor of equilibrium. This essay explores the role that the adoption of the use of male/female color differentiation may have played in the establishment and promotion of pharaonic ideology.

While it is not possible to trace all the steps in the development of the Egyptian political system—since during the formative years of Dynastic Egypt, i.e., the Late Pre-Dynastic and Early Dynastic periods (3200 B.C.E-2600 B.C.E.) material evidence is fragmentary—some conclusions can be drawn. After a period in which rival kingdoms vied for supremacy, Egypt was eventually unified under one ruler. As Rice notes "... three outstanding achievements must be set to Egypt's account at this time which represent an extraordinary level of creative accomplishment: these are the institution of divine kingship, the concept of the unified political state and the construction of monumental funerary architecture."[10] The major evidence for social structure and artistic production for this period comes from graves at the most important sites (Hierakonpolis, Naqada, el-Amra, Mahasna, Abydos, Mattmar, Gerza, and Minshat Abu Omar).[11]

---

[10] Rice, *Egypt's Making*, 72.
[11] T. A. H. Wilkinson, *Early Dynastic Egypt* (New York: Routledge, 1999), 29.

**Fig. 1-1. Pair Statue of Ptahkhenuwy and his wife.
Egyptian Old Kingdom, Dynasty Five[12]**

Pottery is the most plentiful source for iconography during this period, although it is limited both in color palette (red paint on buff clay) and range of motifs. The images depicted include schematically rendered outline figures of boats, human figures, and, occasionally, landscape. Men and women are distinguished not by color but by shape. Women are usually shown as broad-hipped figures, nude from the waist up and wearing a long skirt. They often hover above the boats with upraised arms.

---

[12] Photograph © 2008, Museum of Fine Arts, Boston. Pair statue of Ptahkhenuwy and his wife, Egyptian, Old Kingdom, Dynasty Five, about 2460-2323 B.C.E. Findspot: Egypt, Giza tomb G 2004. Painted limestone. Height: 70.14 cm. (27 5/8 in.). Museum of Fine Arts, Boston. Harvard University-Boston Museum of Fine Arts Expedition, 06.1876.

Men are usually shown with triangular chests, narrow waists, and erect phalluses.[13]

Analogous figure types are found in the clay figurine repertoire. These early clay figurines are very simply shaped—arms, legs, torsos, and neck are all formed from long rolls of clay. Their pinched, un-detailed faces resemble a bird's beak. The waist is very narrow. The figurines are not differentiated by skin color—all figures are the red color of the fired clay—but by the indication of the genitals for men (the males wear penis sheaths) and breasts and broader hips for women. The women either wear a skirt with no top or are nude with the separation between the legs indicated only by an indentation.[14]

The only context provided for these figurines is their funerary provenance and the iconography of the vases—the range of activities which male and female figures are shown performing in the scenes on the vases. These scenes are ambiguous and subject to a variety of interpretations. Female figures are always shown as larger than males and are usually shown with raised arms. Proposed identifications include dancers, mourners, fertility figures, or goddesses.[15] The raised arms could certainly support the mourner or dancer identification. Nudity could argue for fertility figures, although recent scholarship suggests that we are often too quick to identify any prehistoric female figure as related to fertility.[16] The larger size of the female figures is significant, especially given the fact that, in the later canon of Egyptian art, scale is manipulated to suggest importance. The larger the figure, the more important he or she is in a scene. In searching for a high-status female with which to equate these

---

[13] For examples, see A. Capel, "Goddesses: catalogue entry 53a and b," pp. 121-22 in *Mistress of the House, Mistress of Heaven: Women in Ancient Egypt* (eds. A. Capel and G. Mark; New York: Hudson Hills Press, 1996), fig. 53b; and G. Robins, *The Art of Ancient Egypt* (Cambridge: Harvard University Press, 1997), fig. 23.

[14] For examples, see W. S. Smith, *Ancient Egypt as Represented in the Museum of Fine Arts, Boston*, (Boston: T. O. Metcalf, 1960), fig. 4; Capel, "Goddesses," fig. 53a; and J. Malek, *Egypt: 4,000 Years of Art* (London: Phaidon, 2003), p. 502, fig. 18, female figurine, Brooklyn Museum of Art, N.Y., from a grave at El-Mamariyz, height: 33.8 cm., collection fund 07.447.

[15] B. K. Hartwig, "Painting," pp. 1-13 in *OEAE* 3, 4-5; B. S. Lesko, *The Great Goddesses of Egypt* (Norman, Okla.: University of Oklahoma Press, 1991), 10-11.

[16] R. Tringham and M. Conkey, "Rethinking Figurines," in *Ancient Goddesses, The Myths and the Evidence* (eds. L. Goodison and C. Morris; Madison, Wisc.: University of Wisconsin Press, 1998), 22-45.

figures, many scholars have identified them as goddesses.[17] Support for
the life-giving aspect of the female goddess comes from a female figurine
found at Naqada by Petrie, which is decorated with images of flora and
fauna, perhaps suggesting that the "goddess" is the source of these
benefits.[18] The pottery and figurine imagery suggests that the not-yet-
unified local chiefdoms had a religious pantheon based on goddesses and
male ithyphallic gods/consorts.[19]

The above discussion indicates a feature of Pre-Dynastic society
significant for our analysis, namely that women played an important role,
at least in the funerary ideology of the period. Pre-Dynastic graves may
provide supporting evidence for a status for women equal to or even more
prominent than that of men at this time. Mortuary analysis of Pre-Dynastic
gravesites suggests equality in tomb size and wealth of offerings between
male and female.[20] There are, however, distinctions in spheres of activity.
At Cemetery N7000 at Naga-ed-Der, Savage identifies eleven artifact
clusters, including objects such as mace heads, beads, and ceramics, which
he interprets as connected to social roles. However, Savage only identifies
these roles by number. Female burials are associated with all eleven, while
male burials are associated with seven. Caution must be used, since some
social roles are only represented by a few burials, but it is noteworthy that
these patterns suggest a broader range of at least symbolic social roles for
women than for men.[21] These observations have important implications
for our study. They indicate a society in which women may be equal to or
even higher than men in status. While funerary ritual may distort reality by
altering or idealizing societal roles,[22] such distortion should be consistent
with the symbolic fabric of a society. The mortuary patterns discussed
above suggest a more equal status for women before pharaonic unification
than after.

The catalyst for change from egality appears to be the consolidation of
Egypt under a central dynastic authority. Silverblatt has shown that a shift

---

[17] Lesko, *Great Goddesses*, 10-13.
[18] Ibid., 15-16, fig. 1.
[19] F. Hassan, "Earliest Goddesses of Egypt: Divine Mothers and Cosmic Bodies,"
pp. 98-112 in *Ancient Goddesses, The Myths and the Evidence* (eds. L. Goodison
and C. Morris; Madison, Wisc.: University of Wisconsin Press, 1998), 101.
[20] S. Savage, "The Status of Women in Pre-Dynastic Egypt as Revealed through
Mortuary Analysis," in *Reading the Body: Representations and Remains in the
Archaeological Record* (ed. A. Rautman; Philadelphia: University of Pennsylvania
Press, 2000), 77-92.
[21] Savage, "The Status of Women," 86.
[22] Ibid.

in the status of women is often a product of state formation.[23] The specific nature of whatever state is formed determines the ideology behind the diminution of women's status and, in particular, the way women are represented. In Egypt, the state emphasizes pharaonic rule, elevating the male pharaoh as a superior force. As Hassan notes, the unification "brought about a dramatic change in ideology, legitimating the role of a national king who incorporated and assimilated earlier deities within a cosmogenic myth that placed him as the descendant and legitimate inheritor of the throne."[24] This ideology of rule presents itself in a new religious framework in which the creator god, Atum, is closely connected with pharaonic political ideology. Atum is often shown wearing the royal Double Crown of Egypt. The crown is a symbol of unification and indicates that kingship, as a concept, is thus an integral and divinely authorized aspect of the universe, ordained by Atum.[25]

While the male principle is dominant, textual and artistic evidence shows that during the Dynastic period goddesses are closely associated with kingship. For example, the upper corners of each side of the Narmer palette depict human-faced cow heads flanking a *serekh* with the name of the king. These figures are usually considered to be representations of a goddess, either the sky goddess Bat or Hathor,[26] the goddesses most closely associated with early kingship.[27] Their emblematic apposition suggests protection; they support the rule and power of the pharaoh.

For this essay, however, the question remains as to whether the absence of the color convention during the Pre-Dynastic period is indeed a reflection of an "egalitarian" situation—and thus ideologically significant—or is simply a function of a limited color palette. A vital piece of evidence in this discussion is the only monumental painting from this period and indeed the earliest yet found in Egypt. The painting from Tomb 100 at Hierakonpolis dates to the Naqada II Period (3500–3200 B.C.E).[28] As the only painted tomb in the cemetery, it is clearly marked as elite and offers important evidence of the development of the iconography of rule.[29]

---

[23] I. M. Silverblatt, "Women in States," *Annual Review of Anthropology* 17 (1988): 427-60.

[24] Hassan, *Earliest Goddesses of Egypt*, 101.

[25] K. Myśliwiec, "Atum," *OEAE* 1, 158-60; Narmer Palette, Cairo Egyptian Museum from Temple of Hierakonpolis; Robins, *The Art of Ancient Egypt*, fig. 25.

[26] Hassan, *Earliest Goddesses of Egypt*, 102.

[27] Ibid.

[28] H. Case and J. C. Payne, "Tomb 100: the Decorated Tomb at Hierakonpolis," *JEA* 48 (1962): 5-18.

[29] Wilkinson, *Early Dynastic Egypt*, 32-33.

The major scene is a procession of six boats. Subsidiary vignettes include hunting (a person pointing a spear at animals), combat (a figure tying and smiting captives, a bound figure with a mace suspended above), and control of animals (a figure flanked by animals, penned animals). These are all activities that can be connected with the emerging role of chieftainship.[30]

Themes, which are staples of later Dynastic Egyptian art, are also present. For example, the boats may represent funerary barques, important in later Egyptian art.[31] Most significant for our study is the use of color in a potentially symbolic manner—some of the figures are painted black and others red. I use the term "potentially symbolic" since, as with Gerzean pottery and figurines, the precise meaning of the scenes is impossible to judge. As noted above, the general theme of the painting seems to be the exercise of authority of some figures over others and also over animals. No specific identification is possible for any of the figures or even for the situations depicted. It may, in fact, be true that the artist did not intend to show an "actual" event.[32]

Nevertheless, color is used with some degree of consistency, not to distinguish male from female but rather as if to depict two distinct groups of people. Several red, white, and green ships carry red passengers and face right. Another ship is painted black, as are its passengers, and it sails in the opposite direction. It is not possible to securely identify any of the figures in the painting as female based on the typical artistic conventions for depicting women shown on the pottery of the period. There are figures placed above the central red boat in a position analogous to that of the women on the pottery, although they do not exhibit the typical upraised arm gesture of the women on the pottery.[33] They are painted red.

The colors used in the Hierakonpolis painting could be symbolic of two ethnic groups. In Dynastic Egyptian art, foreigners are distinguished from Egyptians by their skin color. Nubians are painted black, Asiatics yellow. Thus one possible use of the two colors is a "realistic" depiction of skin color. That is, the black figures could represent Nubians. While there is clear archaeological evidence of Nubian connections during this period

---

[30] B. Midant-Reynes, *The Prehistory of Egypt: from the First Egyptians to the First Pharaoh* (trans. I. Shaw [orig. 1997]; Oxford: Blackwell, 2000), 209-10; B. Adams and K. M. Cialowicz, *Protodynastic Egypt* (Buckinghamshire: Shire Publications, 1997), 36; B. J. Kemp, *Ancient Egypt: Anatomy of a Civilization* (London: Routledge, 1989), 47.

[31] Midant-Reynes, *The Prehistory of Egypt*, 209.

[32] Ibid., 208.

[33] Case and Payne, "Tomb 100," 17.

in the form of non-figural pottery characteristic of Nubian Group A, the total scene does not support an identification of "foreign invasion."[34] Although early scholarship attempted to identify some of the ships as foreign, especially Mesopotamian, more recent work has shown that all are types common to Egypt.[35] Based on analysis of the relationships of figures in the scenes and their activities, Case and Payne suggest that they are in fact rival political or ethnic groups.[36] Yet no group is seen as the victim or victor in every vignette.

A more subtle color use, one which is an important component of color/differentiation in pharaonic times, may be at work here, namely the use of colors to show duality and, by extension, balance between two distinct elements. The true emphasis, as Case and Payne suggest, is on the restoration of harmony symbolized by the presence of alternating black and red figures (antelopes) in the center of the wall and pairs of black and red antelopes elsewhere in the painting.[37] The Hierakonpolis painting would represent a statement of balance. Kemp also sees the painting as a forerunner of later pharaonic symbolism, in which the maintenance of order and balance in the face of the forces of chaos becomes very important. [38]

By Dynasty Four, usually considered the beginning of the Old Kingdom, there is a codification and stabilization of kingly power and its iconography. Color, just as scale and position, is part of a consistent program of representation, which reflects the Egyptian ruling elite's view of status and power and reflects underlying gender roles amplified during the shift to pharaonic rule.

The first preserved examples of male/female color differentiation in Egyptian art belong to this period.[39] The idea of a balanced universe

---

[34] K. M. Cialowiwicz, "Pre-Dynastic Period," pp. 61-65 in *OEAE* 3, 64.

[35] Adams and Cialowicz, *Protodynastic Egypt*, 36.

[36] Case and Payne, "Tomb 100," 17.

[37] Ibid.

[38] Kemp, *Ancient Egypt*, 46.

[39] Examples include Pair Statue of Kate and Hetep-Heres (painted limestone, Trustees of the British Museum, London EA 1181), catalogue no. 82, 290 in D. Arnold and C. Ziegler, "Non-Royal Statuary," in *Egyptian Art in the Age of the Pyramids* (eds. D. Arnold and C. Ziegler; New York: Metropolitan Museum of Art, 1999), 51-56; and Pair Statue of Iai-ib and Khuaut (30.8 cm., Agyptishces Museum, Univeersitat Leipzig 3684), catalogue no. 83, 293 in D. Arnold and C. Ziegler, "Non-Royal Statuary." Neither the state of preservation nor our lack of ability to precisely date Old Kingdom sculpture allow any one piece to be labeled

guaranteed by pharaoh is supported by this differentiation between men and women. The colors chosen, red and yellow/white, were considered opposites. Egyptian literature reveals that a consistent theme in the maintenance of *maat* is unity achieved through the union of opposites. The union of male and female was an important component of this equilibrium. The sun itself was reborn each day through the union of the setting sun (male) and the earth (female).[40]

The union of male and female takes on even greater significance in the context of the afterlife where women were necessary as the catalyst for reproduction, which, in turn, guaranteed the afterlife. The role of woman as catalyst is clearly seen in Egyptian cosmologies. In the Heliopolitan, "Atum is he who (once) came into being who masturbated in On. He took his phallus in his grasp that he might create orgasm by means of it, and so were born the twins Shu and Tefenet."[41] The hand with which he masturbates is personified as a goddess. The creation act is "male" (ejaculation), but Atum is androgynous in the sense that he contains the possibility for both male and female. In this cosmology, Shu and Tefnut are twins, unlike the Classical creation story in which Pandora belongs to a different "race" or the Biblical story in which Adam is created first (Gen 2:7). For the Egyptians, male and female serve as "complementary sources of generation, which make possible the continuing process of generative creation."[42] In the human realm, as well, the male was seen as the locus of fertility. The female was the catalyst for stimulating male fertility.[43] As Roth states, "The responsibility for fertility and creating new life was not laid on the shoulders of women in ancient Egypt, they were instead expected to be sexually aggressive, to begin the process of creation by enticing their male partners to creation."[44] Such stimulation was a guarantee of the afterlife. Many of the motifs found in tomb paintings

---

the first example of male/female color differentiation. It is, however, an established practice by the Fourth Dynasty.

[40] G. Robins, "Dress, Undress and the Representation of Fertility and Potency in New Kingdom Egyptian Art," pp. 31-39 in *Sexuality in Ancient Art* (ed. N. B. Kampen; Cambridge: Cambridge University Press, 1996), 36.

[41] R. O. Faulkner, *The Ancient Egyptian Pyramid Texts* (Oxford: Oxford University Press, 1969), 1248.

[42] V. A. Tobin, "Creation Myths," pp. 469-72 in *OEAE* 1, 469.

[43] A. M. Roth, "Father Earth, Mother Sky: Ancient Egyptian Beliefs About Conception and Fertility," in *Reading the Body: Representations and Remains in the Archaeological Record* (ed. A. Rautman; Philadelphia: University of Pennsylvania Press, 2000), 187-201.

[44] Roth, "Father Earth, Mother Sky," 200.

show women in situations that indicate their role as catalysts. Manniche cites tomb images from the Sixth Dynasty, depicting the tomb owner's wife playing the harp on the marital bed as evidence of the role of women as stimulation for the sex that was considered a necessity for rebirth.[45] Recent studies of banquet scenes in tombs suggest that there is a strong sexual element in these seemingly quotidian scenes. This emphasis on the role of women as stimulator of the sexual union necessary for the afterlife may explain why the majority of statues of women come from funerary contexts. While statues of men are found in temples and shrines as well as tombs, the majority of statues of women are found in tombs.[46] Men's other roles were stressed in statues found in other contexts, but women were presented in the afterlife-specific role of sexual catalyst.[47]

Male/female color differentiation marks the difference in spheres of activity between men and women, but it also serves to emphasize that the combination of these two opposites through sexual union provides for the afterlife and maintains the stable order of the universe. It does not serve simply to contrast degrees of sun exposure, especially since both colors can also be associated with solar imagery. While red could be used to signify the intense radiance of the sun (red was used for amulets of the "Eye of Re," the sun god),[48] yellow was also used to emphasize connection to the sun. The solar disc was often painted yellow. Statues made of red or yellow stone were used for images of pharaohs who wished to be equated with the sun god. Color differentiation is thus an important signifier of ideological roles, not simply a natural reflection of actual roles. Artistic elements, such as male/female color differentiation, are used to form what Shanks (in a discussion of stylistic features in Greek art) has described as "a technology of power" in which "...concepts and practices of the self and body, ideas of the powers and limits which are appropriate to both; ...and aesthetic systems which indicate the appropriateness of action ...may also work to establish metaphorical links."[49] Color differentiation is part of the broader ideological framework promoted to support the establishment of pharaonic rule. The very ubiquity of the color convention in Egypt may be one reason scholars have often accepted it as a given of

---

[45] Manniche, "Sexuality," *OEAE* 3, 274-77.
[46] Robins, "Dress, Undress and the Representation of Fertility and Potency."
[47] Ibid.
[48] R. H. Wilkinson, *Symbol and Magic in Egyptian Art* (London: Thames and Hudson, 1994), 107.
[49] M. Shanks, *Art and the Early Greek State: An Interpretive Archaeology* (Cambridge: Cambridge University Press, 1999), 311.

ancient art and not something with a strong ideological basis. The indoor/outdoor explanation for the difference in skin tone between men and women in Egyptian art has tended to simplify what, as we can see, was a much more complex process, one which used color to support pharaonic ideology and the role of male and female in the correct ordering of the universe.

CHAPTER TWO

A TASTE OF WOMEN'S SOCIALITY: COOKING AS COOPERATIVE LABOR IN IRON AGE SYRO-PALESTINE

AUBREY BAADSGAARD

The nature of the household as physical space and locus of social relationships and activities has been explored in detail and from many perspectives in the ancient Near East. This paper revisits these issues using evidence from Syro-Palestine, a cultural-geographic region located east of the Mediterranean from Syria to Israel-Palestine during the Iron Age, ca. 1200-586 B.C.E. Discussions of the domestic house abound in the literature on Iron Age Syro-Palestine, making it an ideal case study for a re-evaluation of ancient domestic relationships and activities.[1] This heightened attention to the house is a reflection of the abundance of domestic structures and remains in the archaeological record and the prevailing notion that the patriarchal household (*beit 'av*) was the model for all social, political, and economic relationships in the greater ancient Near East.[2]

---

[1] See Y. Shiloh, "The Four-Room House: Its Situation and Function in the Israelite City," *IEJ* 20 (1970): 277-85; idem, "The Casemate Wall, the Four Room House, and Early Planning in the Israelite City," *BASOR* 268 (1987): 3-15; L. E. Stager, "The Archaeology of the Family in Ancient Israel," *BASOR* 260 (1985): 1-35; P. J. King and L. E. Stager, *Life in Biblical Israel* (Louisville, Ky.: Westminster, 2001); A. Faust, "Differences in Family Structure between Cities and Villages in Iron Age II," *TA* 26 (1999): 233-52; idem, "Socioeconomic Stratification in an Israelite City: Hazor VI as a Test Case," *Levant* 31 (1999): 179-89; idem, "Ethnic Complexity in Northern Israel during Iron Age II," *PEQ* 132 (2000): 2-27.

[2] See S. Bendor, *The Social Structure of Ancient Israel: the Institution of the Family (beit 'av) from the Settlement to the End of the Monarchy* (Jerusalem Biblical Studies 7; Jerusalem: Simor, 1996 [Hebrew]); J. Blenkinsopp, "The Family in First Temple Israel," in *Families in Ancient Israel* (eds. L. G. Perdue, J.

In discussing the Iron Age house, also sometimes referred to as the "four-room house," or the "Israelite house,"[3] past research has investigated the details of house layout and the physical relationships between houses to determine the type of domestic unit residing there (extended versus nuclear family) and the nature of activities that took place within and near the domestic structure.[4] This article reconsiders both of these issues using the evidence for one type of domestic activity—cooking—to explore the relationship between the organization and use of space inside houses and the social roles and networks involved in carrying out this task. To reconstruct the domestic activity of cooking, this research examines the spatial distribution of ovens in and near houses at Iron Age sites to look for patterns in the location of ovens and their association with artifacts and other installations. These patterns are then used as a way to explore the social relationships involved in tasks related to food preparation and cooking. As a starting point, based on ethnographic and historic analogy, it is assumed that domestic activities such as cooking were primarily, if not exclusively, performed by women, whose work was based in and near the domestic unit and combined with child rearing and other duties.[5] Better clarification of the association between the physical spaces and relationships of cooking is thus one means of better illuminating the social

---

Blenkinsopp, J. J. Collins, and C. Meyers; Louisville, Ky.: Westminster, 1997), 48-103; C. Meyers, "To Her Mother's House: Considering a Counterpart to the Israelite *Bêt 'āb*," in *The Bible and the Politics of Exegesis: Essays in Honor of Norman K. Gottwald on His Sixty-Fifth Birthday* (eds. D. Jobling, P. L. Day, and G. T. Sheppard; Cleveland: Pilgrim Press, 1991); idem, "The Family in Early Israel," in *Families in Ancient Israel* (eds. L. G. Perdue, J. Blenkinsopp, J. J. Collins, and C. Meyers; Louisville, Ky.: Westminster, 1997), 1-47; J. D. Schloen, *The House of the Father as Fact and Symbol: Patrimonialism in Ugarit and the Ancient Near East* (Winona Lake, Ind.: Eisenbrauns, 2001).

[3] J. S. Holladay, "House, Israelite," in *ABD* 3, 308-18; idem, "Four-Room House," in *OEANE* 2, 337-42.

[4] See C. Meyers, *Discovering Eve: Ancient Israelite Women in Context* (New York: Oxford University Press, 1988); Stager, "The Archaeology of the Family in Ancient Israel."

[5] See M. I. Gruber, "Women in the Ancient Levant," in *Women's Roles in Ancient Civilizations: A Reference Guide* (ed. B. Vivante; Westport, Conn.: Greenwood Press, 1999), 115-52; K. R. Nemet-Najat, "Women in Ancient Mesopotamia," in *Women's Roles in Ancient Civilizations: A Reference Guide* (ed. B. Vivante; Westport, Conn.: Greenwood Press, 1999), 85-114; M. E. Wiesner-Hanks, *Gender in History* (Malden, Mass.: Blackwell, 2001).

networks and relationships existing among women in Iron Age Syro-Palestine.[6]

In its investigation of women's relationships as evident from domestic tasks, this research draws from two bodies of literature: cross-cultural studies of gender and gender roles in the context of household relations and actions;[7] and, work in the field of "household archaeology." This field was first defined by Wilk and Rathje as the study of the formation of task-focused groups living and working together in shared physical spaces.[8] Fundamental to the approach advanced here is the assertion that the household is an idea and set of social relationships and activities that exists only in an active sense. That is, the household has social reality only

---

[6] This paper was completed before the publication of C. Meyers, "From Field Crops to Food: Attributing Gender and Meaning to Bread Production in Iron Age Israel," in *Archaeology of Difference: Gender, Ethnicity, Class, and Other in Antiquity: Studies in Honor of Eric Meyers* (eds. D. R. Edwards and C. T. McCollough; Boston: ASOR, 2007), 67-84.

[7] For examples, see E. Brumfiel, "Weaving and Cooking: Women's Production in Aztec Mexico," in *Engendering Archaeology: Women and Prehistory* (eds. J. M. Gero and M. W. Conkey; Oxford: Blackwell, 1991), 224-51; M. W. Conkey and J. M. Gero, "Programme to Practice: Gender and Feminism in Archaeology," *Annual Review of Anthropology* 26 (1997): 411-37; N. Charles and M. Kerr, *Women, Food, and Families* (Manchester: Manchester University Press, 1988); S. Gregory, "Gender Roles and Food in Families," in *Gender, Power, and the Household* (eds. L. McKie, S. Bowlby, and S. Gregory; New York: St. Martin's Press, 1999), 60-75; R. A. Joyce, "Women's Work: Images of Production and Reproduction in Pre-Hispanic Southern Central America," *Current Anthropology* 34 (1993): 255-74; L. McKie, S. Bowlby, and S. Gregory, "Connecting Gender, Power and the Household," in *Gender, Power, and the Household* (eds. L. McKie, S. Bowlby, and S. Gregory; New York: St. Martin's Press, 1999) 3-22; D. Morgan, "Gendering the Household: Some Theoretical Considerations" in *Gender, Power, and the Household*, (eds. L. McKie, S. Bowlby, and S. Gregory; New York: St. Martin's Press, 1999), 23-41; S. M. Nelson, *Gender in Archaeology: Analyzing Power and Prestige* (Walnut Creek, Calif.: AltaMira Press, 1997); J. Salisbury, *Women in the Ancient World* (Santa Barbara, Calif.: ABC-CLIO, 2001); R. Tringham, "Archaeological Houses, Households, Housework, and the Home," in *The Home: Words, Interpretations, Meanings, and Environments* (eds. D. N. Benjamin, D. Stea, and E. Arén; Avebury: Aldershot, 1995), 79-107.

[8] See R. R. Wilk and W. L. Rathje, "Household Archaeology," in *Archaeology of the Household: Building a Prehistory of Domestic Life; American Behavioral Scientist* 25 (1982): 617-39; see also, a review of literature on household archaeology by J. A. Hendon, "Archaeological Approaches to the Organization of Domestic Labor: Household Practice and Domestic Relations," *Annual Review of Anthropology* 25 (1996): 45-61.

insofar as its members act out the tasks and relationships that define it, creating and participating in the social definition of the house and engaging directly with questions of meaning, ideology, and social divisions of power and responsibility.[9] This understanding of the house requires that studying its physical spaces, activities and social relationships must be done concurrently since each mutually creates, defines, and depends on the other. From this perspective, exploring the relationships among women within the household is crucial to understanding the divisions of labor and space that were part of its creation and persistence as a fundamental social institution.

Nature of the Iron Age Household

To better understand the organization of Iron Age households and the role of gender in the organization and practice of domestic activities, previous research on the nature of the Iron Age house as social unit, physical structure, and locus of domestic activities is briefly reviewed. In Iron Age society, basic social units were comprised of classic patriarchal families, with patrilocal residence and patrilineal descent the accepted customs.[10] Some scholars see the patriarchal ordering of families as the all-prevailing, principle organizing system in Syro-Palestine and the Eastern Mediterranean, including politically, socially, and within the domestic unit.[11] Others question whether the patriarchal model for Iron Age Syro-Palestinian family structure reflects modern interpretations of patriarchy, stressing either ideologies of male dominance and authority over women or institutionalized male power, more than past realities.[12] Indeed, in reference to evidence from archaeological, written, and

---

[9] See R. E. Blanton, *Houses and Households: A Comparative Study* (New York: Plenum Press, 1994); Hendon, "Archaeological Approaches to the Organization of Domestic Labor," 46; R. M. Netting, R. R. Wilk, and E. J. Arnould, *Households: Comparative and Historical Studies of the Domestic Group* (Berkeley: University of California Press, 1984); C. Meyers, "Material Remains and Social Relations: Women's Culture in Agrarian Households of the Iron Age," in *Symbiosis, Symbolism, and the Power of the Past: Canaan, Ancient Israel, and Their Neighbors from the Late Bronze Age through Roman Palaestina* (eds. W. G. Dever and S. Gitin; Winona Lake, Ind.: Eisenbrauns), 425-44.

[10] See Stager, "The Archaeology of the Family in Ancient Israel," 20.

[11] See Schloen, *The House of the Father as Fact and Symbol.*

[12] C. Meyers, "Hierarchy or Heterarchy? Archaeology and the Theorizing of Israelite Society," in *Confronting the Past: Archaeological and Historical Essays on Ancient Israel in Honor of William G. Dever* (eds. S. Gitin, J. E. Wright, and J. P. Dessel; Winona Lake, Ind.: Eisenbrauns, 2006), 245-54.

ethnographic sources, it is clear the assumption that patriarchy implies male rulership and power over women, has little support.[13] Rather, the evidence reveals that women's roles and powers crosscut household and clan divisions through formal and informal networks.[14] These networks were crucial for maintaining political and economic stability among and between families and communities and entail female power over and control of certain technologies, such as bread and textile production. Thus it seems that Iron Age society might be better understood as a flexible heterarchy, an organizational system with multiple and overlapping individuals and groups existing in different kinds of power relationships.[15]

While the rigid, patriarchal ordering of families is a matter of recent dispute, so too is the makeup of the family unit living together in domestic units. Based on the small size of residential dwellings, most researchers consider the nuclear family comprised of a couple and their children to have been the standard living arrangement,[16] while others argue that larger extended family households better fit the biblical evidence.[17] Stager's model puts nuclear families in individual houses and extended families in residential compounds made up of several houses arranged around shared courtyards.[18] Faust maintains that the social makeup of residential dwellings was dependent on the size and location of the domestic structure itself, with nuclear families living together in smaller houses in urban settings, and extended families living in larger houses located in the countryside.[19] Sites in the Jordanian highlands, for example, were certainly big enough to accommodate large, complex domestic groups.[20] Schloen suggests that patrilocal joint families consisting of three to four couples

---

[13] P. A. Bird, *Missing Persons and Mistaken Identities: Women and Gender in Ancient Israel* (Minneapolis: Fortress, 1997).

[14] Meyers, "Hierarchy or Heterarchy," 247.

[15] See also J. E. Levy, "Gender, Heterarchy, and Hierarchy," in *Handbook of Gender in Archaeology* (ed. S. M. Nelson; Lanham Md.: AltaMira Press, 2006), 219-46.

[16] See Y. Shiloh, "The Population of Iron Age Palestine in the Light of a Sample Analysis of Urban Plans, Areas, and Population Density," *BASOR* 239 (1980): 25-35; Holladay, "House, Israelite;" idem, "The Kingdoms of Israel and Judah: Political and Economic Centralization in the Iron IIA-B (1000-750 BCE)," in *The Archaeology of Society in the Holy Land* (ed. T. Levy; London: Leicester University Press, 1997), 368-98.

[17] See Blenkinsopp, "The Family in First Temple Israel."

[18] Stager, "The Archaeology of the Family in Ancient Israel," 26.

[19] Faust, "Differences in Family Structure."

[20] For examples, see B. Routledge, "Seeing through Walls: Interpreting Iron Age I Architecture at Khirbet al-Mudayna al-Aliya," *BASOR* 319 (2000): 37-70.

and their children best fit both the biblical evidence and estimates for the population density of Iron Age villages.[21] Both Schloen and Stager acknowledge that family size regularly expanded and contracted as part of the normal life cycle, as the addition and loss of family members through birth, marriage, and death changed individual families' requirements for living space.[22] Sometimes renovation and expansion projects were undertaken to meet these changing needs. Given the variety in the size and shape of the Iron Age domestic house (see below), it is probable that the size of families did vary considerably across Iron Age sites, with the social makeup of individual units changing according to the various phases of the household cycle and to other social and economic factors.[23]

As a physical structure, the Iron Age house was a simple dwelling, typically consisting of four rooms, including three parallel, long, roofed rooms, and a central room that served as open (or perhaps roofed) courtyard space, separated from the side rooms by stone pillars and sometimes by walls.[24] Behind and perpendicular to the three parallel rooms was a back or broad room. Considerable variations existed. Some houses had only two parallel rooms with a broad room, or two rooms with no broad room, or additional rooms added to the front or side. Houses could be one or two stories, and roofs also served as usable space. According to Holladay, each room in the house had clearly defined uses. Side rooms were used as stables, central courtyards as the locus for domestic activities such as food processing and cooking, back or broad rooms for storage, and second stories and roofs for seasonal sleeping quarters.[25] Differences in the size, number and orientation of rooms, as well as the distribution of objects within them, however, point to considerable variation in the use of space within the Iron Age house, perhaps related in part to the variety of the social units living there.

A range of domestic activities took place inside or in close proximity to the house. These tasks included general housekeeping, childcare, tending of gardens and small animals, textile production, and food

---

[21] Schloen, *The House of the Father*, 135.

[22] Ibid., 136; Stager, "The Archaeology of the Family in Ancient Israel," 23.

[23] See Faust, "Differences in Family Structure between Cities and Villages;" idem, "Socioeconomic Stratification in an Israelite City."

[24] Shiloh, "The Four-Room House;" idem, "The Casemate Wall, the Four Room House."

[25] Holladay, "House, Israelite;" idem, "The Four-Room House."

preparation.[26] According to ethnographic sources, these domestic tasks were carried out primarily by women with the assistance of older children, while men tended to agriculture and herded livestock. Activities such as food preparation and textile production involved a complex series of tasks, most of which took place in courtyards, on roofs, and sometimes in communal areas or public streets. Food preparation was particularly time-consuming, as it required processing grains, making dough, and baking bread.[27] Meyers estimates that women spent a minimum of ten hours a day engaged in domestic labor, two alone in grain processing. Other duties such as the manufacture and maintenance of processing and baking facilities and the procurement of fuel for fire also demanded considerable time and attention.[28]

According to ethnographic and historic studies of small-scale farming communities, carrying out domestic activities often involves cooperative labor among women.[29] These cooperative relationships, known as "women's networks," are rarely noted in public discourse or in historical writings, but nevertheless provide critical social linkages among women. Similar to the *bayt*, which serves as the locus for household relationships in contemporary Middle Eastern societies,[30] Iron Age women's networks were organized around kinship ties, according to family of birth and family of marital affiliation.[31] Women's cooperative labor involved sharing facilities and tools including grinding implements, ovens and looms, and also sharing knowledge about the procedures, materials and settings for completing domestic tasks. Interaction among women in cooperative networks was also the means for forming and maintaining intra-community alliances among women.

[26] Meyers, "The Family in Early Israel;" idem, "Women and the Domestic Economy of Early Israel," in *Women in the Hebrew Bible* (ed. A. Bach; New York: Routledge, 1999), 33-44.
[27] L. A. Moritz, *Grain-Mills and Flour in Classical Antiquity* (New York: Arno Press, 1979).
[28] Meyers "The Family in Early Israel," 25-27.
[29] K. S. March and R. L. Taqqu, *Women's Informal Associations in Developing Countries* (Boulder, Colo.: Westview Press, 1986); C. Meyers, "Women in the Neighborhood (Ruth 4:17): Informal Female Networks in Ancient Israel," in *Ruth and Esther: A Feminist Companion to the Bible* (ed. A. Brenner; Sheffield: Sheffield Academic Press, 1999), 110-29.
[30] A. Menely, *Tournaments of Value: Sociability and Hierarchy in a Yemeni Town* (Toronto: University of Toronto Press, 1996).
[31] M. Mundy, *Domestic Government: Kinship, Community, and Polity in North Yemen*, (New York: Tauris Publishers, 1995).

Some evidence for the existence of cooperative women's networks has been recovered from Iron Age archaeological and historic sources. Meyers cites evidence for communal bread preparation such as a grinding trough from Iron I Tel Dor that resembles Aegean terracotta models showing several women kneading dough in a single, long trough and iconography and texts from Greece and Egypt depicting women collectively grinding grain and carrying out other domestic tasks.[32] Other evidence comes from the location and distribution of facilities used for domestic activities in shared or open spaces such as courtyards between houses, public streets, or public buildings (see discussion below). Ethnographic accounts also point to the existence of women's cooperative networks. In contemporary northern Jordan, for example, seven to ten women, each representing a separate household, share ovens for baking.[33] The Hebrew Bible mentions the use of one oven by multiple women; such sharing is demanded during times of social upheaval when "ten women will bake in one oven" (Lev 26:26).

Cooking as Domestic Activity

While domestic activities are myriad, this research focuses on one type of activity, cooking, since historic and ethnographic studies of cooking are abundant, and ovens, the most obvious feature associated with cooking, are present in virtually all Iron Age domestic dwellings. Because they are permanent features, oven location and association with objects, walls and other features can be determined and provide insight into the spaces and objects used for cooking. This discussion of cooking begins with a discussion of oven construction and use, and then considers the time, space, and materials required for using them. Next, evidence for the spatial distribution of ovens from several Iron Age sites is presented and used to reconstruct the dynamic connection between women's social relationships and cooking space in the Iron Age.

---

[32] See Meyers, "Women in the Neighborhood;" idem, "Material Remains and Social Relations;" E. Stern, J. Bero, A. Bilboa, I. Sharon, and J. Zorn, "Tel Dor, 1994-1995: Preliminary Stratigraphic Report," *IEJ* 47 (1997): 29-56; and J. Wilkens, "Food Preparation in Ancient Greece: Representations of Gender Roles in the Literary Evidence," in *Representations of Gender from Prehistory to the Present* (eds. M. Donald and L. Hurcome; New York: St. Martin's Press, 2000), 118-36.
[33] A. McQuitty, "Ovens in Town and Country," *Berytus* 38: 53-72.

Ovens: Basics of Form and Use

The term "oven" applies to installations used for cooking and for baking bread.[34] Ovens are cooking installations not open to the air (as is a hearth) but rather partially or completely enclosed. Air is allowed in only through one or more controlled openings. Two kinds of ovens are described in Iron Age contexts. Their construction and use are known from historic and ethnographic research.[35] Both types of ovens consist of beehive-shaped installations made of clay tempered with straw, chaff, sheep/goat hair, and small rocks.[36] Top openings are covered by ceramic lids. The *tabun* (Arabic for oven) has a hollow, flat interior level with the ground and is frequently lined with small stones or potsherds. Fuel of dried dung cakes heaped against the outside heat the interior surface, where bread or other foods are baked. When not in use, dung completely covers the outside of the oven to conserve heat and allow for later use of the oven by others.[37]

In the *tannur* (biblical Hebrew for oven), a wood fire on the bottom produces heat to bake dough slapped up against the oven's interior walls. The *tannur* can be either above ground or semi-subterranean; in either case, a base of pebbles and a mantle of potsherds encircle the exterior walls to aid in heat retention. In modern examples, the *tannur* is heated only when required and is not covered except when in use. For example, Kramer describes the *tannur* in a modern Iranian village as made of unbaked clay set into the floor to a depth of about 1.5 m. Rims are flat, wide, and flush with the floor.[38] The *tannur* may be lined with clay mixed with salt and/or goat hair to minimize cracking. The term *tannur* appears fifteen times in the Hebrew Bible, seven in reference to an oven used in baking bread (Exod 8:3; Lev 2:4, 7:9, 11:35, 26:26; Hos 7:4, 6-7). In some instances, such as that found in Exod 8:3, it is mentioned alongside other food processing equipment such as a kneading-trough.

According to McQuitty, the two types of ovens may be distinguished archaeologically by two principle methods: the clay walls, as the walls of the *tabun* are sun-dried while those of the *tannur* are fired; and the surface construction of the oven bottom, which for the *tannur* is sunk into the ground, and for the *tabun* is at ground level. The location and distribution

---

[34] Ibid., 55-56.

[35] Ibid.; S. Avitsur, "The Way to Bread," *Tools and Tillage* 2 (1972-1975): 228-41.

[36] McQuitty, "Ovens in Town and Country," 57.

[37] Avitsur, "The Way to Bread," 240.

[38] C. Kramer, *Village Ethnography: Rural Iran in Archaeological Perspective* (New York: Academic Press, 1982).

of ashes and fire marks are also useful indicators of whether the oven was heated from within (*tannur*), or from without (*tabun*). Iron Age ovens more closely resemble the *tannur*, although some also appeared to have functioned like the *tabun*. Along with these two types of oven, wood-fired pit ovens, and ovens made of ceramic vessels turned upside down and placed in small pits sealed with mud plaster, were also used. In modern Jordan, the choice of oven appears to be related to functional considerations (size, location, etc.), although available technology and cultural traditions about size and appearance influenced oven type and style in the recent past. In modern villages, ovens have a 3-15 year lifespan, after which new ones are built in the same locations, or in more convenient areas.[39]

Oven Location and Distribution

Ethnographic insights help to reconstruct the location and distribution of ovens and the implications such locations had for the organization of cooking. In Kramer's analysis of rural, Iranian households, all domestic compounds had kitchens with ovens sunk into the floor next to bins and upright looms. All ovens were found on the first floor of houses, since the depth of the level of the oven was greater than the thickness of the first floor ceiling. Many houses had more than one oven. The ideal was to have a least two: one in the kitchen and one in the courtyard for use in warm weather. Not every household met this objective, due to patterns of air circulation, which restricted areas suitable for ovens. Other domestic chores such as tending small animals, milk processing, and weaving took place alongside cooking in outdoor courtyards.[40]

Kramer suggests oven number is a reliable index of family size and makeup if it is assumed that each woman used her own, separate oven.[41] Since building and using ovens is kept to a minimum to reduce fuel consumption and minimize smoke dispersal, women from different households may be forced to share ovens. Ovens could also be rebuilt, moved, or abandoned in response to changes in family size, thus leaving evidence for more than one oven in a kitchen, even if only one was used. In cases where household compounds have more than one oven, usually

---

[39] McQuitty, "Ovens in Town and Country," 56-57.
[40] Kramer, *Village Ethnography*, 100.
[41] C. Kramer, "An Archaeological View of a Contemporary Kurdish Village: Domestic Architecture, Household Size, and Wealth," in *Ethnoarchaeology: Implications of Ethnography for Archaeology* (ed. C. Kramer; New York: Columbia University Press, 1979), 139-63.

only one or the other is in use during any given cooking event. This rule applies even as household size increases and heightens the demands for more cooking facilities. Even wealthy families do not use more than one oven.[42]

In the village of Qal'a, southern Iraq, a bread oven (*tenor*) is an essential feature of household compounds. Ovens are confined to a small courtyard (*harim*) in front of dwelling units that are separate and closed off, either by walls or carpets hung over ropes, to the larger courtyard open to the guesthouse. Ovens are a feature of every household complex, and are sometimes also found in open areas outside dwellings.[43] In rural villages in western Iran, all living rooms have a hearth used for cooking and heating.[44] Ovens are located in roofed courtyard space in the front of houses (known as *aywan*) and in open courtyards, stables and utility rooms. Along with an oven, every household has a set of standard food preparation and storage equipment, stored against or in small niches in the living room walls. Essential items include a *saj*, or iron plate for cooking bread, as well as cooking vessels and utensils, and large storage chests.[45]

In contrast to other ethnographic examples, where cooking occurred in bottom stories or courtyards, cooking and other domestic tasks take place on the roof or in second story rooms in the village Tell-i Nun in southwestern Iran.[46] Here, all houses are built around unroofed, shared courtyards used for the milking and feeding of animals. Bottom stories stable animals in winter and serve as general storerooms during other seasons. Upstairs rooms are slightly smaller than the lower story and the extra space is used as small, unroofed work areas for cooking, drying grains, and washing.

Along with these examples of cooking in domestic houses are ethnographic examples of communal or public bakeries. In modern Jordan, for example, ovens can be located in small bake houses, small rooms in courtyards, or at the edge of villages. Old houses or rooms may also be used as communal bake houses.[47]

---

[42] Kramer, *Village Ethnography*, 120.

[43] H. Nissen, "Survey of an Abandoned Modern Village in Southern Iraq," *Sumer* 24 (1968): 107-13.

[44] P. J. Watson, *Archaeological Ethnography in Western Iran* (Tucson, Ariz.: University of Arizona Press, 1979).

[45] Watson, "*Archaeological Ethnography*," 161.

[46] L. Jacobs, "Tell-i-Nun: Archaeological Implications of a Village in Transition," in *Ethnoarchaeology: Implications of Ethnography for Archaeology* (ed. C. Kramer; New York: Columbia University Press, 1979), 175-91.

[47] McQuitty, "Ovens in Town and Country," 70.

The Process of Food Preparation: Time, Space and Materials

Cooking in ovens is only one stage of food preparation and must take place at the end of a long sequence of preparing grain or other foods for baking. The entire process of cooking thus involves a set of equipment such as grinding, mixing, and serving implements and vessels, and requires the time and space necessary to carry out the full sequence of food preparation.[48] In contemporary traditional Middle Eastern societies, the designation of equipment used for cooking and the time and space in which to do it is linked to social ideals of gendered space and relationships. In terms of space, the designation of certain parts of the house for domestic activities is strictly regimented according to gender and age. In most instances, ovens and other cooking equipment are found in secluded women's space. These "kitchen" areas are kept separate from living rooms used by men for entertaining guests, from upper floors, and from public streets.[49] In ancient Greece, the entire house was designated as women's space and relegated to domestic tasks, and men were considered household guests.[50]

Designating time for cooking is also a fundamental consideration. Since food preparation places extraordinary demands on women's time, it is often done simultaneously with other domestic tasks. Among the Rwala Bedouin, for example, women prepare food while watching children, carding, spinning, and weaving, and entertaining guests. Tasks such fuel gathering, meal planning, and the grinding of grain, all of which take considerable time, have to be done in advance of cooking.[51] Seasonal variations put temporal and spatial constraints on women's activities. For example, cooking and many of the other tasks associated with food preparation have to be moved to indoor kitchens from unroofed courtyards during the winter rainy season.[52]

The heavy demands cooking placed on women's time is the result of the complex process of food preparation, which includes procuring and preparing ingredients, baking, presentation, and consumption of the final product. Both ethnographic observations and replicative experiments

---

[48] McKie, "Connecting Gender, Power, and Household," 7.

[49] Kramer, *Village Ethnoarchaeology*, 102; Jacobs, "Tell-i-Nun," 179.

[50] M. Jameson, "Private Space and the Greek City," in *The Greek City: From Homer to Alexander* (eds. O. Murray and S. Price; Oxford: Clarendon Press, 1990), 171-95.

[51] W. Lancaster, *The Rwala Bedouin Today* (Prospect Heights, Ill.: Waveland, 1997), 72.

[52] Kramer, *Village Ethnoarchaeology*, 100.

demonstrate that bread preparation followed multiple and complex steps beginning with soaking fully ripe grains, milling and grinding the grain into flour, and making and baking dough.[53] Each of these steps required access to multiple features and implements ranging from stored grain, grinding implements (mortars, querns), cooking vessels (baking trays and pots), and baking ovens (*tabun* and *tannur*). The Hebrew Bible mentions some of the implements used in food preparation, such as a griddle (*mahăbat*) (Ezek 4:3), as well as a basin (*kiyyôr*), kettle (*dûd*), cooking jug (*qallaḥat*) and cooking pot (*pārûr*) (1 Sam 2:13-14).

According to the foregoing discussion, cooking is one of many complex steps of food preparation. It involves ovens built into the floors of kitchens and courtyards and occurs within socially defined constraints of space and time. With these basics of both the process and the social relationships of cooking in mind, the evidence for cooking from Iron Age contexts will now be provided, followed by an analysis of the nature of the Iron Age household, which has been gained by examining this evidence.

Ovens from Iron Age Contexts

From the previously reviewed details of cooking, it is possible to outline some expectations for the evidence of cooking from Iron Age contexts and to determine how this evidence might provide insight into the connection between women's social relationships and the physical spaces of cooking. Expectations for the evidence of cooking in the Iron Age are as follows:

1. Ovens in the Iron Age are expected to be of the *tannur* type, consisting of clay ovens slightly excavated into the floor with evidence of burning on the inside.

2. Ovens should be located in domestic contexts and found within secluded women's space or "kitchens" located in interior rooms and courtyards and away from public streets.

3. Ovens should also be located in exterior courtyards to accommodate seasonal weather changes and patterns of smoke dispersal, and also to facilitate the sharing of ovens by women from multiple households.

4. Ovens should be associated with other food processing tools and implements such as storage bins, grinding facilities, and cooking vessels. Ovens should also be found near objects and features associated with other domestic activities such as weaving, in which women would have been engaged while cooking.

---

[53] Avitsur, "The Way to Bread."

To determine how the evidence fits with these expectations, a total of 235 ovens from eighteen Iron Age sites, spanning contexts dating from the Iron I (1150 to 900 B.C.E.) and the Iron II (900 to 586 B.C.E.) periods were examined (see Table 2-1). Recorded features include location, size, construction method, and associations. Location is the position of ovens inside or outside structures and their proximity to walls and features. Size and construction method are examined through measurements of diameter and height (above floor surface) taken from published reports and plans, as available. The features and small finds found in close association with ovens are recorded to determine whether cooking occurred in those areas used for other domestic purposes.

Due to inconsistencies in the reported data, ovens were not grouped according to construction technique. Some site reports call all ovens *tannurs* (Tel Masos), others use *tabun* (Gezer, Tell el-Far'ah [N]), and some merely call them ovens (Tell es-Sa'idiyeh, Beer-Sheba), clay ovens, cooking facilities, or even circular clay features. Some features described as ovens were merely circular depressions in the floor or large pits filled with ash, and others were the upper part of an upturned store jar encircled by small stones. Gunneweg describes two ovens at Tel Masos, in a way that suggests they functioned as *tabuns*, although one appears to have traces of burning on the inside (a hallmark of the *tannur*).[54] Despite confusion over terminology, most ovens from the Iron Age resemble the *tannur* in form and use.

---

[54] J. Gunneweg, "The Ovens of the First Campaign," in *Ergebnisse der Ausgrabungen auf der Hirbet el Masas (Tel Masos) 1972-1975* (eds. V. Fritz and A. Kempinski; Wiesbaden: Harrassowitz, 1983), 106-12.

Table 2-1. List of Iron Age sites with ovens used in analysis

Sites	Date	Number of ovens	Reference
Beer-Sheba	Iron I-II	18	Aharoni 1973; Herzog 1984
Deir 'Alla	Iron II	51	van der Steen 1991; Ibrahim and van der Kooij 1997
Gezer	Iron I-IIB	17	Dever et al. 1974
Hazor	Iron IIA-IIC	22	Yadin et al. 1958, 1960, 1961
Tel Batash	Iron I	11	Mazar 1997
Tel 'Ira	Iron II	8	Beit-Arieh 1999
Tel Masos	Iron IA-IB	10	Gunneweg 1983; Givon 1996; Fritz and Kempinski 1983
Tel Miqne	Iron II	3	Gitin 1997
Tell Beit Mirsim	Iron IIB	4	Albright 1943
Tell en-Nasbeh	Iron II	2	McCown 1947
Tell es-Sa'idiyeh	Iron IIB-IIC	32	Pritchard 1985
Tell Qasile	Iron I, IIA	8	Maisler 1950/51
Tel Qiri	Iron I, II	3	Ben-Tor 1987
Tell Zeror	Iron II	10	Ohata 1970
Tell el-Far'ah (N)	Iron II	36	Chambon 1984
Total		**235**	

Most Iron Age ovens consist of circular clay installations excavated 15-30 cm into the floors of houses, and encircled with *wadi* pebbles. Some ovens from Deir 'Alla, Tel Masos, and Tell es-Sa'idiyeh were placed on stone platforms found directly on the stone pavement of side rooms. The sides of ovens were enclosed with small stones and pottery sherds for support and insulation, and some were plastered on the outside with mud or lime plaster. One well-preserved oven from Taanach was a beehive-shaped installation with triple-layered walls insulating a core formed of

potsherds.[55] The source of heat (whether exterior or interior) is not well
reported, although the location of ash in relation to the oven (inside or
outside) is mentioned in a few cases. Examples from Deir 'Alla have
traces of burning and hollowing out of the inside, suggesting that ovens
were fired from inside and bread baked against the inside wall.[56] Some
covers of Iron Age *tannur* type ovens have been located at Deir 'Alla and
Tel Masos. The Deir 'Alla covers consist of flat, disc-shaped pieces of
unbaked clay, while at Tel Masos, a possible cover with a handle was
found in association with an oven.[57] Ovens at Deir 'Alla were rebuilt one
or more times in the same location.[58]

Variation existed in oven form and function across different Iron Age
sites, and these differences can be linked to temporal trends in oven
building techniques. For example, Gunneweg and van der Steen report that
the construction of ovens simplified from the Iron I to the Iron II period.[59]
Early Iron Age ovens most commonly exhibit a "sandwich wall"
construction with two concentric walls of clay and a layer of sherds and
mud between for insulation. Ovens from the Iron II lose this "sandwich
wall" type of construction and have only single walls, such as described at
Tell el-Far'ah (N), Tell es-Sa'idiyeh, and Tel Masos.[60]

In terms of spatial location, more ovens were found inside houses (55
percent) than in any other context (see Table 2-2). Ovens were also found
in exterior courtyards (21 percent), streets, open areas, and paved areas (13
percent), and in public buildings (5 percent). The existence of cooking
facilities both inside and outside of houses fits well with the expectation
that ovens should be found in multiple enclosed and open locations in
order to accommodate seasonal changes and patterns of smoke dispersal,
as well as the sharing of cooking facilities by women from multiple
households. Ovens from open and public areas have a larger average
diameter than those from domestic structures, further evidence that these

[55] P. W. Lapp, "The 1966 Excavations at Tell Ta'annek," *BASOR* 185 (1967): 2-39.
[56] E. J. van der Steen, "The Iron Age Bread Ovens from Tell Deir 'Alla," *ADAJ* 35 (1991): 135-53.
[57] Gunneweg, "The Ovens of the First Campaign," 108.
[58] van der Steen, "The Iron Age Bread Ovens from Tell Deir 'Alla," 153.
[59] Gunneweg, "The Ovens of the First Campaign," 111; van der Steen, "Iron Age Ovens from Deir 'Alla," 139.
[60] For Tell el-Far'ah (N), see A. Chambon, *Tell el-Far'ah I, L'Age du Fer* (Paris: Editions Recherche sur les Civilisations, 1984); for Tell es-Sa'idiyeh, see J. B. Pritchard, *Tell es-Sa'idiyeh, Excavations on the Tell, 1964-1966* (Philadelphia: University of Pennsylvania Press, 1985); for Tell Masos, see Genneweg, "The Ovens of the First Campaign."

larger facilities were shared across the community (see Table 2-3).
According to van der Steen, oven size is also related to its proximity to
roofed space and to season of use. [61] Ovens in roofed spaces, such as
rooms inside houses, tend to be smaller than open-air ovens, and were
probably used during cold weather months. Large ovens located in open
areas were preferred during the summer.

Table 2-2. Frequency of ovens in different contexts

Contexts	Number of ovens	Percent
Domestic Houses	112	55.2
Courtyards	42	20.7
Public Buildings	10	4.9
Open Areas	21	10.2
Paved Areas	1	0.5
Streets	5	2.5
Casemate Rooms	3	1.5
Pits	2	1.0
Unknown Buildings	2	1.0
Storerooms	1	0.5
Other Rooms	4	2.0
Total	**203**	**100.0**

Table 2-3. Average diameter of ovens in different contexts

Location	Average diameter	Size rank
Domestic Houses	55 cm	4
Courtyards	63 cm	1
Public Buildings	60 cm	3
Street/Open Spaces	61 cm	2
Casemate Rooms	42 cm	5

[61] van der Steen, "The Iron Age Ovens from Tell Deir 'Alla."

As predicted, across all sites, the objects and features found in association with ovens were mostly of a domestic character, evidence that cooking occurred in concert with other domestic tasks (see Table 2-4 for list of oven associations by site). Ash and occasional cooking pots have been found inside ovens (such as two examples at Deir 'Alla), while ash pits near ovens show that ovens were periodically cleaned. Other

Table 2-4. Associations of ovens by site

Site	Oven associations
Beer-Sheba	store jars, cooking pots, ground stone tools, loom weights, storage bins, iron tools
Gezer	pits, ash heap, kiln
Hazor	cooking pot, gaming board, inscription, shelf, silo, storage jar
Tel Batash	ash, stone-lined pit, store jars, cooking pots, loom weights
Tel 'Ira	ground stone tools, plastered installation, iron tools, loom weights
Tel Masos	clay platform, ash
Tell en-Nasbeh	dye vat
Tell es-Sa'idiyeh	ash pit, ground stone tools, stone shelf/table, storage bin, loom weights, iron slag, cloth impression
Tell Qasile	ground stone tools, store jars, oil press, loom weights
Tell el-Far'ah (N)	cooking pots, store jars, storage bins, ground stone

associated finds include grinding implements, loom weights, pottery (storage and cooking vessels), and storage bins. Less frequently associated with ovens are installations such as a silo near an oven in a paved space at Hazor, an oil press alongside an oven in a domestic unit at Tell Qasile, a dye vat located next to an oven in a domestic context at Tell en-Nasbeh, a basin, trough and cistern in the same part of a courtyard as the oven at Taanach, and a gaming board and pottery inscription near an oven from a public building at Hazor.[62] Loom weights were commonly found in houses with ovens at Tell es-Sa'idiyeh.[63]

According to the evidence just reviewed, the expectations that the *tannur* type oven was preferred in Iron Age contexts, that ovens should be more common inside domestic units than other areas, and that ovens should be associated with other domestic features and artifacts, are all met. What remains to be determined is how ovens were distributed spatially within individual domestic units and if this distribution points to the existence of "secluded women's space" or separate kitchen areas used only by women in accordance with expectations based on ethnographic models. To examine the evidence for the existence of such women's space, the spatial distribution and associations of ovens from three sites were examined in detail: Tell es-Sa'idiyeh, Tell el- Far'ah (N), and Beer-Sheba.

At Tell es-Sa'idiyeh, all houses share a similar ground plan, consisting of two long rooms separated by pillars with a transverse back room.[64] The houses are similar in size and attached by means of common, exterior walls. Two rows of houses were organized such that they share common back walls, with entrances facing opposite directions onto prepared, cobbled roadways. Excavations in Iron II levels uncovered some thirty ovens including nine from Str. VII (825-790 B.C.E.), six from Str. VI (790-750 B.C.E.) and fifteen from Str. V (750-730 B.C.E.; Table 2-5). In all strata, ovens are found in long rooms, but with no apparent regularity in terms of position within these rooms. In the plan of Str. V, however, it is clear that most ovens are positioned next to or near entryways into houses, as for example in Houses 11, 12, and 27 (Fig. 2-1). The one exception is House 9, whose oven is situated towards the back of the long room. However, even in this case, the oven is visible from and easily accessible from the entrance. Other ovens are found in courtyards between houses, such as the four ovens located between Houses 29 and 27. House 27 also has an interior oven, but the three other houses (6, 8, and 10) facing this courtyard lack interior ovens, and perhaps shared the facilities in the

---

[62] See Y. Yadin, Y. Aharoni, R. Amiran, T. Dothan, and J. Perrot, *Hazor I* (Jerusalem: The Magnes Press of the Hebrew University of Jerusalem, 1958); Y. Yadin and Y. Aharoni, *Hazor II* (Jerusalem: The Magnes Press of the Hebrew University of Jerusalem, 1960), 148; B. Maisler, "The Excavations at Tell Qasile: Preliminary Report," *IEJ* 1 (1950): 139; W. F. Badé, *Tell en-Nasbeh Excavated under the Direction of the Late William Frederic Badé* (Berkeley: The Palestine Institute of the Pacific School of Religion and the ASOR, 1947), 217; Lapp "The 1966 Excavations at Tell Ta'annek," 14.
[63] See Pritchard, *Tell es-Sa'idiyeh.*
[64] Ibid.

nearby courtyard. The overall spatial distribution of ovens from Tell es-
Saʻidiyeh in highly accessible areas near entryways or in shared courtyards
spaces does not provide evidence for secluded spaces or kitchens used by
women as part of cooking but rather the opposite, that ovens were situated
in areas of high social traffic where facilities could easily by shared by
women from multiple domestic units.

Table 2-5. Location and position of ovens from Tell es-Saʻidiyeh

Stratum	House	Location	Position
VII	House 51	House-Front Room	SE corner
VIIB	House 60-62	House-Long Room	SW corner
VIIB	House 60-62	House-Long Room	SW corner
VIIA	House 60-62	House-Long Room	W wall
VII	House 64	House-Long Room	SW corner
VII	House 65	House-Long Room	NE corner
VII	House 66	House-Long Room	NW corner
VII	House 66	House-Long Room	NW corner
VII	House 66	House-Long Room	NW corner
VI	House 33	House-Long Room	SW corner
VI	House 35	House-Long Room	NE corner
VI	House 37-39	Courtyard	E of house
VI	House 41	House-Long Room	NE corner
VI	House 43	House-Long Room	Center, E wall
VI	House 43	House-Long Room	N, E-W wall
V	House 5	House-Long Room	NE corner
V	House 7	House-Long Room	S wall
V	House 9	House-Long Room	SW corner
V	House 11	House-Long Room	E wall
V	House 12	House-Long Room	SW corner
V	House 16	House-Front Room	Next to wall between long rooms
V	House 16	House-Front Room	Next to wall between long rooms
V	House 25	House-Long Room	NE corner

V	House 25	House-Long Room	N wall
V	House 27	House-Long Room	Paved area, NE corner
V	House 29	House-Back Room	
V	Between Houses 27, 29	Courtyard	SE corner
V	Between Houses 27, 29	Courtyard	W
V	Between Houses 27, 29	Courtyard	N
V	Between Houses 27, 29	Courtyard	N
IV		Open Area	
IV		Open Area	
IV		Open Area	

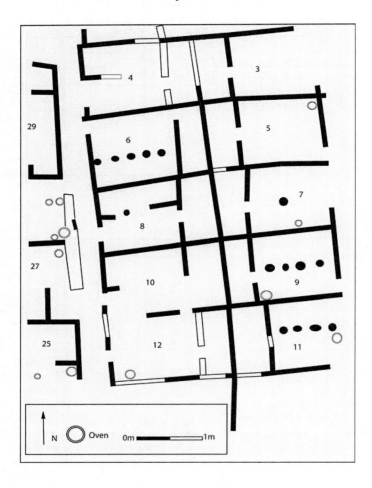

Fig. 2-1. Plan of houses from Level V at Tell es-Saʻidiyeh.[65]

[65] Pritchard, *Tell es-Saʻidiyeh*, fig. 179. Used by permission, University of Pennsylvania Press.

Tell el-Far'ah (N) has six major phases dating to the Iron Age. The best preserved remains come from the two destruction levels of phases VIIb and VIId, dated to the ninth and eighth centuries B.C.E. (Table 2-6).[66] At least fifteen complete four-room houses (including the palatial complex) were uncovered, seven in Stratum VIIb. Houses were similar in size and had two rows of pillars, a central courtyard, and a number of smaller rooms in the back. Many had side rooms on one or both sides of central rooms with cobbled floors. The spatial distribution of ovens in houses is similar to that found at Tell es-Sa'idiyeh, with most having one or two ovens in areas of easy access, such as near the entrance to the building, as in House 442 and House 440 (Fig. 2-2). An exception to this pattern is House 161, whose oven is located in a secluded back room. The plan of the house appears to have been altered, however, and the entrance moved from facing an alleyway to leading to an inner courtyard. Thus, even in this case, the original location of the oven was near the entrance of the structure. Houses without ovens were positioned in such a way as to facilitate easy access to ovens in nearby houses or courtyards. House 410A, for example, lacked an oven near the entrance, but two ovens were positioned in a courtyard immediately to the north of the house. Similarly, an easy route led between House 436 and the entrance of House 410A, went through extra side rooms and into a space with an oven from a neighboring house.

Other examples of multiple households sharing ovens are found in Str. VIId at Tell el-Far'ah (N). For example, two and possibly three houses (362, 366, and "appendage to 366") have back exits facing one courtyard, which contains an oven. Most of the household finds were not discovered in the houses themselves, but rather in the courtyards near ovens, suggesting that domestic spaces were defined by features and facilities such as ovens rather than by walls or rooms in houses.

---

[66] See Chambon, *Tell el-Far'ah (N)*.

Table 2-6. Location and position of ovens from Tell el-Farʻah (N)

Stratum	House	Locus	Location	Position
VIIb	161	159	House-Back Room, Left	SW corner
	436	417	House-Back Room, Right	S wall, center
		433A	House-Back Room, Left	W side, center
	440	440	House-Courtyard	SW corner, near entrance
	442	442A	House-Side Room, Right	SE corner, near door to courtyard
	442	442A	House-Side Room, Right	SE corner, near door to courtyard
	442	429	Exterior Courtyard	S of entrance
		429	Exterior Courtyard	S of entrance
VIId	148	125	Palace-Side Room	NW corner next to courtyard
	148	125	Palace-Side Room	NW corner next to courtyard
	362	342	House-Back Room, Outside	Next to exterior wall
	362	342	House-Back Room, Outside	Next to exterior wall

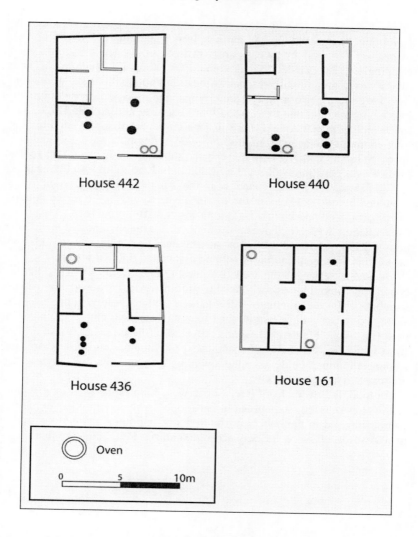

House 442

House 440

House 436

House 161

Oven

0   5   10m

Fig. 2-2. Plan of Houses 442, 440, 436, and 161 at Tell el-Far'ah (N)[67]

---

[67] Chambon, *Tell el-Far'ah I*. Reproduction courtesy of Culturesfrance–ERC, ©ADPF-ERC–Ministère des Affaires étrangères, Paris.

At Beer-Sheba, the nineteen ovens found in domestic units show no patterning in location. In the earliest Iron I settlement (Str. VIII), two ovens were located in pits apparently used for domestic purposes and sleeping. In Str. VII-VI, ovens came from domestic contexts.[68] These ovens varied greatly with respect to location and position; six were from right long rooms, two from left long rooms, one from an interior courtyard inside a house, and one from a courtyard between houses (see Table 2-7). In several instances, ovens were in smaller rooms made by partitioning long rooms. One oven from Building 2358 was in a partially enclosed space called a "cooking corner," and the other in the back of two rooms formed by a partition wall separating the right long room into two spaces. An additional oven was found near the front of the back, right room separated by two columns in the center of the room, and in the middle of three partitioned spaces in a right long room of Building 1651. Also from Iron I strata were two ovens from open courtyards located near two houses. One was found on a rock surface near open pits, and the other in the center of an open courtyard with no associated finds or features.

A small section of the Iron II domestic area in the Western Quarter contained three houses of the three-room variety, their back rooms forming part of the casemate wall.[69] Like at Tell es-Sa'idiyeh, these rooms share walls along their longitudinal axis and all have entrances facing a road (Fig. 2-3). Four ovens were uncovered in these houses, all of which were found in well-sheltered spaces next to entrances and near staircases leading to upper landings. One oven was found near the street and entrances to two buildings.

In total, the ovens from Beer-Sheba were found mostly in long rooms in the Iron I period, sometimes in partitioned spaces with other domestic equipment, and in the Iron II in the fronts of buildings near entryways or in courtyards, allowing for easy access to and sharing of cooking facilities.

---

[68] See Y. Aharoni, *Beer-Sheba I: Excavations at Tel Beer-Sheba: 1969-1971 Seasons* (Tel Aviv: Institute of Archaeology, 1973); Z. Herzog, *Beer-Sheba II: The Early Iron Age Settlements* (Tel Aviv: Tel Aviv University Institute of Archaeology, 1984).

[69] Aharoni, *Beer-Sheba I*.

Table 2-7. Location and position of ovens at Beer-Sheba

Stratum	Building	Locus	Location	Position
VIII		1306	Pit	
VIII		1306	Pit	
VIII		2058	Courtyard	Rock surface near pits
VII	2524	2310	House-Long Room, Right	NW corner
VII	2309	1689/308	House-Long Room, Right	SW wall
VII	2358	2080	House-Long Room, Right	W wall
VII	2358	2086	House-Long Room, Right	E "cooking corner"
VII	2313	2613	Courtyard West of Buildings 2354 and 2060	Surface in main courtyard
VI	1651	1311	House-Long Room, Right-Middle	SW wall
VI	1689	1692	House-Long Room, Right	SW wall
VI	1689	308	House-Courtyard	SW corner
VI	2029	2301	House-Long Room, Left	Center
VI	2029	2301	House-Long Room, Left	SE wall
II		38	Near Street and Entrances to Bldgs. 25 and 75	N Side
II	75	94	House-Front Room	NW corner
II	76	124	House-Front Room	SW corner
II		87	House-Long Room	NW corner
II		44	House-Long Room, Back of Divided Room	NE corner

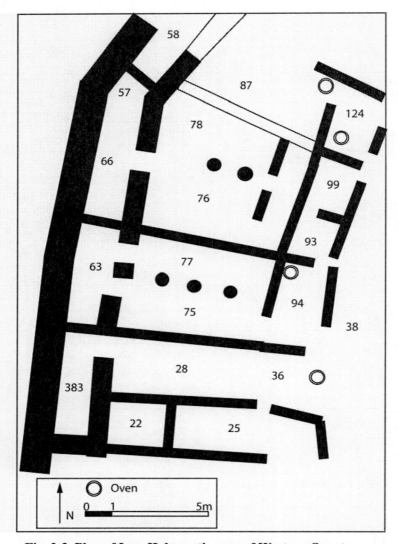

**Fig. 2-3. Plan of Iron II domestic area of Western Quarter
at Beer-Sheba[70]**

[70] Aharoni, *Beer-Sheba I*. Used by permission, Institute of Archaeology, Tel Aviv
University.

Ovens from other Iron Age sites likewise show a great deal of variability in terms of their position within houses and their tendency to be located in areas of easy access near entryways or in shared spaces between houses. Ovens at Tel Masos, for example, were found in a variety of locations such as rooms, courtyards, and streets. Two ovens were found in domestic rooms: one from the main room and one from the southeastern corner of the broad room. Other ovens were found along the northern outer wall of House 2, in an open courtyard, and in a street.[71]

Ovens from Hazor perhaps best illustrate the range of variation in oven location and use. Here, twenty-two ovens were uncovered from public and domestic contexts, most from Area A Iron II strata. In Area A Str. VIII, all ovens are from public contexts.[72] Examples include one oven found in the eastern corner of Pillared Building 71a next to a wall, cooking pot, gaming board, and inscribed sherd in an area called a "domestic quarter." Three ovens were found in small casemate rooms and two ovens in a courtyard between the pillared building and casemate walls. In Area A Str. VI, two ovens were found, one in the second of two back rooms of a domestic complex, and the other in a paved area next to a silo. One oven from Str. V in Area A was found in the central courtyard of a domestic unit and two ovens were found in large rooms in buildings of likely public function next to the pillared building. In Area B Str. VA (Iron IIB), two ovens were found in a courtyard enclosed by two rooms of an unknown function, and one oven in a niche in an alleyway.[73] Str. IV (Iron IIC) had two ovens in domestic rooms, and one in an open area. Ovens from across other areas of the site include one in the western long room of a public tripartite building in Area A Str. X-IX (Iron IIA), and two in Area L, one found in a courtyard between two walls and one from the southeast corner of the back room of a domestic dwelling.

Cooking as Cooperative and Meaningful Women's Labor

Having outlined the evidence for cooking in Iron Age contexts, the task is now to determine how this evidence might shed light on women's roles and relationships, as the primary practitioners of domestic tasks. Associations between ovens and other domestic utensils and features indicate that cooking was carried out by women, in concert with other domestic tasks such as food preparation (soaking and grinding grain,

---

[71] Gunneweg, "The Ovens of the First Campaign," 106-12.
[72] Yadin et al., *Hazor I.*
[73] Yadin and Aharoni, *Hazor II.*

serving food) and weaving. The clustering of domestic objects near ovens, rather than in specific rooms or spaces in houses, indicates that contrary to the typical expectation, walls did not define areas of specialized domestic activities; rather, such activities occurred in relation to facilities and features. Finally, the evidence clearly indicates that ovens were not located in defined or secluded women's spaces, but rather in highly accessible areas near entryways and courtyards that would facilitate visitation and cooperation among women as part of completing domestic tasks. Variation in oven location suggests that women could arrange the spaces used for domestic activities to accommodate such cooperative networks and according to practical and personal considerations.

In total, the evidence presented here makes it clear that patriarchal models of domestic labor in relation to the Iron Age house have not adequately considered the relationship between the spaces of domestic activities and the social roles and networks of women formed during the completion of domestic tasks. Rather, the spatial distribution and association of ovens from Iron Age sites supports Meyers' call for recognizing the existence and importance of women's roles and networks in building and maintaining Iron Age houses and communities and of women's control of certain technologies, such as cooking and bread production, essential for economic survival.[74] Indeed the physical evidence of cooking, in combination with historic and ethnographic insights, highlight women's role in building and maintaining the Iron Age house and the social relationships, physical structure, and activities that defined it. From the evidence reviewed here, it is apparent that the women's activities, roles and relationships were not defined by an all-encompassing patriarchal structure, but were actively created in ways that crosscut and even defined the household structure. The fact that women could arrange domestic spaces and relationships with relative freedom reveals their power over the domestic sphere and their large influence on the structure and activities defining the Iron Age household. Women's informal networks, evident in the sharing of cooking facilities, further reveal their role as active participants in community wide events and relationships and their role in providing crucial structure and cohesion among kinship groups and local neighborhoods. Examples of such community ties are evident in biblical stories such as the naming of Ruth's son by the entire community (Ruth 4:17), sharing a lamb during the Passover feast (Exod

---

[74] Meyers, "Hierarchy or Heterarchy."

12:4), and a widow receiving economic aid from neighbors (2 Kgs 4:3), among others.[75]

Explaining the structure of the Iron Age house with reference to all-encompassing patriarchal models also does little to illuminate the diversity of social relationships and physical spaces that provided the foundations for its existence, or to highlight the meaning and purpose behind women's household activities and relationships beyond their more practical goals. It is clear from the Bible, for example, that women's association with food and food preparation was an important component of or precursor to significant religious and historical events. Preparing and serving bread was the means by which women demonstrated their hospitality, their desire and ability to care for kin, for the poor, or for weary travelers. For women, the giving of food was thus a giving of self, revealing their knowledge and control over food producing technology and procedure and their ability to nourish important household-based and community-wide relationships. Specific examples of women's hospitality through the giving of food include Sarah kneading flour and preparing cakes for the three strangers in Hebron (Gen 18:6), and the widow baking small cakes with the last of her meal and oil for the prophet Elijah (1 Kgs 17:13). In many instances, the preparation and baking of bread immediately preceded or accompanied a significant event, such as the medium at Endor preparing cakes for Saul on the eve of his death on the battlefield at the hands of the Philistines (1 Sam 28:24), and Tamar making cakes for her brother Amnon, before their fateful encounter (2 Sam 13:8).[76]

Ethnographic accounts highlight the religious aspect of women's participation in food preparation.[77] In many rural Near Eastern cultures, for example, women consider common household tasks to be religious performances or rituals, such as elderly Kurdish Jewish women living in Jerusalem who consider all domestic chores as sacred acts referencing religious identity, tradition, and law.[78] Because domestic tasks are sacred, the spaces and facilities involved in their completion are likewise sacred and essential for forming social and spiritual relationships among women,

---

[75] Meyers, "Women in the Neighborhood," 121.

[76] King and Stager, *Life in Biblical Israel*, 62, 65.

[77] C. Meyers, *Household and Holiness: The Religious Culture of Israelite Women* (Minneapolis: Fortress Press, 2005).

[78] See S. S. Sered, "Food and Holiness: Cooking as a Sacred Act among Middle Eastern Jewish Women," *Anthropological Quarterly* 61 (1988): 129-39; idem, *Women as Ritual Experts: The Religious Lives of Elderly Jewish Women in Jerusalem* (New York: Oxford University Press, 1992).

their family and friends, and the divine.[79] These relationships are formed as women share facilities and techniques with other women, instruct children in proper domestic procedures, and prepare food used for religious rituals and celebrations.[80] Success is ensured only if domestic tasks conform to strict procedural and spiritual guidelines similar to those defining formal religious rites. Thus, through domestic performance, women demonstrate their knowledge of social and religious convention even while actively participating in creating and sustaining these same directives.[81]

When combining ethnographic and historic insights with the archaeological evidence for spatial distribution and association of ovens from Iron Age sites, it is possible to glimpse a meaningful, even spiritual aspect of women's lives in Iron Age Syro-Palestine. Rather than existing as a mundane, repetitive task, cooking was one way women acted out social roles, formed informal relationships with each other, and demonstrated their control over a crucial aspect of domestic production. In arranging the spaces used for cooking, women engaged directly with social regulations and issues of gendered divisions of space. By carrying out the daily and necessary task of cooking, women both physically sustained family members and actively participated in the construction and maintenance of the house and the physical spaces, social relationships, and domestic activities that defined it. Women's shared participation in domestic tasks within and across Iron Age communities through informal networks indicates that physical, social, and even spiritual survival was a community-wide concern and ensured only through women's collective labor. Taken together, all the evidence demonstrates that cooking, as women's labor, was a central and indispensable part of maintaining Iron Age communities, and was essential for the formation, existence, and persistence of the individual household, society's most fundamental institution. Better understanding of the spaces and relationships of this everyday task is thus one means of tasting women's sociality, of sensing their active and influential roles in Iron Age society.

---

[79] Sered, "Food and Holiness," 129.
[80] Sered, *Women as Ritual Experts*, 87.
[81] Sered, "Food and Holiness," 132.

CHAPTER THREE

BAKING AND BREWING BEER IN THE ISRAELITE HOUSEHOLD: A STUDY OF WOMEN'S COOKING TECHNOLOGY[1]

JENNIE R. EBELING AND MICHAEL M. HOMAN

Introduction

There has been interest of late in what archaeological data can reveal about ancient Israelite women and their contributions to the household economy. In several recent articles, C. L. Meyers suggests that women gained power in the ancient Israelite household and larger community through control of cooking tasks, specifically their ability to manipulate grain to make bread.[2] Baking in the ancient Near East and Egypt was closely connected to brewing, which was an offshoot of bread production. Beer was a dietary staple in this region consumed by men, women and

---

[1] This paper is an expansion of our presentation in the 2005 American Schools of Oriental Research Annual Meeting session "The World of Women: Gender and Archaeology," chaired by Beth Alpert Nakhai. We sincerely thank Beth for inviting us to contribute to this volume, and for organizing outstanding ASOR sessions that address issues still largely overlooked in our field.
[2] C. L. Meyers, "Having Their Space and Eating There Too: Bread Production and Female Power in Ancient Israelite Households," *Nashim: A Journal of Jewish Women's Studies and Gender Issues* 5 (2002): 14-44; idem, "Material Remains and Social Relations: Women's Culture in Agrarian Households of the Iron Age," in *Symbiosis, Symbolism, and the Power of the Past: Canaan, Ancient Israel, and Their Neighbors from the Late Bronze Age through Roman Palaestina* (eds. W. G. Dever and S. Gitin; Winona Lake, Ind: Eisenbrauns, 2003), 425-44; idem, "From Field Crops to Food: Attributing Gender and Meaning to Bread Production in Iron Age Israel," in *Archaeology of Difference: Gender, Ethnicity, Class and the "Other" in Antiquity: Studies in Honor of Eric M. Meyers* (AASOR 60 & 61; eds. D. R. Edwards and C. T. McCollough; Boston: ASOR, 2007), 67-84.

children of all social classes. However, biblical scholars and archaeologists have focused on wine, not beer[3] because wine is associated with industry, trade, inheritance, ritual and status while beer is associated with the domestic sphere. Moreover, the remains of wine are more common than those concerning beer, because beer was typically produced for immediate consumption, and, unlike wine, it does not improve with age; in general, people traded wine and grain as opposed to beer and grapes.[4]

Overlooked until now is women's role in the production of beer in the Israelite household. In order to demonstrate women's control over brewing in Iron Age (ca. 1200-586 B.C.E) Israel, this article first addresses the connection between women and beer production and consumption in the written and artistic records of the ancient Near East and Egypt. It then turns to the significance of beer goddesses in the region and suggests how women's control over beer production may have influenced the Israelite cult. The chapter then describes the methods used to produce ancient beer and emphasizes its close connection to bread production, while focusing on the archaeological correlates to brewing in Iron Age Israel. It also offers suggestions for identifying beer production activities with female spaces. Ultimately, it demonstrates that women were the primary producers of beer in the Israelite household, and suggests directions for future research into the identification of women's brewing activities in Iron Age households.

Women and Beer in the Ancient Near East and Egypt

Textual Record

A variety of texts connect women to beer production and consumption in the ancient Near East. In texts dating to the third and second millennia B.C.E. Mesopotamia, women are often noted as producers and providers of beer. For example, at the beginning of the *Epic of Gilgamesh*, the prostitute Shamhat, who was sent from the city of Uruk to civilize Enkidu, gives Enkidu bread and beer to mark his transition from the wild to the domestic.[5] Later, the wise tavern keeper Siduri gives Gilgamesh good beer

---

[3] M. M. Homan, "Beer, Barley, and *šēkār* in the Hebrew Bible," in *Le-David Maskil: A Birthday Tribute for David Noel Freedman* (eds. R. E. Friedman and W. H. C. Propp; Winona Lake, Ind.: Eisenbrauns, 2004), 27; idem, "Beer and Its Drinkers: An Ancient Near Eastern Love Story," *NEA* 67/2 (2004): 84-86.

[4] e.g. Homer, *Odyssey*, 2.379-80.

[5] Old Babylonian version, 2.3.6-25; *ANET*, 77.

and even better advice as he journeys to find the secret of immortality.[6] In addition to the literary attestations, numerous economic texts indicate that women ran taverns. Brewing equipment was required for a woman to open a tavern, and such equipment was sometimes among the items given to women as part of their dowries.[7] Interestingly, customers paid for their beer with raw grain, which the proprietor later turned into beer.

Hammurabi's eighteenth century B.C.E. law code regulated beer and documents the important role women played in beer distribution. It stipulated that female tavern keepers needed to price their beer fairly, and if not, they were to be thrown into the water (line 108). It also states that female taverns needed to police their establishments and turn in conspirators (line 109), and that "sisters of a god" (priestesses) could not open a tavern or enter one, lest they be burned to death (line 110).[8] In Mesopotamia, taverns were associated with music, games, prostitutes and the goddess Ishtar.[9]

There are also Egyptian textual accounts of women brewing beer. In the *Destruction of Mankind*, further discussed below, the women of Heliopolis produced beer and dyed it red with ochre to trick the bloodthirsty Hathor-Sekhmet, who was sent by Ra to destroy humankind.[10] The New Kingdom (ca. 1550-1069 B.C.E.) *Instructions of Ani* relates that women made bread and beer at home to feed their families: " [your mother] … sent you to school and you were taught to write, [and] she kept watching over you daily, with bread and beer in her house."[11] Bureaucratic

---

[6] Old Babylonian version, 10.2-3; ibid., 90.

[7] M. Stol, "Beer in Neo-Babylonian Times," in *Drinking in Ancient Societies: History and Culture of Drinks in the Ancient Near East* (ed. L. Milano; Padova: Sargon, 1994), 179-80.

[8] J. B. Pritchard, ed., *The Ancient Near East: An Anthology of Texts and Pictures*, vol. 1 (Princeton: Princeton University Press, 1958), 170.

[9] R. Harris, "Images of Women in the Gilgamesh Epic," in *Lingering over Words: Studies in Ancient Near Eastern Literature in Honor of William L. Moran* (HSS 37; eds. T. Abusch, J. Huehnergard, and P. Steinkeller; Atlanta: Scholars Press, 1990), 219-30; P. Michalowski, "The Drinking Gods: Alcohol in Mesopotamian Ritual and Mythology," in *Drinking in Ancient Societies: History and Culture of Drinks in the Ancient Near East* (ed. L. Milano; Padova: Sargon, 1994), 27-44. There is a long tradition of women being beer providers. For example, note the 5th century C.E. Saint Brigid of Ireland, who gained fame by turning her bath water into beer to satisfy the thirst of a clergyman.

[10] M. Lichtheim, *AEL 2: The New Kingdom*, 199.

[11] Ibid., 141.

titles from literary sources and tomb scenes from the pharaonic period make reference to female as well as male millers and brewers.[12]

Unlike for Mesopotamia and Egypt, there is no historical text from ancient Syria-Palestine that links women to beer production. There is, however, some textual evidence for women drinking beer. For example, female *muḫḫūtu* prophets from eighteenth century B.C.E. Mari, like their male counterparts, appear to have consumed beer to induce ecstatic states and deliver messages to kings from a manifestation of the goddess Ishtar.[13] There are also cases in the Hebrew Bible that accuse Israelite women of drunkenness. The best-known example is when Eli accused Hannah of being drunk at the Tabernacle in Shiloh (1 Sam 1: 12-14). Hannah retorted that she drank neither wine nor *šēkār*, best translated as "beer."[14] In Num 6: 1-4, Yahweh tells Moses that men or women who want to become Nazirites need to separate from wine and *šēkār*. This requirement suggests that there must have been quite a few women who typically did not abstain. Additionally, Deut 14: 26 suggests that beer be drunk at sacrificial meals, and Num 28: 7-10 prescribes the use of beer in Temple ritual.

Artistic Record

The artistic record linking women with beer production and consumption in Mesopotamia and Egypt is long. Sumerian seals depicting banqueting scenes, including one from "Queen" Puabi's tomb at Ur (ca. 2600-2500 B.C.E.), show women in mixed groups or with other women drinking beer out of straws.[15] The remains of three straws–one of reed covered in gold, one of copper encased in lapis lazuli, and one of gold with silver and lapis lazuli–were found in Puabi's tomb, as well.[16] Several early second millennium B.C.E. terracotta plaques show women drinking beer out of a straw while engaged in sexual intercourse. While it has been suggested that these represent tavern or brothel scenes, their original contexts are often unknown.[17]

[12] R. I. Curtis, *Ancient Food Technology* (Leiden: Brill, 2001), 105.
[13] H. B. Huffmon, "Prophecy: Ancient Near Eastern Prophecy," in *ABD*, vol. 5, 477-82.
[14] Homan, "Beer, Barley and *šēkār* in the Hebrew Bible."
[15] M. T. Viviani, "The Role of Alcoholic Beverages in Sumer and Akkad: An Analysis of Iconographic Patterns (4000-2000 B.C.)," *Aram* 17 (2005): 1-50.
[16] Curtis, *Ancient Food Technology*, 218.
[17] Z. Bahrani, *Women of Babylon: Gender and Representation in Mesopotamia* (London: Routledge, 2001), 51-53.

There are many more artistic representations in Egypt. The Fifth
Dynasty (ca. 2494-2345 B.C.E.) tomb of Ti at Saqqara provides the most
complete account of the Egyptian baking and brewing process; in detailed
wall paintings, women are shown alongside men participating in various
processing activities related to baking and brewing (Fig. 3-1).[18]

Fig. 3-1. Beer producing scene from Ti's Tomb[19]

---

[18] L. Epron, *Le Tombeau de Ti*, Memories de l'Institut Francais d'Archeologie
Orientale du Caire 65 (1939), pl. LXVI.
[19] Courtesy of Th. Benderitter, www.osirisnet.net.

Another Fifth Dynasty tomb painting, that of Re'emkuy at Saqqara, depicts women grinding grain and heating bread molds in preparation for brewing beer from malted bread loaves.[20] The earliest examples of three-dimensional models depicting women engaged in activities associated with baking and brewing are among the Egyptian servant statues, which first appear in the Old Kingdom (ca. 2686-2160 B.C.E.). Many depict single women grinding grain or kneading dough, although some depict men carrying out these activities.[21] The First Intermediate Period (ca. 2160-2055 B.C.E.) and Middle Kingdom (ca. 2055-1650 B.C.E.) witnessed the proliferation of tomb models, and many depict detailed bakery and brewery scenes. In several models from the Middle Kingdom tomb of Meketre in Thebes, women are shown grinding grain and kneading dough while men perform other tasks related to baking and brewing.[22]

No iconographic evidence for women's production or consumption of beer has been identified in ancient Israel, although terracotta figurines of individuals grinding grain or kneading dough might depict stages in the brewing process. One such figurine, from a Late Iron Age context at Akhzib (ca. sixth century B.C.E.), shows a person of uncertain sex (likely a woman) standing behind a trough, kneading dough.[23] As will be discussed later, in the ancient Near East and Egypt, beer was often produced from baked bread loaves.

Based on these textual and artistic sources, it can be argued that ancient Israelite women drank beer, but no written or artistic sources directly link them to beer production. However, it is our contention that women dominated beer production in Iron Age Israel, precisely because beer was produced in the same space that bread was produced, and by the same women.

Beer Goddesses

Since women were the brewers of beer in antiquity, it should come as no surprise that the earliest deities associated with alcohol in the Near East and Egypt were female. Hathor–the Egyptian goddess of women *par excellence*–was the goddess of love and happiness and a protector of

---

[20] Curtis, *Ancient Food Technology*, fig. 8.
[21] J. H. Breasted Jr., *Egyptian Servant Statues* (Washington: Bollingen Foundation/Pantheon Books, 1948), pl. 22-24.
[22] H. E. Winlock, *Models of Daily Life in Ancient Egypt from the Tomb of Meket-Re at Thebes* (Cambridge: Harvard University Press, 1955).
[23] Pritchard, ed., *The Ancient Near East*, vol. 1, fig. 22.

women and children, fertility and childbirth. Among her many titles was the "Lady of Drunkenness," and she was the goddess of beer, wine and intoxication. Some inscriptions call her "the inventress of brewing."[24] As part of the annual Feast of Hathor, worshippers drank beer in reenactment of the story of the Destruction of Mankind. In this story, Hathor, in the guise of Sekhmet, goddess of destruction, was tricked into drunkenness during a killing spree initiated by her father, Ra, after consuming beer that had been dyed red with ochre to resemble blood. Hathor-Sekhmet mistook the beer, which had been made by the women of Heliopolis, for the blood of humankind and drank the beer until she passed out and humankind was saved. At the end of the story, Ra transformed this goddess of destruction into Hathor, the goddess of love.[25]

The most important female deity in Mesopotamia–Inanna, later Ishtar–was queen of heaven and earth, fertility, love, war, and alcohol. She was the patroness of tavern keepers, who in early Mesopotamia were usually women (see above). As part of the worship of Inanna, special cakes flavored with wine, beer, and fruits were baked for this "queen of heaven," and in one Sumerian poem, Inanna's genitals are described as "sweet" as "beer."[26]

There were two Sumerian goddesses of beer, Ninkasi and Siris, and "[t]he brewer's craft is the only profession in Mesopotamia which derives divine protection and social sanction from a goddess."[27] The famous *Hymn to Ninkasi* describes the process of brewing beer from loaves of bread.[28] Anchor Brewing Company reproduced this *bappir* bread in 1989, and their experiments showed that the hymn provides a linear account of brewing.[29]

Can we extend the idea of a goddess of beer to ancient Israel? This leads to a consideration of the identification of the Queen of Heaven mentioned in Jer 7 and 44. In Jer 7: 17-18, the prophet rails against the practice of women kneading dough to make cakes for the Queen of Heaven and pouring libations to other gods; in Jer 44: 15-20, the worship of this goddess includes burning incense, pouring libations, and making

---

[24] Curtis, *Ancient Food Technology*, 111.

[25] Lichtheim, *AEL* 2, 197-99.

[26] B. Alster, "Sumerian Love Songs," *RA* 79 (1985): 127-59.

[27] L. F. Hartman and A. L. Oppenheim, "On Beer and Brewing Techniques in Ancient Mesopotamia," (*JAOS* Supp. 10; Baltimore: American Oriental Society, 1950), 12.

[28] M. A. Civil, "A Hymn to the Beer Goddess and a Drinking Song," in *Studies Presented to A. Leo Oppenheim, June 7, 1964* (Chicago: The Oriental Institute of the University of Chicago, 1964), 67-89.

[29] *Sumerian Beer Project*, http://www.anchorbrewing.com/beers/ninkasi.htm

cakes in her image. Although the identification of this deity is still subject to debate, the evidence suggests that she may be a syncretistic deity incorporating the Canaanite goddess Astarte and Mesopotamian Ishtar.[30] The association between bread baking and libation pouring in these passages suggests that beer was the preferred beverage offering of the Israelite Queen of Heaven. Israel's male deity apparently shared a fondness for beer: four *hins* of *šēkār* (≈ 16 liters) were libated to Yahweh weekly (Num 28: 7-10).

Brewing Beer in Antiquity

Ancient brewing methods were quite different from modern ones. It was a relatively straightforward process that required at a minimum barley or wheat, water, and yeast. To make beer, grain was kept moist for a few days so that it would begin to germinate. After this, beer producers in antiquity had two options: heat the germinated grains so that they malted, and then throw these malted grains into water with some yeast and wait a few days; or, grind up the germinated grains and bake the flour into malted bread cakes.

Textual accounts and iconographic representations from the Near East and Egypt indicate that beer was often made from malted bread cakes; these are called *bappir* in the Sumerian *Hymn to Ninkasi*.[31] After the bread cakes were baked, they were crumbled and added to water in other ceramic jars. Several ancient texts, including Eccl 11:1-2, reference "throwing" (*šlḥ*) one's bread into the water to make the brew.[32] Yeast was then added to the mixture or yeast spores in the air would ferment the liquid. A few days later, the beer could be decanted and enjoyed, either plain or flavored with any number of fruits or spices.[33] Since beer does not store well and therefore was made for immediate consumption, the brewing process was ongoing and could be achieved with only one jar.[34] Making beer proved to be an excellent way to make the most of a harvest. By choosing to use grains to make beer rather than bake bread, people greatly increased the caloric intake from their harvest and added protein

---

[30] S. Ackerman, *Under Every Green Tree: Popular Religion in Sixth-Century Judah* (HSM 46; Atlanta: Scholars Press, 1992), 116-17.

[31] Civil, "A Hymn to the Beer Goddess and a Drinking Song."

[32] M. M. Homan, "Beer Production by Throwing Bread into Water: A New Interpretation of Qoh. XI 1-2," *VT* 52/2 (2002): 275-78.

[33] Ibid., "Beer and Its Drinkers: An Ancient Near Eastern Love Story," 91.

[34] Ibid., 86.

and other vitamins to their diet. Furthermore, the small amount of alcohol
killed off bacteria, making it safer to drink than water.

Archaeological Correlates for Baking and Brewing

Since brewing was integral to baking in antiquity, an examination of
the archaeological correlates for bread production, as well as the more
specialized implements required for beer production and consumption, is
required to learn more about the context of baking and the identity of
Israelite brewers. As D. Samuel admits in her study of bread production at
New Kingdom Amarna, identifying the archaeological evidence for
cooking, and specifically baking bread, is a challenge because baking and
cooking are highly complex processes.[35] Not only does the transformation
of grain to bread involve a series of complicated technologies, it also
involves numerous tools and installations that do not always survive in the
archaeological record. New Kingdom Egypt provides evidence for the use
of bread-making tools, including sieves, winnowing baskets, trays, and
paddles, stone mortars, wooden pestles, handstones, querns, brushes, jars,
and pieces of cloth for collecting flour from around grinding areas.[36]
Although it can be assumed that many of the same tools were used to
make bread in ancient Israel, organic items do not survive well in the
climate of Israel.

Using ethnography, ethnohistorical sources from the ancient Near East
(especially passages about grinding and baking in the Hebrew Bible),
iconography, and archaeological material from Iron Age I (ca. 1200-1000
B.C.E.) sites, Meyers identifies the following archaeological correlates of
bread production in ancient Israelite village households: stone grinding
equipment including upper and lower grinding stones, mortars and pestles;
kneading slabs; kneading troughs; ceramic bread pans and griddles; and
cooking installations, including *tabuns*, *tannurs*, and hearths.[37] The only
artifacts closely related to brewing and baking are ground stone tools,
including upper and lower grinding stones, mortars, and pestles, and these
were only used in the early stages of both bread and beer production. The
fact that earlier generations of excavators often overlooked ground stone
tools because their functions were considered to be self-evident, mundane,
and evidence of unimportant "women's work" means that even if their

---

[35] D. Samuel, "Bread Making and Social Interactions at the Amarna Workmen's
Village, Egypt," *World Archaeology* 31/1 (1999): 122.
[36] Ibid.
[37] Meyers, "Having Their Space and Eating There Too."

presence was noted in excavation reports, the tools themselves were often not illustrated.

In general, though, there is a pattern suggesting that sets of ground stone equipment used for small scale grain processing are found in courtyards and roofed areas within Iron Age household units. In some cases, individual families had their own toolkits, while in other excavated examples, groups of tool sets are found together in a room or courtyard.[38] It thus appears that sometimes the arduous task of grinding grain was carried out in groups; Meyers believes that this would have been the locus of important social interactions between women in the village community.[39] Although it is impossible to say with certainty that women were the sole grinders of grain and main bakers of bread in ancient Israel, the artistic, textual, and archaeological evidence–as well as the overwhelming ethnographic evidence–suggest that it was women who were most closely associated with these household activities.[40]

Despite the problems involved in identifying archaeological evidence for women's control of bread making technology, there are a number of archaeological correlates for beer production and consumption that have been identified at Iron Age and earlier sites in Israel: ceramic containers, including "flower pots" for baking bread; beer jugs and bottles; straw tip strainers; and fermentation stoppers. When these items are found in association with the tools (mostly ground stone) required to process grains for making bread, it provides insight into the technology of beer production and its socio-economic context.

Ceramic Containers

Throughout much of Egypt's ancient history, the so-called beer bottle or beer jar was used to store fermenting beer. This vessel has a globular base and narrow neck and is often shown in scenes of beer production, like the Old Kingdom examples discussed above. Moreover, one was found with the inscription "beer" (*ḥnqt*) on it.[41] In Israel, they have been found at Deir el-Balah, Beth Shean, and Tel Mor.[42]

---

[38] J. R. Ebeling and Y. M. Rowan, "The Archaeology of the Daily Grind: Ground Stone Tools and Food Production in the Southern Levant," *NEA* 67/2 (2004): 114-15.

[39] Meyers, "Having Their Space and Eating There Too."

[40] Ibid.

[41] Z. E. Szafranski, "Seriation and Aperture Index 2 of the Beer Bottles from Tell El-Dab'a, *Ägypten und Levante* 7 (1998): 96.

[42] Homan, "Beer and Its Drinkers: An Ancient Near Eastern Love Story," 86.

Other Egyptian ceramic forms closely linked to brewing are bread molds and "flowerpots," so named because of their perforated base. On the second register of Ti's tomb from Fifth Dynasty Egypt, bread molds and "flowerpots" are heated in fires, and then a batter is poured into them for baking (Fig. 3-2).[43]

Fig. 3-2. Beer producing scene from Ti's Tomb Detail[44]

Preheated molds prevented the batter from sticking, and the perforated bases on flowerpots allowed for easy extraction of the bread. Prototypes, including Old Kingdom bread molds (*bedja*), were used in producing bread and beer. Baking molds and vats were used in beer production in the Early Bronze I period settlement at 'En Besor in southern Canaan.[45]

Perforated "beer jugs" or side-spouted sieve jugs are well known from the Philistine ceramic assemblage (Fig. 3-3). Derived from Mycenaean IIIc prototypes, this vessel features a filtered spout formed by holes punched into the body at a ninety-degree angle from its handle. It was used for personal drinking rather than serving, as the user would hold the handle and place the spout upon his or her lips.[46] Side-spouted sieve jugs

---

[43] Epron, *Le Tombeau de Ti*, pl. LXVI.
[44] Courtesy of Th. Benderitter, www.osirisnet.net.
[45] R. Gophna and D. Gazit, "The First Dynasty Egyptian Residency at 'En Besor, *TA* 12 (1985): 9-16.
[46] Homan, "Beer and Its Drinkers: An Ancient Near Eastern Love Story," 91.

appear in quantity throughout Iron Age Israel, used for filtering beer, wine or a combination of these. While residue analyses have been inconclusive, other evidence suggests that these vessels were used to filter and serve beer, wine or a mixture of alcoholic beverages.[47]

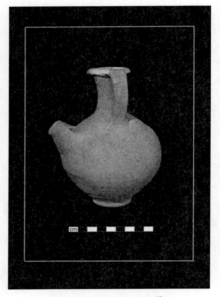

Fig. 3-3. Beer jug[48]

Straw Tip Strainers

As noted above, there are many representations of men and women drinking beer through straws in Mesopotamia and Egypt, and the remains of straws made of reeds and precious materials have been found in Sumer and Egypt. Reed straws do not usually survive in the archaeological record, but a number of perforated bone and metal objects found throughout the Near East have been identified as straw tip beer-strainers (Fig. 3-4). Examples have been found in Middle and Late Bronze and Iron Age contexts in Israel and Syria, and the findspot of a recently identified example at Middle Bronze Age Gesher in the Jordan Valley–inside a jar–

---

[47] Ibid., 92.
[48] Philistine "beer jug" or side-spouted sieve jug from Tell es-Safi. Courtesy of Aren M. Maeir, The Tell es-Safi/Gath Archaeological Project.

corroborates the iconographic evidence for their function.[49]

Fig. 3-4. Straw-tip strainer[50]

Fermentation Stoppers

The function(s) of perforated round clay objects has been debated over the past century (Fig. 3-5). Originally, excavators including Albright, Crowfoot, Kenyon, Macalister, Starkey and Tufnell identified them as loom weights. At Tell Qasîle, B. Mazar discovered about eighty of these objects along with a baking oven and mass quantities of pottery, and he suggested that they were "clay heaters . . . used for keeping food warm."[51] Similarly, S. Yeivin argued they were used to keep heat during the Sabbath, [52] while P. Lapp theorized that they were devises to absorb heat in cultic sacrifices.[53] Others have argued that they were weights used in fishing nets. Now, the theory that they functioned as weights for warp weighted vertical looms dominates archaeological publications.[54]

---

[49] A. M. Maeir and Y. Garfinkel, "Bone and Metal Straw-tip Beer-Strainers from the Ancient Near East," *Levant* 24 (1992): 218-23; A. M. Maeir, "The Bone Beverage Strainers," in *Excavations at Gesher* (AASOR 62; eds. S. Cohen and Y. Garfinkel; Boston: ASOR, 2007): 119-23.

[50] Bone straw-tip strainer from Gesher, Middle Bronze II. Courtesy of Yosef Garfinkel. Photographer Gabi Laron.

[51] B. Maisler (Mazar), "The Excavations at Tel Qasîle," *IEJ* 1 (1950-51): 197.

[52] S. Yeivin, *First Preliminary Report on the Excavations at Tel 'Gat': Seasons 1956-1958* (Jerusalem: Ministry of Education and Culture, Department of Antiquities, 1961).

[53] P. Lapp, "The 1968 Excavations at Tell Ta'annek," *BASOR* 195 (1969): 2-49.

[54] G. Friend, *Tell Ta'annek 1963-1968 III/2 The Loom Weights* (ed. K. Nashef; Birzeit: Birzeit University Press, 1998); O. Zimhoni, "The Pottery of Levels III and II/Unbaked Clay Stoppers as Evidence for the Context of Vessels," in *The Renewed Archaeological Excavations at Lachish (1973-1994)*, vol. 4, (ed. D. Ussishkin; Tel Aviv: Emery and Claire Yass Publications in Archaeology, 2004), 1791-92.

Fig. 3-5. Fermentation stoppers[55]

Recently, scholars have begun to question this theory, for a variety of reasons. First, most are far too fragile to have been used as loom weights. Second, while the warp weighted vertical loom was common in Europe, there is little evidence that it was used in Syro-Palestine. Instead, the horizontal ground loom was the most common form of loom in Egypt, Syria-Palestine and Mesopotamia.[56] The third difficulty is that the sides of these objects rarely show string marks, which would be expected in fragile clay objects that hung from threads. Fourth, they weigh much more than typical loom weights. Persian and Hellenistic period weights tended to weigh less than 200 grams, whereas these objects typically weigh in the range of 200-800 grams.[57] Fifth, this wide range in weight is problematic, as a consistent weight would be preferable for producing an even weave. Sixth, the perforations in these objects are most often vertical rather than horizontal. That is to say, when these objects are placed on the ground, the perforation is most often through the top. Loom weights, one would expect, would be designed so that when the object is set down the hole would be in the side. Finally, they are usually found in storerooms, an

---

[55] Fermentation stoppers from Zeitah, 10th-9th century B.C.E. Courtesy of R. E. Tappy and the Zeitah Excavations sponsored by the Pittsburgh Theological Seminary. Photographer M. Homan.
[56] Z. Gal, "Loom Weights or Jar Stoppers?" *IEJ* 39/3-4 (1989): 281-83.
[57] Ibid.

unlikely location for looms.

The best evidence that these perforated clay objects functioned as fermentation stoppers is that several have been found *in situ*, demonstrating that they functioned in such a capacity. At Tell el-Hammah, two stoppers were discovered resting in the mouths of storage jars. The carbonized remains of barley inside the jars indicate that these jars and stoppers were used to ferment beer.[58] At Tel Zeitah, one stopper was found inside a broken jar, where it had fallen when the jar was smashed (Fig. 3-6). Furthermore, the imprint of woven cloth, visible both inside and on the exterior of surfaces surrounding the perforations, suggests that these items functioned as fermentation stoppers. The cloth was placed inside the holes, thus reducing the amount of bacteria, which would spoil the brew,

Fig. 3-6. A fermentation stopper found inside a broken jar.[59]

---

[58] J. M. Cahill, "The Excavations at Tell el-Hammah: A Prelude to Amihai Mazar's Beth-Shean Valley Regional Project," in *I Will Speak the Riddles of Ancient Times: Archaeological and Historical Studies in Honor of Amihai Mazar on the Occasion of His Sixtieth Birthday*, vol. 2 (eds. A. M. Maeir and P. de Miroschedji; Winona Lake, Ind.: Eisenbrauns, 2006), 429-59.

[59] One fermentation stopper from Zeitah was found inside of a broken jar, as seen here. The context is a stratigraphically sealed pit that functioned as part of a late 10th-9th century B.C.E. building that was destroyed sometime in the mid-to-late 9th

but allowing the gasses that form during fermentation to escape. Moreover, the size of the objects often corresponds to the size of the mouths of jars found in close proximity.[60]

Attempts to correlate ground stone tools with the ceramic vessels, straw tip strainers and fermentation stoppers used for brewing beer at Iron Age sites have been difficult because of problems relating to the identification, preservation, and publication of these artifacts. An instructive example can be seen at Tel Qasile. In the eleventh century, Room 168 contained the remains of clay troughs, perhaps used in bread production, not far from a courtyard with a grinding installation. The excavator, A. Mazar, suggested that this complex may have been used for brewing beer. He related ten unbaked clay "loom weights" found throughout rooms in the complex to weaving activities.[61] However, when one considers the context, these "loom weights" should be identified as fermentation stoppers, strengthening the excavator's conclusion that beer was produced in this area. The correlation between these specialized artifacts and female-gendered spaces in Iron Age Israelite houses (see below) awaits a careful study of the published evidence.

Ethnographic Sources and Women's Control of Brewing

Although invaluable for understanding many aspects of ancient Israelite lifeways, there is little useful information about women's baking and brewing activities in the early ethnographic sources from Palestine[62] or in more recently published accounts of Palestinian village life.[63] Likewise, the ethnoarchaeological studies carried out in Iran and other

---

century B.C.E. Courtesy of R. E. Tappy and the Zeitah Excavations sponsored by the Pittsburgh Theological Seminary.

[60] Personal communication, R. E. Tappy, Director of the Zeitah Excavations.

[61] A. Mazar, *Excavations at Tell Qasîle: Part I. The Philistine Sanctuary: Architecture and Cult Objects* (Qedem 12; Jerusalem: Institute of Archaeology, Hebrew University of Jerusalem, 1980), 80.

[62] E.g., S. Avitzur, *Man and His Work* (Jerusalem: Carta/Israel Exploration Society, 1976) [Hebrew]; G. Dalman, *Arbeit und Sitte in Palestina III: Von der Ernte zum Mehl* (Hildesheim: G. Olms, 1964).

[63] E.g., S. Amiry and V. Tamari, *The Palestinian Village Home* (London: British Museum Publications, 1989); Y. Hirschfeld, *The Palestinian Dwelling in the Roman-Byzantine Period* (Jerusalem: Franciscan Printing Press and Israel Exploration Society, 1994).

parts of southwest Asia by Watson,[64] Kramer,[65] Horne[66] and others offer little information that sheds light on ancient baking and brewing.

The primary reason for this lacuna is the fundamental change in grinding technology that has occurred since the Iron Age: a specialized milling apparatus–the rotary millstone–replaced the upper and lower grinding stones known from archaeological contexts in the Middle East. In addition, the Islamic prohibition against alcohol stymied attempts to investigate the production and consumption of alcohol in Middle Eastern societies in the nineteenth and twentieth centuries.

Ethnographic sources can, however, offer insights into the spatial organization of ancient household baking activities, as Meyers has shown.[67] Since iconographic and textual sources from the ancient Near East and Egypt show that beer was often produced from bread cakes, the spatial correlates of brewing in the areas where bread production was carried out can now be identified. In the "four-room houses" found in Iron Age sites in Israel, for example, the central open space on the lower level may have been the main locus of baking and brewing activities. Only careful reconstruction of the findspots of archaeological correlates for bread and beer production from domestic structures can provide definitive identifications for such use of these spaces.

Ethnographic information also allows for the identification of female-gendered spaces in ancient Israelite households, and may even permit the recognition of women's control of household cooking tasks. Meyers, citing Hirschfeld, notes that ethnographic observations made during a 1970's survey of Ottoman-period houses in the Hebron district document the location of bread ovens in courtyards, sometimes serving several households. They reveal that women were not only in charge of bread production, but they also controlled space for household cooking activities.[68] Control of these cooking activities, Meyers believes, gave ancient Israelite women social, personal, and socio-political power in their households and villages.[69]

[64] P. J. Watson, *Archaeological Ethnology in Western Iran* (Tucson, Ariz.: University of Arizona Press, 1979).
[65] C. Kramer, *Village Ethnoarchaeology: Rural Iran in Archaeological Perspective* (New York: Academic Press, 1982).
[66] L. Horne, *Village Spaces: Settlement and Society in Northeastern Iran* (Washington, D.C.: Smithsonian Institution Press, 1994).
[67] Meyers, "Having Their Space and Eating There Too."
[68] Ibid., 24-25; see also Baadsgaard in this volume.
[69] Ibid., 30-32.

Future work on identifying women's control of brewing activities in ancient Israel will include the analysis of domestic spaces where the archaeological correlates of brewing have already been identified. Analysis of recently excavated material at sites such as Tell el-Hammah and Tel Zeitah, where fermentation stoppers have been found in association with jars used for brewing, will allow us to reconstruct household brewing technology. It will also provide insight into the gendered component of this activity and the power women gained as a result.

Conclusion

This paper has shown that women were closely associated with beer production and consumption in the ancient Near East and Egypt since at least the third millennium B.C.E. Although textual and iconographic evidence for women's control of beer production in Iron Age Israel is scant, ways of identifying the archaeological correlates for brewing, especially in female-gendered spaces, have been provided. Although its importance has been overlooked or denied until recently, it is certain that beer was a beverage common in ancient Israel, and even prescribed in Temple ritual (Num 28: 7-10) and drunk at sacrificial meals (Deut 14: 26). The brewing methods known from a variety of ancient Near Eastern and Egyptian sources give insight into both the technology and the social context of brewing, and this information can be used to reconstruct the manufacture and consumption of beer in Iron Age Israel.

Since brewing was an offshoot of bread production, and women were most closely associated with baking, one can conclude that women were the primary producers of beer in the Israelite household. Meyers states that women had a monopoly on the transformation of grains to make bread in the early Iron Age,[70] and to this we add the importance of brewing within the household context. Choosing to brew beer was a relatively easy way for women to increase the caloric and nutritional value of the grains they processed and therefore provide better nutrition for family members. In a future study, we will identify the archaeological correlates of beer production in female-gendered spaces within specific Israelite households, and through this demonstrate not only that women controlled household beer production, but also that the primary interests of women in ancient Israel were food, sustenance, and the preservation of the family.

---

[70] Ibid.

CHAPTER FOUR

BRINGING THE ARTIFACTS HOME: A SOCIAL INTERPRETATION OF LOOM WEIGHTS IN CONTEXT[1]

DEBORAH CASSUTO

Introduction

The changes that took place in women's roles during the latter half of the twentieth century have triggered a widespread academic interest in the study of gender. Part of this phenomenon is the focus on women and women's roles in ancient Israelite society where scholars such as Meyers,[2] Bird,[3] Ackerman[4] and others have been instrumental in bringing the subject to the forefront of academic discussion, endeavoring to ascertain the status of women within Israelite society. The discourses presented by these scholars accentuate the roles of women in cultic, commercial, and household activities. While these groundbreaking studies employ data

---

[1] This article is a revision of a paper delivered at the 2005 Annual Meeting of the American Schools of Oriental Research.
[2] C. Meyers, "Women and the Domestic Economy of Early Israel," pp. 33-43 in *Women in the Hebrew Bible* (ed. A. Bach; New York: Routledge, 1999), 33-34; idem, "Material Remains and Social Relations: Women's Culture in Agrarian Households of the Iron Age," in *Symbiosis, Symbolism, and the Power of the Past* (eds. W. G. Dever and S. Gitin; Winona Lake, Ind.: Eisenbrauns, 2003), 425-44; idem, "Engendering Syro-Palestinian Archaeology: Reasons and Resources," *NEA* 66/4 (2003): 185-97.
[3] P. A. Bird, "Women, Old Testament," in *ABD* 6, 951-57; idem, *Missing Persons and Mistaken Identities: Women and Gender in Ancient Israel* (Minneapolis: Fortress Press, 1997); idem, "The Place of Women in the Israelite Cultus," in *Women in the Hebrew Bible* (ed. A. Bach; New York: Routledge, 1999), 3-19.
[4] S. Ackerman, "Digging Up Deborah: Recent Hebrew Bible Scholarship on Gender and the Contribution of Archaeology," *NEA* 66/4 (2003): 172-84.

retrieved from the archaeological record, their main objective concentrates on interpretation based on Biblical narrative while, at times, incorporating ethnographic comparison. In these cases, use of archaeological data tends to be somewhat limited, merely skimming over the physical remnants of the past; neither their agenda nor their methods have a direct archaeological orientation. Artifacts can, in fact, tell the story of how things once were, if only they would be put to the test. By redirecting the focus towards the finds and the contexts in which they were found we can gain a greater understanding of how they were used and who used them. This paper focuses on the artifacts associated with female activities, namely loom weights and weaving, and engages in some aspects of the intricate problem of gender in Israelite society from a more archaeological perspective.

Division of Labor by Sex

In 1937, G. P. Murdock conducted the first of a series of cross-cultural ethnographic studies, in which he identified a phenomenon he called the "Division of Labor by Sex."[5] This is the idea that women and men in all traditional cultures have significantly different domestic tasks. While many of the types of tasks attributed to each sex vary from culture to culture, there is a tendency in traditional societies for women to be responsible for gathering fuel and greens, fetching water, cooking, laundering, spinning, weaving and sewing. J. Brown emphasizes the compatibility of these activities with the primary task of child rearing, which demands that the mother be able to perform tasks that are close to home and that can be disrupted easily.[6]

Male Artifacts

Since the majority of archaeological projects emphasize the reconstruction of chronology and historical events, the reflection of gender roles in the material culture has not received sufficient attention. Attempts

---

[5] G. P. Murdock, *Social Structure* (New York: Macmillan, 1949); "World Ethnographic Sample," *American Anthropologist* 59 (1957): 664-87; idem, "Comparative Data on the Division of Labor by Sex," in *Culture and Society: Twenty-Four Essays* (ed. G. P. Murdock; Pittsburgh: University of Pittsburgh Press, 1965), 308-10; G. P. Murdock and C. Provost, "Factors in the Division of Labor by Sex: A Cross-Cultural Analysis," *Ethnology* 12 (1973): 202-25.
[6] J. K. Brown, "A Note on the Division of Labor by Sex," *American Anthropologist* 72 (1970): 1073-78.

to identify gender in artifacts bring us promptly to the discovery that the vast majority of artifacts are, in fact, associated with male activities. Ancient public buildings, storehouses, fortifications, roads and dwellings were all designed and built by men. The artisans who produced metal objects such as arrowheads and knives, fine pottery, and inscriptions regularly passed their trades from father to son.

Female Artifacts

Traditionally, the presence of women has been identified in the archaeological record based on discoveries of jewelry and fine cosmetic implements, that is, by artifacts used by women to enhance their appearance. Throughout history women, particularly royal women, have been depicted wearing various pieces of jewelry, i.e. necklaces, bracelets, rings and earrings; men however, have been known to wear specific accoutrements, as well as symbols of status such as signet rings, scarabs, pendants and headdresses.[7] Women used cosmetic implements such as small alabaster jars, mixing and application sticks, mirrors, and elaborately made kohl spoons in the application of rouge and eye paints; here too, however, men, particularly royalty or priests, were also known to have used makeup.[8] In short, the interpretation of jewelry and cosmetic implements as female markers can be ambiguous, as well as misleading as indicators of the general female population.

The commonplace artifacts that reflect domestic female-specific quotidian activities such as weaving, spinning and food preparation would be better suited as indicators of women. Women have long been associated with the crafts of spinning and weaving, particularly within the home. Clusters of loom weights, spindle whorls, cooking pots, grinding stones, mortars and pestles are all indicative of female-specific activities carried out within the home, viz. food preparation and textile production. Cooking pots, grinding stones, mortars and pestles designate the loci of kitchen activities. The loom weights from heavy warp-weighted looms (Fig 4-1) indicate where looms were located and where weaving was carried out. The spatial distribution of these artifacts when "returned" to their find-spots reveals how the women of the house utilized their household space.

---

[7] L. Meskel, "Intimate archaeologies: the case of Kha and Merit," *WA* 28/3 (1998): 363-79; E. E. Platt, "Jewelry, Ancient Israelite," in *ABD* 3, 823-34.
[8] M. Dayagi-Mendels, "Cosmetics," in *OEANE* 1, 67-69; M. Dayagi-Mendels, *Perfumes and Cosmetics in the Ancient World* (Jerusalem: Israel Museum, 1989).

Fig. 4-1. Vertical warp-weighted loom[9]

Weaving as a Gender-Specific Activity

Despite such gender-specificity, additional research has shown a degree of culturally determined variability in such a division of labor, often on a regional and/or environmental basis. Some of these gender-specific tasks are considered "swing" activities and may be performed in some societies by one gender, and in other societies by the other. Weaving, for example, is a "swing" activity meaning that in some societies it was predominantly done by men and in other societies it was predominantly done by women.[10] Cross-cultural data from traditional societies indicate that in Africa weaving is considered a male-specific activity, whereas in traditional communities in Europe and in the Eastern Mediterranean it is a task performed 84 percent of the time by the woman of the house. The relevance of the ethnographic comparanda increases significantly when societies are similar in other ways, i.e. origin, religion, and geographic location. Therefore, the examples used in this study for ethnographic and ethnoarchaeological comparisons are limited to the Middle East and the Mediterranean, and thus to societies that are most likely to resemble the Iron Age II inhabitants of the Southern Levant.[11]

---

[9] Photo courtesy of Orit Shamir, Israel Antiquities Authority.

[10] Murdock and Provost, "Factors in the Division of Labor by Sex," 209.

[11] Murdock and Provost, "Factors in the Division of Labor by Sex," 216-20; Meyers, "Material Remains," 433.

This paper focuses primarily on the contexts of the loom weights, where they were found within dwellings, and which artifacts and associated finds were found in proximity to them. The patterns observed are interpreted employing analogous comparisons to ethnographic and archaeological data. This enables a reconstruction of the use of domestic space, which illuminates the daily lives of its inhabitants, and reflects upon their perceptions of the world, their beliefs and their culture.

Women and Weaving in Antiquity

Evidence of the association between women with weaving in antiquity is abundant. Textual and iconographic documentation depict women weaving in workshops and at home.

Mesopotamia

The earliest iconographic and written records from the eastern Mediterranean and the Near East frequently depict women of any status, from the royal and elite to the poorest factory workers, spinning and weaving.[12] Documents from Mesopotamia show that women were responsible for textile production both domestically and, in several cases, commercially.[13] Mesopotamia was renowned for the quality of its "Akkadian textiles." These woolen fabrics, according to second millennium Akkadian documents, were in high demand in the Anatolian and Assyrian markets, higher even than the local textile products. The women who produced "Akkadian textiles" ran small production centers from their homes. The fine cloths that they made were either sent to their merchant husbands, or sold locally to provide for their households.[14]

---

[12] R. P. Wright, "Technology, Gender, and Class: Worlds of Difference in Ur III Mesopotamia," pp. 79-110 in *Gender and Archaeology* (ed. R. P. Wright; Philadelphia: University of Pennsylvania Press, 1996), 86; E. J. W. Barber, *Prehistoric Textiles* (Princeton: Princeton University Press, 1991), 193.

[13] R. P. Wright, "Technology, Gender, and Class," 99; K. R. Veenhof, "Some Social Effects of Old Assyrian Trade," *Iraq* 39 (1977): 109-18.

[14] J. N. Postgate, *Early Mesopotamia: Society and Economy at the Dawn of History* (London: Routledge, 1992), 213; D. T. Potts, *Mesopotamian Civilization: The Material Foundations*, (London: Athlone, 1997), 235; Veenhof, "Some Social Effects of Old Assyrian Trade," 114.

Egypt

The Egyptians were well known throughout the ancient Near East for their fine linens. From as early as the Old Kingdom, textile production was the exclusive domain of women and, as in other cultures, a prospective wife's weaving aptitude was considered an asset to the household.[15] Funerary wall paintings and a Twelfth Dynasty model of a "weaving workshop" depict women spinning threads, preparing the warp and weaving at the loom.[16] Textual and archaeological evidence indicate that workmen's wives wove in their homes in the workmen's villages at Deir el-Medina and Amarna, probably selling or trading surplus cloth to supplement household costs.[17] The beginning of the New Kingdom introduces men into the predominantly female textile workforce contemporary with the newly developed vertical two-beam loom. It is most likely that this change in gender involvement occurred as part of the commercialization of textile production, a phenomenon, which according to O'Brian,[18] is well known throughout history. However, there is no evidence that such changes would have occurred on the domestic level, as well.[19]

The Aegean

The evidence from the Aegean that links women and weaving is overwhelming. Spinning and weaving were primary activities performed by Greek women, to the extent that the relationship of women to these activities became a powerful metaphor for femininity and a woman's morality. When a female baby was born, the door to the home was decorated with wool.[20] When a tombstone relief described a woman as one

---

[15] G. Vogelsang–Eastwood, "Weaving, Looms, and Textiles," in *OEAE* 3, 488-92; G. Robins, *Women in Ancient Egypt* (Cambridge: Harvard University Press, 1993), 44; E. J. W. Barber, "Textiles: Textiles of the Neolithic through the Iron Ages," *OEANE* 5, 190-95.

[16] Barber, "Ancient Textiles," 85.

[17] Robins, *Women in Ancient Egypt*, 126.

[18] R. O'Brian, "Who Weaves and Why? Weaving, Loom Complexity, and Trade," *Cross-Cultural Research* 33/1 (1999): 30-42.

[19] Robins, *Women in Ancient Egypt*, 104.

[20] K. Carr, "Women's Work: Spinning and Weaving in the Greek Home," *Archéologie des textiles des origins au Ve siècle: Actes du colloque de Lattes, Octobre 1999* (2000): 163.

who "filled her time spinning," it implied that she was a virtuous woman. She may also have been buried with her spindle whorl.[21]

The spindle, the distaff and the loom took on female-specific attributes, such as decency and fidelity.[22] Weaving was the symbol of the virtuous and fastidious woman; we find repeated references to this in the textual record, where Homer's Penelope at the loom is the prototypical loyal wife, devoted to her husband at all costs. The goddess Calypso lived alone on an island and filled her days by working at her loom. Aphrodite was associated with spinning, Athena was the patron of weaving, and the Moirae were present at every birth to spin out the thread of life and to cut it. Vases from the Archaic through the Classical periods in ancient Greece regularly depict women busy at a variety of activities associated with weaving.

Biblical Texts

The Bible throws light upon the traditions of ancient Israel. Biblical references link women with spinning and weaving. When the Children of Israel received orders to build an ark for the Covenant, the women were enlisted to spin the yarn to be woven into cloth (Exod 35: 25-26, 35). In the story of Samson and Delilah, she wove his locks into the warp threads of her loom (Judg 16:13-14); and in 2 Kgs 23:7, women wove the covering for the *ashera* deity. Proverbs 31 describes the virtuous wife who works incessantly at spinning and weaving, in order to provide the best for her family. And, David's curse at Joab (2 Sam 3:29), that his sons shall be spinners, is even more telling of the femininity of textile production: "May [the guilt] fall upon the head of Joab and all his father's house. May the house of Joab never be without someone suffering from a discharge or an eruption, or a male who handles the spindle, or one slain by the sword, or one lacking bread."[23]

---

[21] Ibid., 163.
[22] Ibid., 163-64.
[23] H. A. Hoffner Jr., "Symbols for Masculinity and Feminity: Their Use in Ancient Near Eastern Sympathetic Magic Rituals," *JBL* 85 (1966): 326-34; M. Malul, "David's Curse of Joab (2 Sam. 3:29) and the Social Significance of *m h z y q b p l k*," *AuOr* 10 (1996): 49-67; B. Lang, "Women's Work, Household and Property in Two Mediterranean Societies: A Comparative Essay on Proverbs XXXI 10-31," *VT* 54/ 2 (2004): 188-207.

Method: "Bringing the Artifacts Home"

The process of archaeological excavation removes artifacts from their findspots, a procedure that in effect is a form of destruction. However, in order to interpret the social behaviors and interactions of the ancient inhabitants, artifacts must be "returned" to their original findspots, thus enabling spatial analyses and the identification of gender-specific activity areas.[24] By focusing on the findspots of loom weights and their associated artifacts, we can identify where weaving took place and which activities were performed in conjunction with it.

Iron Age II Levantine "Four-Room" Houses

Throughout the world and throughout time architecture has been understood as a reflection both of function and of geographical requirements influenced by societal values.[25] To paraphrase the first century B.C.E. Classical architect Vitruvius, there is meaning to be found in a building.[26] This suggests that several factors affect domestic design, not the least of which are cultural standards, and by extension, regional styles. One such style, which is of particular relevance to the present study, is the "four-room house." This distinct architectural style is common throughout the southern Levant during the Iron Age, and is associated with the Israelite settlement.[27] The recurrence of this particular

---

[24] Similar studies have been conducted for Iron Age contexts in the region. They include: J. W. Hardin, *An Archaeology of Destruction: Households and the Use of Domestic Space at Iron II Tel Halif* (Ph.D. diss., University of Arizona, 2001); G. van der Kooij, "Use of Space in Settlements–an Exercise upon Deir 'Alla-IX," in *Moving Matters Ethnoarchaeology in the Near East: Proceedings of the International Seminar held at Cairo 7-10 December 1998* (eds. W. Wendrich and G. van der Kooij; Leiden: Leiden University, Research School of Asian and Amerindian Studies, 2002), 63-73.

[25] D. Sanders, "Behavioral Conventions and Archaeology: Methods for the Analysis of Ancient Architecture," pp. 43-72 in *Domestic Architecture and the Use of Space: an Interdisciplinary Cross-Cultural Study* (ed. S. Kent; Cambridge: Cambridge University Press, 1990), 43.

[26] D. J. W. Meijer, "Ground Plans and Archaeologists: On Similarities and Comparisons," pp. 221-36 in *To the Euphrates and Beyond: Archaeological Studies in Honor of Maurits N. van Loon* (eds. O. M. C. Haex, H. H. Curvers, and P. M. M. G. Akkermans; Rotterdam: Balkema, 1989), 221.

[27] Y. Shiloh, "The Four-Room House: Its Situation and Function in the Israelite City," *IEJ* 20 (1970): 180-90; idem, "The Four-Room House-The Israelite Type-House?," *ErIsr* 11 (1973): 277-85 [Hebrew]; E. Netzer, "Domestic Architecture in

style in this context reflects an unambiguous set of cultural norms particular to Israelite society.

Although the architecture differs slightly from site to site, the basic plan remains the same: an elongated central room entered from the outside on its short end, which allows access to one or two parallel elongated rooms on one or both sides, and a rear broad room at the end opposite the entrance. Variations include additional subdivisions of rooms, an entrance room or courtyard and often a row of pillars that divide the entrance room along one or both of the parallel spaces. Scholars differ as to whether the main area of the "four-room" house was an open-air courtyard or an enclosed roofed room.[28] Debates concerning the source of the "four-room" house plan question whether it had functional advantages associated with a previously nomadic society, or it was derived or adapted from Late Bronze Age dwellings.[29] More recently a third proposal suggests that the layout of the "four-room" house reflects the Israelites' ethnic behaviors that evolved from the laws of impurity that applied to the relationship between a man and his wife during her menses. Hence, the spatial division of the dwelling enables a woman to move more freely while avoiding contact with the men of the house.[30] A contextual study of artifacts can shed light on

---

the Iron Age," in *The Architecture of Ancient Israel* (eds. A. Kempinski and R. Reich; Jerusalem: Israel Exploration Society, 1992), 193-201; G. E. Wright, "A Characteristic North Israelite House," in *Archaeology in the Levant: Essays for Kathleen Kenyon* (eds. P. R. S. Moorey and P. Parr; Warminster: Aris and Phillips, 1978), 149-54; S. Bunimovitz and A. Faust, "Ideology in Stone: Understanding the Four-Room House," *BAR* 28/4 (2002): 31-40, 59-60; idem, "Building Identity: The Four-Room House and the Israelite Mind," in *Symbiosis, Symbolism, and the Power of the Past* (eds. W. G. Dever and S. Gitin; Winona Lake, Ind.: Eisenbrauns, 2003), 411-23; A. Faust and S. Bunimovitz, "The Four Room House: Embodying Iron Age Israelite Society," *NEA* 66/1-2 (2003): 22-31; A. Faust, "Burnished Pottery and Gender Hierarchy in Iron Age Israelite Society," *JMA* 15/1 (2002): 53-73.

[28] Shiloh, "The Four-Room House-The Israelite Type-House?," 278; Wright, "A Characteristic North Israelite House," 151; Netzer, "Domestic Architecture in the Iron Age," 196-97; L. Stager, "The Family in Ancient Israel," *BASOR* 260 (1985): 1-35, 15; P. M. M. Daviau, "Domestic Architecture in Iron Age Ammon: Building Materials, Construction Techniques, and Room Arrangement," pp. 113-36 in *Ancient Ammon* (eds. B. MacDonald and R. W. Younker; Leiden: Brill, 1999), 128-29.

[29] F. Braemer, *L'architecture domestique du Levant à l'Âge du Fer* (Paris: Protohistoire du Levant, 1982); J. S. Holladay, "House, Israelite," pp. 308-18 in *ABD* 3, 309; idem, "Four-Room House," pp. 337-42 in *OEANE* 2, 337.

[30] Bunimovitz and Faust, "Ideology in Stone;" Faust and Bunimovitz, "The Four Room House."

domestic gender-interactions and their meanings, including the ways in which inhabitants of the "four-room" house used their space, and divided their activity areas.

Test Case: Iron Age II Dwellings at Timnah/Tel Batash

The test case presented here is based on the publication of the dwellings at Timnah/Tel Batash, in Israel's Shephelah–Lowlands.[31] These publications, which include extensive descriptions of the material finds, the stratigraphy and the plans and sections, are well suited to the application of the "returning the artifacts home" method. Of the several buildings excavated by A. Mazar and G. L. Kelm between 1977 and 1989, significant concentrations of loom weights were found in four buildings from Stratum II, dated to the destruction at the beginning of the sixth century B.C.E. Three of these are prime examples of Iron Age II houses of the "four-room" category: Building 743 in Area D and Buildings F607 and F608 in Area F. [32] These buildings are characterized by the typical row of monolithic pillars that divided the largest space of the building into two separate oblong areas, and the broad room at the back of the house, which was subdivided as well.

---

[31] A. Mazar, *Timnah (Tel Batash) Final Reports I: Stratigraphy and Architecture* (Qedem 37; Jerusalem: Hebrew University, 1997); A. Mazar and N. Panitz-Cohen, *Timnah (Tel Batash) Final Reports II: The Finds from the First Millennium BCE* (Qedem 42; Jerusalem: Hebrew University, 2001).

[32] Mazar, *Timnah (Tel Batash) Final Reports I*, 205-11, 240-44; Mazar and Panitz-Cohen, *Timnah (Tel Batash) Final Reports II*, 163-85; D. C. Browning, "Loomweights," in *Timnah (Tel Batash) Final Reports II: The Finds from the First Millennium BCE* (Qedem 42; A. Mazar and N. Panitz-Cohen; Jerusalem: Hebrew University, 2001), 248-58.

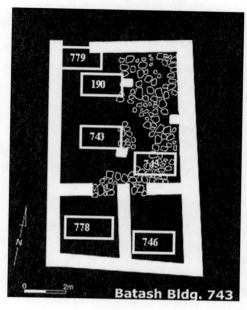

Fig. 4-2. Timna/Tel Batash Building 743[33]

The majority of artifacts from Building 743 were found in Locus 743, the entrance room of the main section of the house divided by stone pillars from the eastern section, where a cluster of forty-one loom weights was found along the western wall (Fig. 4-2). The provenance of this assemblage designates where the loom was located at the time of the building's destruction. In addition to the loom weights several bowls, kraters, juglets, store jars, and grinding tools were found reflecting the domestic nature of this room.

Locus 181 and Locus 745, east of the central pillars, had significantly fewer artifacts. It has been suggested that Locus 181, a paved section divided by pillars, was used as a stable for housing small domestic animals.[34] The paved floor facilitated cleaning and the collection of dung used for burning fuel.

---

[33] Adapted with permission from Mazar and Panitz-Cohen, *Timnah (Tel Batash) Final Reports II*, 166.
[34] Mazar, *Timnah (Tel Batash) Final Reports I*, 210.

The material remains of Rooms 778 and 746, the southern rooms in the rear of the house, included kitchen utensils (bowls, juglets, cooking pots, grinding stones and storage jars), as well as a scarab, three loom weights, and an arrowhead that may have come from the destruction of the site. The character of this assemblage indicates that these areas were used for dining and living quarters.[35]

The character of the loom weight finds in Building 743 can be divided into two categories: (1) loom weights found in small groups or in scattered contexts; and (2) those found in a single large cluster. It is difficult to determine whether the loom weights found in small groups or scattered contexts were actually used as loom weights at the end of the Stratum II occupation. It is possible that they were dispersed from their original location by the destruction. Alternatively, they may have had other secondary uses, such as stoppers for wine jars.[36] The cluster of loom weights found in Locus 743, on the other hand, undeniably represents a warp-weighted loom, given the large number of loom weights and their proximity to one another. The character of the assemblage found in this area points towards an activity area that included food preparation (i.e. a mortar, a pestle, a grinding stone, cooking pots and kraters), spinning (two spindle whorls), and weaving. This area is unmistakably identifiable as a multifunctional area where the women of the dwelling conducted their gender-specific quotidian activities.

Buildings F607 and F608 in Area F belong to Stratum II as well (Fig. 4-3), and share a plan similar to that of Building 743. However, distinct from Building 743, each of these buildings contained an oven located in the main section of the building. In Building F607, the area east of the pillars was only partially paved and included several built installations: a stone vat, an oven made of stone and plaster with burnt remains, and a hollow pit containing burnt ash. A trough constructed between the two pillars shows that the paved section of the building was used for keeping small domestic animals. The area west of the trough produced only one bowl, one krater and one jug. In contrast, the assemblage found in the southwestern corner of this section includes a few loom weights, bowls, storage jars, a lamp, a juglet, a mortar, and a krater, indicating that this part of the building was not used as a stock hold for domestic animals.

---

[35] Mazar and Panitz-Cohen, *Timnah (Tel Batash) Final Reports II*, 165.
[36] Z. Gal, "Loom Weights or Jar Stoppers?," *IEJ* 39 (1989): 281-83.

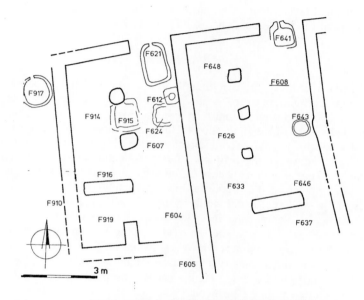

Fig. 4-3. Timnah/Tel Batash Buildings F607 and F608[37]

Locus F607, located between the oven and the ash pit, produced the majority of artifacts. A group of forty loom weights was found, as well as several bowls, jugs, four cooking pots, a few storage jars, juglets, kraters, a grinding stone, an ash pit and an oven. The character, quantity and variety of the assemblage suggests that it was a multi-functional area in which both food preparation and textile production were carried out.

In Building F608 as well, the western section is paved with cobblestones, suggesting its function as a stable. Animal bones found among the burnt debris that covered the paved floor may be the remains of animals, trapped within the destruction inferno. Beyond the paved area, a plaster floor surrounded the basin at the threshold, and the majority of artifacts were found on it, in the vicinity of the oven. The assemblage from this area contained cooking pots, bowls, a large grinding stone, storage jars and two flattened stones that, according to the excavators, may have been used for making bread. The assemblage clearly shows that food was

---

[37] Adapted with permission from Mazar and Panitz-Cohen, *Timnah (Tel Batash) Final Reports II*, 171.

prepared and heated here. The cluster of some thirty loom weights found nearby points to the site of household textile production.

Discussion

Reconstruction of the dwellings from Tel Batash/Timnah shows that the main concentrations of artifacts, particularly implements used for weaving and food preparation, were consistently found in one of the two elongated rooms of the domestic dwellings. More specifically, they were found in the main activity room, directly accessed by the main threshold to the house. However the artifacts' locations within these main activity rooms were not consistent. These differences demonstrate the influence of individual choice in the organization of household space. As I. Hodder notes, "[i]n each particular context, beliefs and material symbols are negotiated and manipulated in different ways as part of individual and group strategies."[38] A case can be made for the variability of formation processes in these findings. However, when this method is used on dwellings from other sites, which may or may not have undergone the same abandonment processes, certain patterns become apparent. The most evident of these is that when concentrations of loom weights are found within a dwelling, they are consistently found in proximity to implements used for the preparation of food.

Ethnographic studies report that the woman's half of the Bedouin tent is where all tasks related to laundry, food preparation, cooking, storage, spinning, bathing and child rearing are conducted.[39] Women in the Bedouin village of Ed-Dhahiriya are responsible for determining how the spaces within their houses are used, and where things are kept.[40] Ethnographic and ethnoarchaeological studies in Iran and Afghanistan, conducted by C. Kramer and P. J. Watson, document specific examples in which household looms are located in the kitchens, where women also prepare food.[41] In

---

[38] I. Hodder, *Symbols in Action: Ethnoarchaeological Studies of Material Culture* (Cambridge: Cambridge University Press: 1982), 217.

[39] L. L. Layne, "Village Bedouin: Patterns of Change from Mobility to Sedentism in Jordan," pp. 345-73 in *Method and Theory for Activity Area Research* (ed. S. Kent; New York: Columbia University Press, 1987), 356-60.

[40] Y. Hirschfeld, *The Palestinian Dwelling in the Roman-Byzantine Period* (Jerusalem: Franciscan Printing, 1995), 182.

[41] C. Kramer, "An Archaeological View of a Contemporary Kurdish Village: Domestic Architecture, Household Size, and Wealth," pp. 139-63 in *Ethnoarchaeology: Implications of Ethnography for Archaeology* (ed. C. Kramer; New York: Columbia University Press, 1979), 147; *Village Ethnoarchaeology*

ancient Israelite dwellings, these multi-functional gender-specific areas were found in the elongated front rooms, where the majority of the household's daily activities were conducted. The woman working in this central location had access to all she might require from the various adjacent rooms. Thus, she could procure products from storage and tend to domestic animals, while simultaneously keeping an eye on her children and on all her family's needs.

As a corpus, this evidence reveals that Iron Age II domestic life in the Land of Israel focused on the woman's centrality in the household, since it was she who determined where food preparation and weaving took place. Inasmuch as these took place in the most central room of the house, the woman is understood to have "manned" a position that controlled access to all the other rooms within the dwelling. These findings indicate that Israelite homes differed from those of societies that restricted women's social contact, and which situated women and their activities in the more isolated rooms. In all likelihood, it was the woman of the Israelite household who decided upon the order and location of the space in which she carried out her quotidian domestic tasks. This strong female presence in the center of the dwelling may be the archaeological evidence of what is described in Prov 31, where the "virtuous woman" is portrayed as running the household and tending to all her family's daily needs, while her husband and sons were active outside the domestic domain.

(New York: Academic Press, 1982), 99-100; P. J. Watson, *Archaeological Ethnography in Western Iran* (Tucson, Ariz.: University of Arizona Press, 1979), 21.

CHAPTER FIVE

INFANT MORTALITY AND WOMEN'S RELIGION IN THE BIBLICAL PERIODS[1]

ELIZABETH ANN R. WILLETT

The Problem of Infant Mortality in the Ancient Near East

The skeletal analysis of human remains from archaeological excavations in the eastern Mediterranean region confirms biblical clues to Israelites' preoccupation with fertility, infant mortality, and short female lifespan. The difficult subsistence environment of the hill country, with its dependence on unreliable rainfall and a large labor force for successful agriculture, forms the background of the fertility aspects of Canaanite and Israelite religions. Limited female longevity and a high rate of infant mortality presented major obstructions to population stability or growth. Israelites and Babylonians considered women at risk during pregnancy and childbirth and their infants at risk until they were weaned.[2] The extreme danger period for mothers and newborns coincides with the forty-day state of impurity that survives in the Jewish, Christian, and Islamic religions.[3]

---

[1] This article is a revision of a paper presented at the 2001 Annual Meetings of the American Schools of Oriental Research and the Society of Biblical Literature, and an article published in *DavarLogos* 1/1 (2002): 27-42.

[2] K. van der Toorn, *From Her Cradle to Her Grave: The Role of Religion in the Life of the Israelite and the Babylonian Woman* (Sheffield: Sheffield Academic Press, 1994), 25-26.

[3] E. Lichty, "Demons and Population Control," *Expedition* 13/ 2 (1971): 23.

Archaeological Evidence for High Infant Mortality
and Short Female Lifespan

During the whole time span from Upper Paleolithic to the nineteenth century C.E. in the Near East, most women died before menopause,[4] living on the average only to age thirty.[5] Plagues and military conquests launched the Iron Age with as much as a four-fifths reduction in population,[6] and studies show very high infant mortality for 1150-650 B.C.E. Because of endemic disease and poor socioeconomic conditions, of the average 4.1 births per female, only 1.9 survived. From 650-300 B.C.E., this improved to 4.6 births per female, with 3.0 survivors.[7] Data from the excavation of Roman period Meiron in Upper Galilee indicate that 50 percent of the individuals identified within the *kokhim* and central chamber died before age 18, and 70 percent of those childhood and adolescent deaths occurred within the first five years of life.[8] Osteological analysis of communal burials at other excavations in Israel and Jordan produced similar results.[9] On average, 35 percent of all individuals died before age five.[10] High infant mortality kept nuclear families small enough to live in the familiar

---

[4] J. L. Angel, "Ecology and Population in the Eastern Mediterranean," *World Archaeology* 4/1 (1972): 102.

[5] C. L. Meyers, *Discovering Eve: Ancient Israelite Women in Context* (New York: Oxford University Press, 1988), 112-13.

[6] Ibid., 70.

[7] Angel, "Ecology," 95.

[8] P. Smith, E. Bornemann, and J. Zias, "Human Skeletal Remains," in *Excavations at Ancient Meiron, Upper Galilee, Israel 1971-72, 1974-75, 1977* (eds. E. M. Meyers, J. F. Strange, and C. Meyers; Cambridge, Mass.: ASOR, 1981), ch. 7.2.

[9] For a comparative chart and references see P. Bikai and M. Perry, "Petra North Ridge Tombs 1 and 2: Preliminary Report," *BASOR* 324 (2001): 59-78. For earlier reports from Lachish and Jericho, see M. Giles, "The Human and Animal Remains: The Crania," in *Lachish III: The Iron Age* (ed. O. Tufnell; London: Oxford University Press, 1953), 405-9; idem, "The Human and Animal Remains: The Crania," in *Lachish IV: The Bronze Age* (ed. O. Tufnell; London: Oxford University Press, 1958), 318-22; D. L. Risdon, "A Study of the Cranial and Other Human Remains from Palestine Excavated at Tell Duweir (Lachish) by the Wellcome-Marston Archaeological Research Expedition," *Biometrika* 31 (1939): 99-166; D. R. Hughes, "Report on Metrical and Non-metrical Aspects of E.B.-M.B. and Middle Bronze Human Remains from Jericho," in *Excavations at Jericho*, vol. 2 (ed. K. M. Kenyon; London: British School of Archaeology in Jerusalem, 1965), 664-85.

[10] Meyers, *Discovering Eve*, 112.

four-room house.[11] Even without an epidemic, families would have had to produce almost twice the number of children they wanted in order to achieve optimal family size.

Biblical Evidence for Anxiety about Infant Mortality and Female Lifespan

Biblical clues affirm anxieties about infant mortality and female lifespan in Iron Age Israel. Jacob's wife Rachel characterizes the archaeological statistics in that she has trouble conceiving, then dies during her second childbirth (Gen 30:1-2; 35:16-17). The biblical creation and flood narratives instruct couples to be fruitful and multiply (Gen 1:28; 9:1, 7). Meyers traces the origin of the Gen 2-3 narrative to Israelite families' survival and population problems, and she interprets what are traditionally perceived as curses, as prescriptives for men to sweat working the ground six days a week and women to "increase their toil and pregnancies."[12] The Lev 27 table of economic worth assigns adolescent women less economic value than adult women, probably because at puberty they became susceptible to the mortality of childbearing. The demographic situation in early Iron Age Transjordan encouraged taking virgins as war trophies, even after the Midianite Baal Peor crisis (Num 25:1-8; 31:9-18). When Israelite kings and military men married women from Egypt, Phoenicia, Syria, Moab and Ammon, they imported their family religions with them.

Egyptian Fears of Child-Stealing Spirits

Biblical stories of Joseph and the Exodus emphasize the problems Egypt had with plagues and famine (Exod 7:14-12:30). The sixteenth century B.C.E. Berlin Papyrus 3027 contains incantations for mothers and children that exhibit Egyptian fears of child-stealing spirits:

Another (charm).
May you flow away, he who comes in the darkness and enters in furtively, with his nose behind him, and his face reversed, failing in what he came for!
May you flow away, she who comes in the darkness and enters in furtively,

---

[11] D. C. Hopkins, "Life on the Land: The Subsistence Struggles of Early Israel," *BA* 50 (1987): 182.
[12] Meyers, *Discovering Eve*, 105.

with her nose behind her, and her face turned backwards, failing in what
she came for!
Have you come to kiss this child? I will not let you! Have you come to
silence (him)? I will not let you set silence over him! Have you come to
injure him? I will not let you injure him! Have you come to take him
away? I will not let you take him away from me![13]

Mesopotamian Child-Stealing Demons

Scanty diet and medical care, along with poor sanitation, forced the rate
of miscarriages, stillbirths, infant mortality, and women's death in
childbirth just as high in Mesopotamia, and spawned its mythology of
child-stealing demons.[14] Textual and iconographic examples that begin
with third millennium B.C.E. Sumerian texts, continue through Akkadian
and early Babylonian Bronze Age cultures, and culminate in seventh
century Neo-Assyrian Iron Age inscribed amulets, attest that Babylonians
and Assyrians guarded against them through family religious practices and
prayers to protect mother and child (Fig. 5-1). Texts indicate that women
stood a deity figurine in their household shrines and recited incantations to
protect themselves and their infants against being sickened by Lamashtu
and Lilith, preying female spirits who represent the fear of pre- and
neonatal mortality:

> ... not a midwife, she wipes off the babe.
> She keeps counting the months of women with child;
> she is continually blocking the door of the woman in labor,
> She seizes... the babe from the arm of the nurse.
> The twin gods who saw her
> and made her go through the window,
> made her slip away past the cap of the door pivot
> bound her with ...
> She strangles the babes,
> the weak ones she gives water of ... to drink.
> Who carried fat, she slew the fat;
> who carried milk, she slew the milk;
> the nurses who opened widely,
> who spread a little their strong elbows,
> she has bitten;

---

[13] "Magical Protection for a Child," (trans. A. Erman; *ANET*, 328; A. Erman,
Zaubersprüke für Mutter und Kind, APAW, 1901, recto i 9-ii 6; K. Sethe,
Aegyptische Lesestücke, 2nd ed. (Leipzig, 1928), 51-52; translated in G. Roeder,
Urkunden zur Religion des alten Aegypten (Jena, 1923), 116-19.
[14] Lichty, "Demons and Population Control," 23.

...away with your breast from here![15]

Fig. 5-1. Bird-like *lamashtu*[16]

In these texts, the goddess-demon strangles newborns or kills them indirectly by biting the nurse's breast to "slay" its fat and milk, then substituting her own poison. Women could protect themselves through goddesses who opposed the child-stealer: "may the goddess Annunitu crush the ... snatcher-demon *lamashtu*;" or, by wearing jewelry like the "fourteen stone beads (as charms) against the *lamashtu*"(CAD 9:66).

Syrian Child-Protecting Amulets Derived from Mesopotamian Practices

Babylonian religious practices and magical objects spread to northern Syria and occur at Ugarit. Family gods, goddesses and protective spirits, as distinguished from deceased ancestors,[17] protected the members of the household, and especially the interests of women and infants. Logically, family interests differ from or supplement national interests. Personal religion reflects concerns with the everyday physical welfare of individual

---

[15] J. J. A. van Dijk, A. Goetze, and M. I. Hussey, *Early Mesopotamian Incantations and Rituals* (YOS, Babylonian Texts 11; New Haven: Yale University Press, 1985), 26, 49.

[16] F. Thureau-Dangin, "Rituel et amulettes contre Labartu," *RA* 18/4 (1921): 161-98.

[17] K. van der Toorn (*Family Religion in Babylon, Syria, and Israel: Continuity and Change in the Forms of Religious Life* [Leiden: Brill, 1996], 168) distinguishes between deceased ancestors and family gods on the basis of *Ugaritica V*, 148.

family members. While kings chose gods from the higher echelons of the pantheon, ordinary citizens approached city and national deities through intermediaries who belonged to their extended families and neighborhoods, who honored them with daily prayers and offerings in domestic shrines rather than in the large state temples. Texts as well as archaeology indicate that these shrines consisted of incense altars and offering platforms located in the streets of residential neighborhoods or in the courts or living rooms of private houses, where families burned incense or oil to invoke their personal gods and goddesses and to frighten away unwanted supernatural beings.

Figurines invited the family deity or the deity's emissaries, male *šedu* and female *lamassu* spirits, to come into the house to protect its residents:

> You write on the magic figurine's side, "This is the one who makes the favorable *šedu*-spirit and the favorable *lamassu*-spirit come in" (*CAD* 9:63; *KAR* 298:36).[18]

The term *lamassu* refers to a benevolent goddess that Neo-Babylonian art depicts introducing worshipers into the presence of important deities.[19] Cognate with *edu,* Deut 32:17 and Ps 106:37 mention *šedim* that receive Israelite sacrifices.

Excavations and texts reveal that Assyrians and Babylonians placed figurines on guard in the courtyards or bedrooms of their houses, hung or buried them near doorways, or stood them on roofs.[20] For example, they buried one of the protective god Lahmu, with "Get out, evil demon!" and "Come in, good demon!" inscribed on his arms in a seventh century B.C.E. foundation at Assur.[21] The figurines that Assyrians put in their house windows or buried beneath thresholds at Nineveh and Nimrud had names like "the one who drives away the Asakku-demon,"[22] which is another name for the child-stealer.

Epigraphers dated two limestone plaques from Arslan Tash in Syria (whose West Semitic dialect approximates Hebrew), to the early seventh century B.C.E., when Assyria controlled Israel. Grotesque figures on the

---

[18] E. Ebeling, ed., *Keilschrifttexte aus Assur juristischen Inhalts* (Osnabruck: Zeller, 1968 [orig. 1927]), 972.
[19] J. Black and A. Green, *Gods, Demons, and Symbols of Ancient Mesopotamia: An Illustrated Dictionary* (London: British Museum, 1992), 115.
[20] F. A. M. Wiggermann, *Mesopotamian Protective Spirits: The Ritual Texts* (Groningen: Styx, 1992); E. Reiner, "Plague Amulets and House Blessings," *JNES* 19 (1960): 148-55.
[21] Black and Green, *Gods, Demons, and Symbols.*
[22] Lichty, "Demons and Population Control," 24.

plaques gobble small humans whose shape, proportions and lack of clothing replicate Assyrian relief depictions of young children carried by their mothers when Sennacherib captured them.[23] One text exemplifies the Near Eastern concept that demons drain their victims' body fluids while they are sleeping.[24] Scholars like Albright and Cross translated the other text as relying on the god El Olam (the Eternal One) and his consort Asherah for protection:

> Incantations: O Fliers, goddesses...
> The house I enter, you shall not enter
> And the court I tread, you shall not tread.
> The Eternal One has made a covenant with us,
> Asherah has made (a pact) with us. [25]

The expression "make a covenant," familiar from the Bible, combines the notions of a pact of protection by superior powers and a ban on those that threaten. This plaque illustrates a family naming protective deities to keep night demons from their house.

At fourteenth-thirteenth century B.C.E. Ugarit, the large number of terracotta and precious metal deity figurines and their distribution in the houses east of the royal palace and in the south residential district, underscore the importance of household-based religion.[26] Private citizens

---

[23] For drawings of the plaques, see R. du Mesnil du Boisson, "Une tablette magique de la région du moyen Euphrate," in *Mélange syriens offerts à M. René Dussaud* (Bibliotéque archéologique et historique 30; Paris: Guenthner, 1939), 1.423; A. Caquot and R. du Mesnil du Boisson, "La second tablette ou 'petite amulette' d'Arslan Tash," *Syria* 48 (1971): 391-406. For the reliefs, see P. Albenda, "Western Asiatic Women in the Iron Age: Their Image Revealed," *BA* 46/2 (1983): 82-88.

[24] T. H. Gaster, "A Hang-up for Hang-Ups: The Second Amuletic Plaque from Arslan Tash," *BASOR* 209 (1973): 18-26; F. M. Cross, "Leaves from an Epigraphist's Notebook," *CBQ* 36 (1974): 486-94.

[25] F. M. Cross and R. J. Saley, "Phoenician Incantations on a Plaque of the Seventh Century B.C. from Arslan Tash in Upper Syria," *BASOR* 197 (1970): 42-49; W. F. Albright, "An Aramaean Magical Text in Hebrew from the Seventh Century B.C.," *BASOR* 76 (1939): 5-11; D. Pardee ("Les documents d'Arslan Tash: authentiques ou faux?," *Syria* 75 [1998]: 15-54), while differing on readings of the deity names, defends the authenticity of these inscriptions.

[26] See, for example, M. Yon, "Ugarit: History and Archaeology," *ABD* 6, 695-706; idem, "The Temple of the Rhytons at Ugarit," in *Ugarit, Religion, and Culture* (eds. N. Wyatt, W. G. E. Watson, and J. B. Lloyd; Münster: Ugarit-Verlag, 1996); J.-C. Courtois, "Ras Shamra," *Dictionnaire de la Bible Supplement*, vol. 9 (Paris: Letouzey & Ane, 1979).

at Ugarit, like those of Assyria and Babylonia, replicated the furnishings and rituals of major sanctuaries in their family shrines in less elaborate form and with less expensive materials in order to invoke the deities upon whom they depended for daily care. Sacred texts found throughout the neighborhoods—wisdom tablets, a medical ritual for a pregnant woman, conjurations against various evils including demons and evil eyes— indicate that knowledge and practical use of the Babylonian literary tradition was not limited to rare scribal specialists. Practitioners at the household level assisted their family members or neighbors to deal with normal human life situations and perceived dangers.

A text defying Lamashtu from one house shows the longevity of women's tenacious combat of infant mortality, as it is nearly identical to Neo-Assyrian child-stealing texts.[27] Also from Ugarit comes the tiny cuneiform cylinder archaeologists found on an infant's skeleton in a Greco-Persian period grave.[28] The Lamashtu texts expel the child-stealer by naming god and goddess pairs.

Asherah Assists El/Yahweh to Protect Families

Near Eastern deities generally worked in teams of the national god and his associates. For example, the inscription from northern Syria against child-stealing night demons names Baal and his wives.[29] Greco-Roman period and later Jewish and Christian incantations against Lilith name a form of Yahweh (Yahu, Iao, or Shaddai) and one or more mythologized biblical characters such as Solomon, Michael, or the Virgin Mary as Yahweh's agent-protectors.[30]

---

[27] M. J. Nougayrol, "Nouveaux textes d'Ugarit en cuneiformes babyloniens," in *Academie des inscriptions et belles-lettres. Comptes rendus des seances de l'annee 1963. Avril-Juin* (Paris: Librairie C. Klincksieck, 1964), 135; M. J. Nougayrol, "La Lamaštu à Ugarit," in *Ugaritica VI* (Mission de Ras Shamra 17; ed. C. F. A. Schaeffer; Paris: Guethner and Mission archeologique de Ras Shamra, 1969), 404-405.

[28] Ibid., 394-403.

[29] Cross and Saley, "Phoenician Incantations."

[30] E. R. Goodenough, *Jewish Symbols in the Greco-Roman Period*, 4 vols. (New York: Pantheon, 1953-4); T. H. Gaster, *The Holy and the Profane: Evolution of Jewish Folkways* (2nd ed.; New York: Morrow, 1980); J. A. Montgomery, "Some Early Amulets from Palestine," *JAOS* 31 (1910-11): 272-81; idem, *Aramaic Incantation Texts from Nippur*, vol. 3 (University of Pennsylvania, The Museum, Publications of the Babylonian Section; Philadelphia: University Museum of Archaeology and Anthropology, 1913).

Biblical as well as other Levantine texts indicate that in both Canaanite and Israelite religions, the goddess Asherah served El as personal assistant. The Israelite culture, although distinctive socio-economically, developed from Canaanite prototypes. Texts like Aqhat and Kirta probably comprised a "Canaanite Bible" that expressed the worldview of the West Semitic people inhabiting the Galilee and northern Transjordan. Although discovered at thirteenth century Ugarit, they unfold among toponyms like Lake Galilee, Mt. Hermon, and Udumu in Bashan. Thus, when Israel split from Judah and established its religious centers with Bull El, Asherah and Baal, it appealed to long-standing traditions of the region.[31]

Israelites attributed Northwest Semitic and Egyptian imagery for several goddesses to Asherah. Her role as mediator in the Ugaritic Baal Cycle survives as one of her primary functions in Israelite religion. Asherah's stylistic tree in Yahwistic shrines and the formula "by his *asherah*" indicate that she was the means of approaching Yahweh, as well as the vehicle of his protection. The Khirbet el-Kôm inscription credits Yahweh with rescuing Uryahu from his enemies through Asherah, and the Kuntillet 'Ajrud apotropaic symbols and inscriptions that ask "Yahweh and his *asherah*" for blessing appear to request protection for travelers.[32]

Ugaritic, as well as biblical, narratives allude to El as child-giver and child-claimer.[33] Although Ugaritic Asherah acts primarily as mother,[34]

---

[31] B. Margalit, *The Ugaritic Poem of AQHT: Text, Translation, Commentary* (Berlin: de Gruyter, 1989), 473-75.

[32] For description, translations, and interpretations of the Khirbet el-Kôm inscription, see J. Naveh, "Graffiti and Dedications," *BASOR* 235 (1979): 27-30; A. Lemaire, "Les inscriptions de Khirbet el-Qom et l'Ashérah de YHWH," *RB* 84 (1977): 595-608; W. G. Dever, "Recent Archaeological Confirmation of the Cult of Asherah in Ancient Israel," *Hebrew Studies* 23 (1982): 37-43; Z. Zevit, "The Khirbet el-Kom Inscription Mentioning a Goddess," *BASOR* 255 (1984): 39-47. For the Kuntillet 'Ajrud inscriptions, see Naveh, "Graffiti and Dedications;" W. G. Dever, "Asherah, Consort of Yahweh? New Evidence from Kuntillet 'Ajrud," *BASOR* 255 (1984): 21-37; J. M. Hadley, "Some Drawings and Inscriptions on Two Pithoi from Kuntillet 'Ajrud," *VT* 37 (1987): 180-211; O. Keel and C. Uehlinger, *Gods, Goddesses, and Images of God* (trans. T. H. Trapp; Minneapolis: Fortress Press, 1998 [orig. *Göttinnen, Götter, und Gottesymbole*. Freiburg: Herder, 1992]), 225-48.

[33] Biblical passages that suggest El/Yahweh is child-giver and child-claimer include Gen 16:2, 17:16, 21:1-2, 30:2; Exod 13:1-2, 12-13; Judg 13:5; Ruth 4:12-14; 1 Sam 1:11; Job 1:21; 2 Kgs 16:3, 21:6; Mic 6:6-7; Isa 30:33; Ezek 20:25-26, 31. Although archaeology has never documented child sacrifice in the Levant, there is ample evidence for the practice in Phoenician colonies like Carthage.

[34] J. Day, "Asherah in the Hebrew Bible and Northwest Semitic Literature," *JBL* 105/3 (1986): 389.

when El promises Kirta an heir after seven childless wives, Kirta vows to
give Asherah silver and gold,[35] indicating that Asherah assists El in
promoting family fertility. Fragments of a Kuntillet 'Ajrud wall inscription
presuppose a similar partnership; this Hebrew text promises that Yahweh
will enrich and do good to the inscriber of the votive prayer; as a result
they will give offerings to Asherah.[36] Biblical texts agree that it is as a
deity that Asherah receives ritual offerings from the Israelites when they
employ the Hebrew verb *'bd,* "worship, serve" (Judg 3:7; 2 Chr 24:18).[37]
Other biblical passages connect incense altars with *asherim* (Isa 17:8;
27:9).[38]

House Shrines Protected Israelite Families

Beginning in the earliest Iron Age settlements and continuing under the
United and Divided Monarchies, neighborhood cult rooms and semi-
private house shrines substantiate the tradition of offering incense and
gifts to personal deities to invoke their protection of the family.[39] Icons
and the apparatus for burning incense and oil, pouring libations, and
gifting grain and luxury items are often placed on benches. Houses at Tell
el-Far'ah (N), Beer-Sheba, Tell Halif, and Tell Masos provide examples of
artifacts and furniture that families employed in household rituals.[40]

---

[35] *KTU* 1.14-16.

[36] For the inscription see G. I. Davies, *Ancient Hebrew Inscriptions: Corpus and
Concordance* (Cambridge: Cambridge University Press, 1991), 80; Keel and
Uehlinger, *Gods, Goddesses,* 244.

[37] Isa 19:21 clarifies the meaning of *'bd* when it says that the Egyptians will "*'bd*"
Yahweh "with sacrifices and grain-offerings."

[38] Although scholars agree that most biblical references to *asherim* refer to real or
artificial cultic trees, they differ on the extent to which the trees represent a deity
associated with Yahweh.

[39] Although specific examples here are from Israelite sites, archaeologists also
have found house shrines at Transjordanian Ammonite sites like Jawa and
'Umayri. See P. M. M. Daviau, "Family Religion: Evidence for the Paraphernalia
of the Domestic Cult," in *The World of the Arameans II: Studies in History and
Archaeology in Honour of Paul-Eugène Dion* (JSOTSup 325; eds. P. M. M.
Daviau, J. W. Wevers, and M. Weigl; Sheffield: Sheffield Academic Press, 2001);
L. G. Herr and D. R. Clark, "Excavating the Tribe of Reuben," *BAR* 27 (2001): 47.

[40] For descriptions of the common Iron Age four-room house, see L. E. Stager,
"The Archaeology of the Family in Ancient Israel," *BASOR* 260 (1985): 1-35; J. S.
Holladay, Jr., "Four-Room House," in *OEANE* 2, 337-42; J. S. Holladay, "Israelite
House," in *ABD* 3, 308-18. For a compilation of religious objects found at various
sites in ancient Israel see idem, "Religion in Israel and Judah Under the Monarchy:

Studies on gendered division of labor in pre-modern societies demonstrate that men's activities usually center on food production and community leadership, while women tend to manage the household economy, including food processing and clothing production.[41] Biblical and other ancient Near Eastern texts, stone reliefs and paintings portray women as spinners and weavers in industrial contexts as well as in the homestead subsistence setting of early Israel (Fig. 5-2).[42] Women's

---

An Explicitly Archaeological Approach," in *Ancient Israelite Religion* (eds. P. D. Miller, P. D. Hanson, and S. D. McBride; Philadelphia: Fortress, 1987), 249-99; Z. Zevit, *The Religions of Ancient Israel: A Synthesis of Parallactic Approaches* (London: Continuum, 2001).

[41] The Prov 31:10-31 description of a good wife reflects this division of labor: the wife "keeps her eye on the conduct of her household" (v. 27), whereas "her husband is well known in the assembly, where he takes his seat with the elders of the region" (v. 23). For ethnographic and historical studies on the gendered division of labor, see C. Hastorf, "Gender, Space, and Food in Prehistory," in *Engendering Archaeology: Women and Prehistory* (eds. J. M. Gero and M. W. Conkey; Oxford: Blackwell, 1991), 132-62; R. Harris, "Independent Women in Mesopotamia?" in *Women's Earliest Records: From Ancient Egypt and Western Asia* (ed. B. S. Lesko; Atlanta: Scholars Press, 1989); J. M. Gero, "Feasts and Females: Gender Archaeology and Political Meals in the Andes," *Norwegian Archaeological Review* 25/1 (1992): 15-30; L. H. Dommasnes, "Male/Female Roles and Ranks in Late Iron Age Norway," in *Were They All Men? An Examination of Sex Roles in Prehistoric Society* (eds. R. Bertelson, A. Lillehammer, and J.-R. Naess; Stavanger, Norway: Arkeologist Museum I Stavanger, 1991); J. C. Lowell, "Reflections of Sex Roles in the Archaeological Record: Insights from Hopi and Zuni Ethnographic Data," in *The Archaeology of Gender: Proceedings of the Twenty-Second Annual Conference of the Archaeological Association of the University of Calgary* (eds. D. Walde and N. D. Willows; Calgary: Archaeological Association, University of Calgary, 1991).

[42] Proverbs 31 describes the Israelite matriarch's activities of weaving, spinning, and sewing more fully than her other activities; verses 14-15 emphasize her labor in food preparation. See also 2 Kgs 23:7; Exod 35:25-26; and for an exception, see Exod 35:34-35. A painting from the Middle Kingdom Khnum-hotep tomb at Beni Hasan, Egypt (2052-1778 B.C.E.) shows women spinning thread and weaving on a loom (P. Newberry, *Beni Hasan* [1893], pl. 29). *Ugaritic Text* 51.2: 3-4 mentions the goddess Asherah's spindle. Asherah threatens to stab Baal with it in the Hittite Elkunirša myth from the second half of the second millennium, and other Hittite texts and a stela from Marash picture spindles and mirrors as women's characteristic accessories (H. A. Hoffner, "The Elkunirsa Myth Reconsidered," *Revue Hittite et Asianique* 23, fasc. 76 [1965], 5-16). Records from ancient Sumer indicate that women did the milling, oil pressing, and weaving (M. van de Mieroop, "Women in the Economy of Sumer," in *Women's Earliest Records: From Ancient Egypt and Western Asia* [ed. B. S. Lesko; Atlanta: Scholars Press

implements connected with food preparation and textiles frequently occur with incense altars and figurines in the archaeological record of Israelite house rooms. Often jewelry and accessories that women used to deflect evil forces accompany their weaving and cooking tools.[43]

The early Iron Age settlement at Tell Masos included four-room-type houses as well as the larger Canaanite-style House 314.[44] Four figurines typical of votives deposited in the Hathor temple at Timna demonstrate that the House 314 family revered a protective goddess. Residents likely used the hearth, mudbrick structure, and courtyard bench for metalworking and associated religious rituals. Perhaps a woman with a newborn child slept in Room 331, which held three incense burners, three oil-burning lamps, a bead, shells from the Red Sea, and an ivory lion head that symbolized the powerful protector goddesses of the Egypto-Canaanite pantheon.

The benches, careful plastering, and potsherd paneling suggest that Room 169 in House 167 functioned as a shrine. Artifacts found in and around the house hint at luxury votive offerings, and a bone scaraboid carved with animals and a limestone lion head connote the goddess Asherah. Throughout the later seventh to early sixth century rooms at Tell Masos, excavators found female and animal figurines, lamps, and a furniture model among women's textile and food processing tools, illustrating the importance of household religion to women's daily life.

1989]; A. Zagarell, "Trade, Women, Class, and Society in Ancient Western Asia," *Current Anthropology* 27/5 [1986]: 415-30; K. Maekawa, "Female Weavers and Their Children," *Acta Sumeralogica* 2 [1980]: 81-125). The *Hurpu* incantation tablets from the library of Assurbanipal at Nineveh depict the goddesses Ishtar and Uttu spinning a thick multicolored thread (*Hurpu* 5-6:144-153; E. Reiner, *Hurpu: A Collection of Sumerian and Akkadian Incantations* [Osnabrück, Germany: Biblio, 1970], 34). For general discussions of women's economic activity, see C. Meyers, *Discovering Eve*; idem, "Women and the Domestic Economy of Early Israel," in *Women's Earliest Records: From Ancient Egypt and Western Asia* (ed. B. S. Lesko; Atlanta: Scholars Press, 1989), 265-78; idem, "The Family in Early Israel," in *Families in Ancient Israel* (eds. L. G. Perdue, J. Blenkinsopp, J. J. Collins, and C. Meyers; Louisville, Ky.: Westminster John Knox, 1997), 1-47.

[43] For archaeological details and analysis, see E. A. R. Willett, *Women and Household Shrines in Ancient Israel*, (Ph.D. diss., Univ. of Arizona, 1999).

[44] Archaeological information on Tell Masos is from V. Fritz and A. Kempinski, *Ergebnisse der Ausgrabungen auf der Hirbet El-Msas (Tel Masos) 1972-1975* (Wiesbaden: Otto Harrassowitz, 1983).

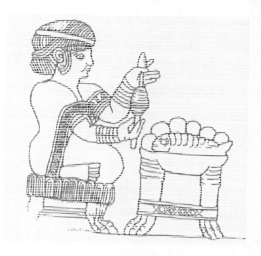

Fig. 5-2. Lady spinning[45]

Although the Bible speaks of royally-established worship sites at Bethel, Dan, and elsewhere (1 Kgs 12:28-31), Israelite families at tenth century Tell el-Far'ah (N), biblical Tirzah, did not confine their religious activities to these public shrines, because most included either a female or an animal figurine in their household commodities.[46] The prophet Ahijah refers to this when he informs Jereboam's wife that it was because Israelites made *asherim* that her son becomes ill and dies at Tirzah (1 Kgs 14:15). Artifacts like the ivory pendant, the cow nursing calf motif, and the blue jewelry plaque represent rituals the Near Eastern heritage associated with preventing infant mortality.[47] No specifically male tools or

---

[45] The drawing of lady holding a spindle and a bundle of fibers she is about to spin into thread from an 8th-7th century B.C.E. Susa stone relief (National Museums of France, Louvre #SB2834) is an original drawing prepared for the author by C. Marlett. A photograph of the relief appears in M. Pézard and E. Pottier, *Catalogue des Antiquités de la Susiane*, (n.p.: 1926), pl. 13; and in Lesko, *Women's Earliest Records*, 212.

[46] Archaeological information on this site is from A. Chambon, *Tel El-Far'ah 1: L'Age du Fer* (Paris: Editions Recherches sur les civilisations, 1984).

[47] In *Women and Household Shrines in Ancient Israel*, and "Hathor, Asherah, Divine Eye Motifs and the Judean Pillar-based Figurines" (paper presented at the Annual Meeting of the Society of Biblical Literature, 2000), I show that the jewelry that biblical texts like Isa 3:18-21 mention negatively appears as women's amulets in Near Eastern apotropaic and mythological texts. Excavations in Egypt,

92   Chapter Five

weapons accompany these; on the other hand, items like household pottery and a spindle whorl confirm women's interest in them. In the northeast section of town, in House 440 excavators discovered a nursing female figurine, a horse head from a zoomorphic vessel, an alabaster pendant, and six beads from the courtyard floor near an oven, a female with frame-drum figurine next to a stone bench, and a model sanctuary. House 436 included luxury votive objects; House 442 contained an incense burner and Cypriot bowls; and House 427 produced bovine and female figurines. The houses from tenth century Tell el-Far'ah (N) illustrate Israelite women's religion.

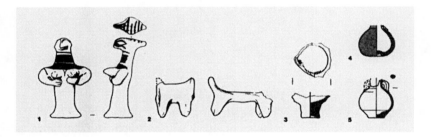

Fig. 5-3. Figurine, model chair, miniature lamp, and juglet from Beer-Sheba, House 25[48]

In the eighth century houses at Beer-Sheba, several figurines occurred with lamps or incense burners.[49] Model chairs that represent the lap of the child-protecting goddess appeared with figurines and incense burners in Houses 25, 808 and 430, ordinary domestic dwellings.[50] Excavators found

Syria-Palestine, and Mesopotamia provide examples of these inscribed amulets, divine eye-motifs and other magical jewelry, often associated with women's graves and women's cooking and weaving implements.

[48] *Beer-Sheba I: Excavations at Tel Beer-Sheba, 1969-1971 Seasons* (ed. Y. Aharoni; Tel-Aviv: Institute of Archaeology, Tel-Aviv University, 1973), pl. 71. Used with permission of Institute of Archaeology, Tel-Aviv University.

[49] Incense burners commonly occur in cultic texts and cultic loci with the role of attracting the pleasure and protection of good deities while repelling evil. Although some archaeologists dispute a religious function, suggesting that incense was used merely to cover the malodor of animal residues, the ubiquity of incense burners in small neighborhood shrines without animal sacrifice altars affirms their cultic significance.

[50] Archaeological information on this site is from Aharoni, *Beer-Sheba I*; Z. Herzog, A. F. Rainey, and S. Moshkovitz, "The Stratigraphy of Beer-Sheba and the Location of the Sanctuary," *BASOR* 225 (1977): 49-58.

a female figurine, a couch model, and a miniature lamp topped with burned incense particles on the paved floor of Room 25, among cooking pots and domestic dishes (Fig. 5-3).

Next to Room 25, Courtyard Kitchen 36, lined with structures resembling offering shelves, adjoins Front Room 94, the site of a woman's oven and cooking pots that held a lamp and a zoomorphic figurine fragment. Stationing a figurine in a house space that fronts the street guards access to the entire house, and lighting a lamp to attract the beneficent deity and deflect evil ones are rituals that Near Eastern women habitually practiced. House 430 included two miniature cuboidal altars, and its front room housed a female pillar-base figurine and model chair.

At Tell Halif (Lahav) a fenestrated incense stand and female figurine head between beveled stone blocks were found with ordinary household pottery and stone and bone utensils in the broadroom of an eighth century four-room house.[51] Fish bones and carbonized remains of grapes, cereals, and legumes, as well as an oven in the courtyard just outside the room, indicate that this was a food preparation and storage area. This Israelite house shrine at Lahav affords another example of an incense-burning altar and a female figurine associated with a woman's work area.

These houses from Israelite settlements reveal the cultic artifacts and furniture that families employed in protective household rituals: incense burners or offering structures to invoke deities, and apotropaic jewelry and accessories that repel child-stealing demons, clustered with women's food processing equipment. Similar items come from houses at Lachish, Tell en-Nasbeh, and Tell Beit Mirsim.

Pillar-Base Figurines as Prayers for Protection

The common Israelite and Judean pillar-base figurines consist of heads with prominent eyes, heavy breasts emphasized by encircling arms, and conical bodies (Fig. 5-4). Since most come from houses, women likely used them as votives in family religion to invoke the goddess Asherah to ensure successful child rearing.[52] Votives represent a contract between a

---

[51] J. D. Seger, "Tel Halif. Notes and News," *IEJ* 43/1 (1992): 6-70; P. Jacobs, "Iron Age Halif Revisited," *Lahav Newsletter* 51 (1992); J. W. Hardin, "Understanding Domestic Space: An Example from Iron Age Tel Halif," *NEA* 67/ 2 (2004): 71-83.

[52] So W. G. Dever, "The Silence of the Text: An Archaeological Commentary on 2 Kings 23," in *Scripture and Other Artifacts* (eds. M. D. Coogan, J. C. Exum, and L. E. Stager; Louisville, Ky.: Westminster John Knox, 1994), 150-51; W. G.

person and their deity and stand as tokens of the agreement to provide offerings if the deity protects them or answers a request. Biblical women frequently made vows (Num 30), often in connection with progeny issues. For example, Hannah vowed to dedicate her son to Yahweh if he provided her with one (1 Sam 1:11), and King Lemuel's mother calls him "the son of my vow" (Prov 31:2). The vow was a convenient medium of religious expression for women, since it could be practiced outside the sphere of religious and political authority structures.[53]

A votive figurine may represent either the deity or the votary,[54] or dually identify the goddess as an ideal woman and portray the female worshiper expressing herself in the image and likeness of the goddess.[55] At either end of the scale, the pillar figurine represents a female. The Israelites who made and revered the figurines clearly associated their blatant femaleness with a goddess rather than with Yahweh. If the figurine represents the votary, the votary is obviously a woman and not a man. Representing an Israelite woman, the large breasted pillar-figurine might mean: "This is me—a woman with watchful eyes and full breasts for my infant." Or, "This is what I want—Please guard my child and my milk from being sickened by demons." Or, representing the goddess: "This is you. I invoke your name over this child. This figurine invites you to guard the doorway from child-stealers while I sleep." The meaning of votive figurines leads us to believe that women manufactured them and used them in their homes to protect themselves and their children.[56]

Dever, *Did God Have a Wife? Archaeology and Folk Religion in Ancient Israel* (Grand Rapids, Mich.: Eerdmans, 2004).

[53] J. Berlinerblau, The Vow and the "Popular Religious Groups" of Ancient Israel: A Philological and Sociological Inquiry (JSOTSup 210; Sheffield: Sheffield Academic Press, 1996).

[54] M. Morden, "Cult from Clay: The Evidence of the Terracottas from the Lower Sanctuary of the East Acropolis of Idalion" (paper presented at the 1997 Annual Meeting of the American Schools of Oriental Research, to be published in the *University of Arizona Expedition to Idalion Vol. 1: the Hellenistic Levels of the Temple Terrace*, SIMA.)

[55] Keel and Uehlinger, *Gods, Goddesses*, 108; M. E. L. Mallowan, "Excavations at Brak and Chagar Bazar," *Iraq* 9 (1947): 209.

[56] A workshop in the village of Narok, southern Kenya, provides an ethnographic parallel. Only women work there, sculpting only statues with female fertility symbolism, perceived as containing powers or spirits of female fertility. Women buy them and set them in their homes to ensure their own fertility. The figures are not made for tourist shops (U. Avner, personal communication). M. Conkey assumes that "in most instances, those who use certain tools and facilities in their tasks are likely to be those who are *primarily* (but not exclusively) engaged in the

Biblical texts describe women's religious activities in their homes and sometimes mention family support. At Endor, a woman consulted the dead Samuel, and then prepared King Saul a meal (1 Sam 28:7-25). Huldah prophesied to the high priest and king's cabinet in her home (2 Kgs 22:14-20). Women baked cakes, burned sacrifices, and poured wine offerings to the "Queen of Heaven" (Jer 7:18; 44:19). Some sewed wristbands and donned head coverings to predict future events (Ezek 13:18-23). A woman's house was the center of her religious as well as her economic activity.

The Prov 31 woman kept the night lamp burning and managed household enterprises including real estate, employees and textile manufacture. Strict division of labor places a high value on women's work and makes it likely that women supervised religious duties in settings in which they predominated. Abigail (1 Sam 25) exemplifies the independence and power sagacious women had as household managers. Without informing her husband, she collected foodstuffs and sent them to David, whom she dissuaded from blood revenge through argumentation, blessing, and taking blame as if, as Brenner puts it, "the real responsibility for the household is hers."[57]

---

manufacture and maintenance of them" ("Contexts of Action, Contexts for Power: Material Culture and Gender in the Magdalenian," pp. 57-92 in *Engendering Archaeology: Women and Prehistory* [eds. J. M. Gero and M. W. Conkey; Oxford: Blackwell, 1991], 78). Also, from J. Gero: "We suspect, moreover, that women were especially visible and active in household contexts where they played significant roles in household production and household management.... Almost ironically, women can be expected to be most visible and active precisely in the contexts that archaeologists are most likely to excavate: on house floors, at base camps and in village sites where women would congregate to carry out their work.... Since the user of a tool is in the best position to judge its adequacy, it makes sense that women produced many of their own tools, and indeed it would be most inefficient for them to rely on men for these needs" ("Genderlithics: Women's Roles in Stone Tool Production," pp. 163-93 in *Engendering Archaeology: Women and Prehistory* [eds. J. M. Gero and M. W. Conkey; Oxford: Blackwell, 1991], 169-70).

[57] A. Brenner, *The Israelite Woman: Social Role and Literary Type in Biblical Narrative* (Sheffield: JSOT Press, 1985), 40.

Fig. 5-4. Pillar-base figurines from houses at Tell Beit Mirsim[58]

The forty-two Roman-era Aramaic texts from Nippur that Montgomery cataloged affirm women's leadership in household rituals designed to protect aspects of the domestic welfare of a married couple and their children, house, property and cattle, including measures against child-stealing demons. Frequently, women procured the incantations without reference to their husbands, and Jews as well as Mandaeans and Greeks required the household mother's name in each text.[59] The Talmud reflects this role for women when it stipulates that "all repetitive incantations are in name of the mother."[60] In an ethnographic parallel, every home in Yerani, a poor subdivision of Athens, has a shelf for icons and other sacred substances, with an oil lamp suspended in front of it. Although the

---

[58] W. F. Albright, *The Excavation of Tell Beit Mirsim. 3. The Iron Age* (AASOR 21-22; New Haven, Conn.: ASOR, 1943), pl. 31. Courtesy of the American Schools of Oriental Research.
[59] Montgomery, *Aramaic Incantation Texts*, 49.
[60] *b. Shab.* 66b.

iconostási is found in a multi-purpose room and does not take up any floor area, through its concentrated spiritual presence, the house becomes a temple. The family is its religious community and the woman of the house fulfills the role of intercessor, patterned on the divine Mother. She cares for the spiritual needs of family members, as does the priest in the community's church. Although the husband may be "head of the family," she is paradoxically its central figure through her association with "essential objects" and hence the sacred dimension.[61]

Conclusion

The symbolism of a child-protecting figurine or amulet and its accompanying ceremony remain basically the same through the centuries, although the divine names change as it adapts to different religious cultures.[62] Egyptian and Mesopotamian child-stealing beliefs continue in Greco-Roman period rituals against Lilith. The she-demon appears in Greek as Gogol. The legend of a demon confronted by an archangel or saint figure who forces her to tell her names and return the infants she has stolen occurs on a Syriac scroll from Urmi, Persia that binds "an evil spirit in the form of a hateful woman" who was "the suffocatress of children and women." It repeats in *The Testament of Solomon*, the pseudepigraphic folktale from the first centuries C.E. that fuses astrological and mystical beliefs that Gnostics adopted from Jewish, Egyptian, Assyrian and Greek teachings. A second century C.E. Jewish tomb, at Irbid southeast of Lake Galilee, held an amulet that calls on God to send his angel to protect a young woman and her unborn child from the "lilith" hiding in her bed canopy. Women's preventive measures against supernatural damage to their young children and breast milk reflect long-standing traditions for dealing with poor milk supply and high infant mortality.

Burial statistics that show a high rate of infant mortality and short female life span explain ancient Near Eastern people's preoccupation with human fertility and child-stealing spirits. For agrarian families, this was a life and death issue because producing sufficient progeny assured necessary field labor as well as old-age security. While biblical texts validate a centralized national cult involving a male priesthood and

---

[61] R. Hirschon, "Essential Objects and the Sacred: Interior and Exterior Space in an Urban Greek Locality," in *Women and Space* (ed. S. Ardener; Oxford: Berg, 1997), 81, 85.

[62] M. Gaster, "Two Thousand Years of a Charm against the Child-Stealing Witch," in *Studies and Texts in Folklore, Magic, Mediaeval Romance, Hebrew Apocrypha, and Samaritan Archaeology*, vol. 3 (New York: Ktav, 1971).

community religious celebrations dependent on male participation,
household archaeology reveals an undergirding family system that utilizes
the technical wisdom and agency of women. Women's ritual for
maintaining adequate lactation and preserving the lives of their newborn
infants invested them with societal worth and complementary religious
power for sustaining a heterarchical culture in a manner that negates
images of an Israelite patriarchal hierarchy. Although the Bible is largely
silent on this essential socio-religious leadership function of women, we
can learn much about it from the archaeology of Iron Age houses and from
remnants of other ancient eastern Mediterranean cultures.

CHAPTER SIX

MUT'A MARRIAGE IN THE ROMAN NEAR EAST: THE EVIDENCE FROM PALMYRA, SYRIA

CYNTHIA FINLAYSON

Introduction

In her most recent book, *Women in the Middle East-Past and Present*, N. R. Keddie noted:

> There is scarce documentation concerning women from pre-Islamic times until about the fourteenth century C.E., which, along with the controversial nature of documentation, means that what is written about these periods is often more speculative than are writings about recent times. Few extant texts about the Middle East were written before the third Islamic century, and until recently, texts overwhelmingly reflect views of elite men about women, rather than direct material about how women lived and thought.[1]

Given the lack of authoritative documentary evidence on women's daily lives, scholars must look at the physical evidence emerging from the archaeological record and utilize comparative anthropological and art historical approaches to understand the complex roles of women in the ancient and classical Near East (c. 5000 B.C.E.-330 C.E.).[2] These efforts are not only essential for a more balanced understanding, but also necessary given the importance of these time periods as cultural paradigms in the eras prior to Islam. This article investigates the social positions of Aramaean/Arab women in the late classical era in Greater Syria. It utilizes the archaeological and art historical evidence emerging from the funerary art of Palmyra/Tadmor, particularly focusing on the phenomenon of *mut'a*

---

[1] N. Keddie, *Women in the Middle East Past and Present* (Princeton: Princeton University Press, 2007), 9.
[2] Ibid., 4.

or temporary marriage (Fig. 6-1). This evidence is examined in conjunction with descriptions of "Saracen women" (a term coined by Rome to describe both the nomadic and some settled tribes of Greater Syria and Arabia) as recorded in Roman-era texts, along with pre-Islamic gendered traditions as described in the medieval period. Given the challenges to historical accuracy inherent in the classical and medieval literary sources, the importance of the physical evidence supplied by the Palmyrene funerary portraits from Syria cannot be overstated.[3] The funerary portraits of Palmyra present us with some of the most important extant examples of inscribed personal images from the classical Near East (Fig. 6-2).[4] They surpass the Fayyum collections of Hellenistic and Roman Egypt due to the information that the Syrian examples reveal through their inscriptional dedications and family genealogies recorded in Palmyrene Aramaic.[5] As personalized artifacts created to symbolize both the physical and metaphysical nature of the soul, these portraits reveal how certain women from Aramaean/Arab contexts, of the first through the late third centuries C.E., perceived their own statuses and identities. Additionally, they divulge clues about the perception of women within this tribally based Aramaean/Arab urban community and point to the possible existence of multiple forms of marriage. The Palmyrene portraits, sculpted by local artisans for the aristocratic families of the Tadmor Oasis, have the potential to provide tangible physical evidence that addresses issues of women's status in the pre-Islamic era. The social context is also significant since classical Palmyra represented an era characterized by the evolution

---

[3] For the challenges of historicity with regard to the textual evidence, see D. Spellberg, *Politics, Gender, and the Islamic Past: The Legacy of ʿAʾisha bint Abi Bakr* (New York: Columbia University Press, 1994), 2.
[4] Previous studies of South Arabian inscriptions (E. Glaser ["Polyandrie oder Gesellschaftsehen bei den alten Sabäern," *Beilage zur Allgemeinen Zeitung* 276/7, 1897]; D. Nielsen [*Handbuch der altarabischen Altertumskunde*; Copenhagen: n.p., 1927]; F. Hommel [*Ethnologie und Geographie des alten Orients*; Munich: n.p., 1926]) appear to confirm the practice of polyandry in southern Arabia before the advent of Islam. See also R. Spencer, "The Arabian Matriarchate: An Old Controversy," *Southwestern Journal of Anthropology* 8/4 (1952): 478-502; 490-91. These examples do not, however, include the study of viable portraiture with inscribed genealogies.
[5] S. Moscati, *The Semites in Ancient History: An Inquiry into the Settlement of the Beduin and Their Political Establishment* (Cardiff: University of Wales Press, 1959), 120. The proper names in the Palmyrene inscriptions are mostly Arab, while the script and official language are Palmyrene Aramaic.

of Aramaean and Arab tribal entities from nomadism and semi-nomadism to urbanism based on caravan and other trade ventures.[6]

One of the most revealing social manifestations of a woman's role in any society is the institution of marriage. Marriage encompasses critical cultural perceptions of self identity, community and social status, legal access to property, land ownership and inheritance, the legitimacy or non-legitimacy of sexual activity and resultant progeny, possible participation in or denial of religious roles and most importantly, the manner in which the procreative powers of women are controlled for the perceived benefit of a society over and against the personal inclinations of the individual. The social engines that attempt to control the procreative powers of women thus often define the very identity and status of women within a particular cultural paradigm. In the words of S. Haeri, "A culturally specific signifier, marriage constitutes its own 'language,' the knowledge of which enables one to appreciate a particular form of social organization, its structure, and the meaning of gender relations within it."[7] The constructs of marriage are thus invaluable indicators of the roles and status of women both in antiquity and in the Islamic world. Inasmuch as Islam has allowed for various forms of marriage, it may be that women's roles and status in Islam evolved from former social constructs.[8]

Speaking broadly, Islam has historically permitted both permanent (*nikah*) and temporary (*mut'a/mot'a*) or usufruct marriage. Each requires a contract or agreement between the participating parties, thus differentiating it from sexual relationships involving prostitution.[9] *Mut'a,* or temporary marriage, is of special significance in this study, given its potentially unique cultural manifestations. Its practice becomes a valuable marker of perceptions of women's sexual and procreative autonomy. The pre-Islamic origins of temporary marriage as a venue for understanding the roles of women in the ancient and classical Near East have not been adequately

---

[6] See Spencer, "The Arabian Matriarchate," 478-502, for a discussion of the impact of Islam on urbanism and the potential changes in women's status in Arab societies.

[7] S. Haeri, *Law of Desire: Temporary Marriage in Shi'i Iran* (Syracuse, N.Y.: Syracuse University Press, 1989), ix.

[8] Spencer, "The Arabian Matriarchate," 480. See also, J. Esposito, *Women in Muslim Family Law* (Syracuse, N.Y.: Syracuse University Press, 1982), 12. Esposito lists the types of conjugal relationships that may have existed in pre-Islamic Arabia and Greater Syria, i.e. patrilineal/patrilocal, patriarchal, matrilineal/matrilocal, uxorilocal, polyandrous, and polygamous, and suggested that the probable predominant pattern was patrilineal/patrilocal.

[9] Haeri, *Law of Desire*, 1.

explored.[10] These matters will be explored with the Palmyrene portraits as the focus of inquiry.

The existence of *mut'a* marriage practices among the nomadic pre-Islamic tribes of the Near East seems confirmed by the famous account of Ammianus Marcellinus (ca. 330 C.E.) to a Greek family at Antioch. In a derogatory fashion, he wrote about the Saracen tribes of the desert steppes:

> Their life is always on the move, and they have mercenary wives, hired under a temporary contract. But in order that there may be some semblance of matrimony, the future wife, by way of a dower, offers her husband a spear and a tent, with the right to leave him after a stipulated time, if she so elect.... And it is unbelievable with what ardor both sexes give themselves up to passion....[11]

If this account is accurate, it is significant that it was the woman who offered the dower to the male, and it was also the woman who retained the right to terminate the relationship rather than be bound by a fixed contract. While it may not be possible to distinguish the exact type of *mut'a* practiced by certain women at Palmyra, it might be possible to ascertain whether or not *mut'a* existed in some forms, and which types of women practiced it. This is important for understanding the status of women in the late Classical period in the Saracen Near East.

Mut'a Marriage and Previous Studies Related to the Status of Women in the Pre-Islamic Near East

In her work on temporary marriage in Shi'i Iran, Haeri stated that *mut'a* simply refers to a "marriage of pleasure" of pre-Islamic practice; however, the meaning of *mut'a* is more complex and multivalent.[12] The term *mut'a* derives from the Arabic verb stem *mata'a* or *mut'a,* meaning "to carry away, take away, to be strong, firm, solid; to make to enjoy; to furnish, equip, supply; to gratify the eye; to enjoy, savor, relish."[13] The action of the verb, to "carry away, or take away," may hint at the

---

[10] The focus of modern scholarship with relation to *mut'a* marriage has emphasized the Islamic eras and the decades just before Muhammad.

[11] Ammianus Marcellinus, *Ammianus Marcellinus* (trans. J. C. Rolfe; Cambridge: Harvard University Press, 1935-1939), vol. 1, XIV. 3. 1-4, pp. 27-29. The Arabs in this context were known by the Romans as "Saracens" or "Scenitic Arabs."

[12] Haeri, *Law of Desire*, 1.

[13] J. M. Cowan, *Arabic-English Dictionary: The Hans Wehr Dictionary of Modern Written Arabic* (Ithaca, N.Y.: Spoken Language Services, 1976), 890.

association between pre-Islamic desert raiding and the capture of women,
or the sexual conquests of women often referred to in pre-Islamic poetry
such as that of Imru al-Qais. Modern definitions include "enjoyment,
pleasure, delight, gratification, recreation, compensation paid to a divorced
woman under Islamic Law, temporary marriage, usufruct marriage
contracted for a specified time and exclusively for the purpose of sexual
pleasure," and, interestingly, a recreation center is today called *al-makan
al-mut'a*, literally a "place of pleasure or enjoyment" in modern standard
Arabic.[14] Other sources note that the term *mut'a* was utilized in two
distinct ways in Fatimid texts (909-1171 C.E.) discussing Islamic legal
opinions on marriage and divorce. *Mut'at al-talaq* indicated a compulsory
"present/gift" or "gratification" given by a husband upon the divorce of a
wife, while *mut'at al-hajj* was a compensation paid to one who performed
the *hajj* to Mecca on behalf of another.[15]

    The study of *mut'a* marriage as practiced in the pre-Islamic and
Islamic Near East is not a new area of inquiry for Western scholars. One
of the first individuals to point to the importance of *mut'a* marriage in
early Islamic contexts was the Scottish Orientalist, William Robertson
Smith. In 1889, this accomplished Hebrew and Arabic scholar published
his famous book entitled *Religion of the Semites*. This work eventually
became the foundation for later research in comparative religion and
anthropology, greatly influencing scholars such as Emile Durkheim and
Sigmund Freud. Somewhat lesser known but more revolutionary was
Robertson Smith's earlier study of Semitic Arab family organizations,
Kinship and Marriage in Early Arabia, published in 1885.[16] *Kinship and
Marriage* represented an intensive study of kinship groupings and
traditions among Arab clans and tribes and revealed the importance of
women's roles in the development of the political and social fabric of both
pre-Islamic and Islamic Arab societies. Many of the book's positions,
especially those relating to gender scholarship, began to break down
Western stereotypes surrounding the perceived "exotic" (i.e., sexual) roles
of Near Eastern women. Robertson Smith's mastery of Arabic allowed
him access to early Islamic and medieval Arabic texts and enabled him to

---

[14] Ibid.
[15] A. Fyzee, "Aspects of Fatimid Law," *Studia Islamica* 31 (1970): 81-91; 86. See
also Y. Rapoport, "Matrimonial Gifts in Early Islamic Egypt," *Islamic Law and
Society* 7/1 (2000): 16-21.
[16] W. Robertson Smith, *Kinship and Marriage in Early Arabia*, was first published
in the United States and Canada in 1903, and reprinted in 1966 (Boston: Beacon
Press). An earlier book by G. A. Wilken, *Het Matriarchate bij de oude Arabieren*
(Leiden: n.p.,1884), is also noteworthy.

present an unprecedented analysis of the political dynamics of women, marriage and power in the evolution of Arab societies. Robertson Smith was criticized by later scholars for over-emphasizing the importance of the phenomenon of *mut'a* marriage within early Arab tribal structures.[17] Subsequent Western scholars have also discussed the existence of *mut'a* in the pre-Islamic period shortly before Islam and its practice in later Islamic eras. The most recent comprehensive studies are by Haeri (1989) and Gribetz (1994).[18] Significantly, my on-going research at the Late Hellenistic and Roman-era site of Palmyra strongly refutes many of the earlier criticisms of Robertson Smith's emphasis on the importance of *mut'a* in pre-Islamic contexts. At the same time, the evidence from Palmyra also helps to correct some of Robertson Smith's assumptions with regard to the earlier practices of *mut'a* in pre-Islamic Greater Syria and Arabia. While Robertson Smith discussed the evidence for *mut'a* marriage in early Arab social structures, he only hinted at the importance of *mut'a*

---

[17] See E. L. Peters, "Preface," pp. vii-ix in W. Robertson Smith, *Kinship and Marriage in Early Arabia* (Boston: Beacon Press, 1966). Also, T. Nöldeke, "Über W. Robertson Smith's Kinship and Marriage in Early Arabia," *ZDMG* 40 (1886): 148-87.

[18] Haeri, *Law of Desire*; A. Gribetz, *Strange Bedfellows: Mut'at al-nisâ and Mut'at al-hajj: A Study Based on Sunnî and Shi'î Sources of Tafsir, Hadîth, and Fiqh* (Berlin: Klaus Schwarz, 1994). See also R. Nager, "Religion, Race, and the Debate over *Mut'a* in Dar es-Salaam," *Feminist Studies* 26 (2000): 661-90; W. Ende, "Ehe auf Zeit (*mut'a*) in der innerislamischen Diskussion der Gegenwart," *Die Welt des Islams,* New Series 20/1-2 (1980): 1-43; D. von Denffer, "Mut'a: Ehe oder Prostitution?," Beitrag zur Untersuchung einer Institution des sî'tischen Islam, *ZDMG* 128 (1978): 299-325; A. F. Beeston, "Temporary Marriage in Pre-Islamic South Arabia," *ArSt* 4/19 (1977): 21-25; I. K. A. Howard, "*Mut'a* Marriage Reconsidered in the Context of Formal Procedures," *JSS* 20/1 (1975): 82-92; F. R. Castro, *Materiali e Ricerche sul Nikah al-Mut'a* (Rome: Fonti imamite, 1974); M. Muslehuddin, *Mut'a (Temporary Marriage)* (Lahore: Islamic Publications, 1974); G. Stern, *Marriage in Early Islam* (London: Royal Asiatic Society, 1939); D. M. Donaldson, "Temporary Marriage in Iran," *The Muslim World* 26/4 (1936): 358-64; C. S. Hurgronje, *Mekka in the Latter Part of the 19th Century: Daily Life, Customs and Learning of the Moslims of the East-India Archipelago* (trans. J. H. Monahan; London: Luzac, 1931); M. Hartmann, *Der islamische Orient: Band II, Die arabishche Frag* (Leipzig: n.p., 1909); J. Redhouse, "Notes on Professor Tyler's 'Arabian Matriarchate,' Propounded by Him as President of the Anthropological Section, British Association," *JRAS* 17 (1884-1885): 277-78; E. B. Tyler, "Presidential Address," *Transactions, British Association for the Advancement of Science, 54th Meeting* (Montreal: n.p., 1885): 899-910.

marriage as a gender-based political and economic tool.[19] A careful examination of the archaeological and art historical record at Palmyra, with a special focus on the evidence provided by the female funerary portraits with their accompanying genealogies, in conjunction with Roman accounts of the region, adds new insights concerning the important roles of women in the pre-Islamic Near East. A better understanding of the practice of *nikah* and *mut'a* marriages in the ancient Near East not only assists in helping to explain the widespread regional power exerted by the Palmyrenes from the first to the mid-third centuries C.E. (despite their relatively low population base), but also sheds light on the rise of Palmyra's last viable ruler, the powerful warrior queen Zenobia/Bat (daughter of) Zabbai who challenged the might of imperial Rome itself (Fig. 6-3). The *mut'a* marriage arrangement was of social, economic, and political importance, and was a practical solution to the harsh environmental and political dangers within Greater Syria. As practiced prior to the Islamic period, it represents a functional remnant of an earlier nomadic tribal existence in which matriarchal social customs were more prevalent.[20]

Marriage Options as a Response to Conditions in the Near East before the Advent of Islam

In the past, nomadic, semi-nomadic and settled societies of the Near East faced political, economic and environmental challenges that often threatened the survival of the individual and thus the efficacy of the clan, tribe and community. In order to cope with these challenges, early Semitic-speaking groups including the Aramaean, Hebrew, and emerging Arab societies of the Levant, Greater Syria, and Arabia relied on a range of marriage and adoption options in order to ensure the birth of children and the viability and power of the individual, clan, and tribe.[21] Such

---

[19] Robertson Smith, *Kinship and Marriage in Early Islam*, xi, 29, 38-39, 80-81, 102-3, 116, 126-27.

[20] The debate over the extent of matriarchal customs within early Aramaean and Arab tribes is on-going. See fns. 4, 6 and 17 for a few of the major sources. See also Appendix 6-I.

[21] The exact number and types of such marriage arrangements, as they existed before Islam, are unknown. See Esposito, *Women in Muslim Family Law*, 12-13. At Palmyra, patriarchal marriage and temporary matriarchal marriage are evident, as this article discusses. Variations of temporary (*mut'a*) marriage seem to have been numerous both before the advent and at the beginning of Islam. These types could have included: 1) the temporary lending of a wife to a male guest to meet

options were necessary given the severe climate, armed confrontations, diseases, and the resultant high adult, infant, and child mortality rates of the region. Additionally, members of nuclear families were often separated for long periods of time due to caravan ventures, war, or economic necessity.

Other ancient cultures also developed social contrivances to address the need for viable offspring, or the more appropriate channeling of human sexual desires. For example, the ancient Spartans initiated laws with relation to infertility within its family structures. These laws were driven by the stresses put upon the Spartan population base due to the military nature of its society. Given Sparta's communally-based social structure and the conscription of all healthy males from age six through their early thirties for military service, Spartan society faced issues of a declining indigenous population due to low birth rates, plague, injury, the age of thirty or above for males at marriage (and thus declining sexual potency), and other factors.[22] Thus, Spartan law provided that if a man could not produce his own heir, an outside male could be temporarily contracted to impregnate his wife in order to produce legitimate offspring.[23] Additionally, if a Spartan male favored another man's wife due to her modesty, social virtues and the beauty of her children, that male could make a contract with the woman's husband to "borrow her" in order to produce children with her for his own line.[24] The Spartan women involved in such

---

customs of hospitality; 2) the temporary marriage of a male to a female during long caravan or military ventures, which took the male away from immediate family. Such an arrangement not only met sexual needs, but offered a temporary sanctuary of protection and support through the family of the temporary wife; 3) temporary marriage for the sexual pleasure of one or both partners. This was also a more acceptable social solution to societies with high numbers of widows or widowers due to famine, war, or disease; 4) temporary marriage contracted by a single woman with a male partner to produce offspring that would build up the woman's clan; and, 5) temporary marriage of a wife to a male other than her husband due to the impotency of the husband in order to produce offspring within the husband's lineage.

[22] W. G. Forrest, *A History of Sparta 950-192 B.C.* (New York: Norton, 1958), 51-55.

[23] Ibid., 136c for the stresses on Spartan populations and their impact on Spartan inheritance laws. For Spartan customs associated with an outside male impregnating another's wife to not only allow offspring for the married couple's family, but also on occasion to contract another's wife to raise up his own independent offspring, see Plutarch, *Plutarch's Lives* (trans. J. Dryden; New York: Random House, 1988), 61.

[24] Ibid.

temporary relationships were not from the lowest levels of Spartan society, but rather were from the highest social strata and, given Plutarch's account, representative of the best of Spartan virtues.[25]

According to the Hebrew Bible, Israelite society provided for the Levirate marriage. In this case, a man was obliged to marry the widow of his deceased brother and to raise any children that resulted from that union in his brother's name.[26] In both ancient Sparta and Israel, the concern was to produce heirs for the patriarchal side of the family, males for military service and economic productivity, and to provide for the widow or other unwed women in the family, especially in old age.[27] By contrast, certain types of *mut'a* marriages as they were practiced in pre-Islamic Arab Near Eastern contexts were concerned with preserving the number of offspring associated with an individual woman, and with guaranteeing children for the woman's extended family and clan. This presupposes a concern with the rights and economic and political needs of both the patriarchal and matriarchal sides of a family.[28] Additionally, various forms of *mut'a* marriage may have provided a more socially controlled and accepted venue for channeling human sexual needs in situations where primary spouses were separated for long periods of time, or when populations contained large numbers of widows or widowers due to war, famine or devastating disease.

In pre-Islamic Syrian tribal contexts, *mut'a* or temporary marriage manifested itself in various forms. Some forms of *mut'a* were characterized by the woman choosing a mate for a contracted period of

---

[25] Ibid.

[26] See Gen 38:8, Deut 25:5-10, Ruth 4:1-1; see also Matt 22:24.

[27] Ibid.

[28] The importance of respecting legitimate concerns of both the male and female's clan or family can be seen especially at Palmyra in tomb contexts, where the custom of having dual portraits is often found for deceased women. When the woman has been the spouse in a patrilocal marriage, one portrait exists in the tomb of her husband, while another portrait appears in the tomb of her parents, in order to respect the clan associations of both sides of the families that are linked by marriage. See also Robertson Smith, *Kinship and Marriage in Early Arabia*, 80-81; Abu al-Faraj 'Ali ibn al-Husayn al-Isbahani, *Kitab al-Aghani* (Cairo: Dar al-Kutub, 1927-1961), 16, 106; Abu-Tammam, *Kitab al-Hamasa*, (Calcutta: Laysay fi D'ar al-Am'arah, 1856), 729; and Marcellinus, *The Works of Ammianus Marcellinus*, vol. 1, XIV.1-4. All of the above note situations in pre-Islamic Greater Syria and Arabia in which a married woman retained her location of residence with her clan or tribe and/or owned and controlled her residence with the male as an invited guest. The male spouse might have been dismissed from the marriage and sexual access to the wife at the wife's whim.

time, in order to produce living offspring.[29] The resultant child belonged
solely to the mother and was accorded legitimacy by its mother's clan and
tribe.[30] Such an arrangement built up the woman's clan but also made it
possible for the woman to become the founder of her own family, clan,
and tribe.[31] This type of *mut'a* marital arrangement contrasts significantly
with the *nikah al-mut'a* marriage, in which a man initiates negotiations for
a wife for hire for a short period of time. *Nikah al-mut'a* was also a pre-
Islamic pagan practice, which some Muslim scholars believe was
condemned during the early decades of Islam.[32] Others disagree, and
suggest that Muhammad and the *Quran* sanctioned the practice.[33] If early
Islam accepted *nikah al'mut'a*, at the same time Shi'a Islam eventually de-
emphasized other types of *mut'a* marriages, favoring the arrangement that
built up the lineage of the male participant. Significantly, many scholars
including Robertson Smith assumed that women of a clan or *hayy* who
engaged in a temporary marriage arrangement at the advent of Islam must
have been from a lower social strata, possibly even harlots or "others who
were ineligible for regular marriage," or women of a lower class status.[34]
Since there is conflicting evidence by the time of the Prophet Muhammad
with regard to this question, the evidence from pre-Islamic Palmyra is
essential in understanding the historic and cultural roots of the practice in
the late Hellenistic and Roman periods and thus before the advent of Islam.[35]

---

[29] See Robertson Smith, *Kinship and Marriage in Early Arabia*, 29, 38-39, 202-3.
These examples, taken with the conditions described by the marriage of Queen
Zenobia of Palmyra with the Palmyrene general and senator Odainat discussed in
this study and cited in the *Scriptores Historiae Augustae, trig. tyr.* (trans. D.
Maggie; London: W. H. Heinemann and NY: Putnam, 1932) 30, 103, and 12-22
seem to indicate that a woman could contract for a husband to produce children for
her own lineage or to formalize a temporary sexual relationship.
[30] Ibid.; Robertson Smith, *Kinship and Marriage in Early Arabia*, 29.
[31] Ibid.
[32] See Appendix 6-I for a listing of sources pertinent to the debate over *nikah al-
mut'a* within Islam. In addition to published sources, Appendix 6-I includes a
website listing, which is representative of the current on-going debate between
Shi'i factions and Sunni Islam. Some of these websites are valuable since they
contain English translations of Arabic texts that are often difficult for Western
scholars to find and access. I am indebted to my esteemed colleague, Dr. Hashim
al-Tawil, for the website sources.
[33] Ibid.
[34] See Peters, "Preface," viii-ix; as well as Robertson Smith, *Kinship and Marriage
in Early Arabia*, 127-28.
[35] For conflicting evidence about *mut'a* marriage at the time of the Prophet
Muhammad, see Robertson Smith, *Kinship and Marriage in Early Arabia*, 289-90,

At the Oasis of Palmyra/Tadmor, an eclectic mix of Phoenician, Mesopotamian, Parthian, Persian, Hellenistic Greek and Roman artistic and religious influences melded with an already evolving Aramaean and Arab nomadic tribal heritage to create a cultural milieu whose funerary customs resulted in a unprecedented opportunity to trace the relationships among individuals within family and tribal groups and to look at their religious preferences. Palmyra's wealth supported the construction of tombs with funerary portraits, which also hosted inscribed genealogies. Additionally, for women, the utilization of multiple types of female headdresses and hair arrangements make their portraits important depositories of information associated with familial ties, cultic associations, and family, clan and tribal history (Fig. 6-4).[36]

Palmyra's Importance, and the Complex Roles of Palmyrene Women

By the late first century C.E., Palmyra, Syria (known previous to Roman incursions in the Near East as Tadmor), was already eclipsing Nabataean Petra to the south in present-day Jordan as the premier trade emporium of the Near East. Palmyra acted as one of the major transport hubs and caravan staging regions for exotic goods coming from China, India, the Persian Gulf, southern Arabia and Afghanistan as they made their way to the consumer ports of the western Mediterranean Basin and Roman Asia Minor. From these locations, goods were sold and transported to Rome itself and throughout the vast Roman Empire, finding their way

---

where Robertson Smith discusses the suggestion made by early Islamic historians that Khadija, Muhammad's first wife, was born to her parents through a *mut'a* marriage arrangement between her mother and her father. In addition, Khadija's relationship with the Prophet Muhammad indicates that women had the right to initiate all types of marriage arrangements (both *mut'a* temporary marriages and patrilocal long-term marriages) with male partners during the era before the advent of Islam (i.e., Khadija proposed to her younger employee, Muhammad, who in turn accepted her offer of a long-term marriage). This seems to have been done without the permission of any male guardian from Khadija's side of the family, suggesting that she was free to make this arrangement for herself. It additionally suggests that she was able to own a major caravan enterprise, which hired male employees. See Appendix 6-I for sources relevant to the on-going debate concerning *mut'a* marriage at the advent of Islam.

[36] C. Finlayson, "Veil, Turban and Headpiece: Funerary Portraits and Female Status at Palmyra," *Les Annales Archéologiques Arabes Syriennes* 45-46 (2002-2003): 221-35.

even beyond Rome's boundaries to Northern Europe and Africa. Silk, pearls, spices, bronze statues, textiles, slaves, prostitutes, precious and semi-precious jewels, and gold were only a few of the commodities bought and sold along a vast network of intricate caravan hubs linked by tribal agreements often sealed with marriage alliances.[37] Both Petra and Palmyra shared a strong tribal heritage enriched over time by direct trade contacts with the Phoenician city-states, Persia, and the Hellenistic dynasties of Ptolemaic Egypt and Seleucid Syria, as well as Asia Minor. With the Roman absorption of Nabataean Petra to the south in 106 C.E., Palmyra emerged as the premier trade conduit of the northern Syrian desert and as an important client kingdom of Rome, charged with maintaining the safety and vitality of the trade routes to the East and Dura Europos on the Euphrates, and the integrity of the boundaries of the Eastern Roman Empire against the Parthians and emerging Sassanian Persian Empire. Palmyrene camel corps and archers were famous for their prowess throughout the Roman world.[38] These political and military responsibilities, in addition to the manpower necessary to maintain caravan and trade initiatives as far east as Gandhara, India and Afghanistan, placed population pressures on the clans and tribes of the Tadmor Oasis. With so many men involved in these endeavors, the women of Palmyra maintained an importance within their society that stemmed from practical necessity. Additionally, nomadic tribal customs in the region dictated that women and children had to join men in the defense of the family, clan and tribe in situations of military necessity.[39]

    With these economic and military responsibilities came increased wealth. From the late first century B.C.E. to the capture of Palmyra in 272/273 C.E. by the Roman Emperor Aurelian, Palmyrene families built and embellished extravagant tombs for members of their immediate and extended households. They also sublet *loculi* or burial slots to friends and fellow citizens. Due to the religious influences of Egypt by way of Phoenicia, as well as trade with Mesopotamia through the Euphrates corridor, Palmyrenes adopted an eclectic mix of religious assumptions

---

[37] J. Chabot, "Remarque sur le Tarif de Palmyre," *JA* 12 (1918): 301-17. Also, J. Teixidor, "Le tariff de Palmyre, I: un commentaire de la version palyrénienne," *AuOr* 1 (1983): 235-52; J. F. Matthews, "The Tax Law of Palmyra: Evidence for Economic History in a City of the Roman East," *JRS* 74 (1984): 157-80. For marriage alliances and their importance in Palmyra, see Finlayson, "Veil, Turban, and Headpiece," (2002-2003).

[38] M. Colledge, *The Art of Palmyra* (London: Thames and Hudson, 1976), 231-33.

[39] Robertson Smith, *Kinship and Marriage in Early Arabia*, 295. See also fns. 57, 76 for other women warriors.

regarding the afterlife, which included the importance of funerary portraits to seal the burial *loculi* of the deceased. Almost more important for the Palmyrenes than these beautiful sculptures, however, were the genealogical inscriptions that accompanied portrait depictions of the mummified bodies of their loved ones. Within the Palmyrene metaphysical paradigm, these inscriptions tied the living members of the family and clan to their deceased relatives in the next life, and allowed the soul to be identified and maintained in the dimensions beyond the known world.[40] This belief system stemmed from Egyptian/Phoenician and Mesopotamian influences melded with Aramaean and Arab pantheons and cultic traits.[41] It is significant that the first deity mentioned in an inscription as associated with pre-Classical Tadmor was the great Mesopotamian goddess of fertility, fate, and rejuvenation, Ishtar.[42] By the Hellenistic and Roman periods, all the major male and female deities of Palmyra were associated with cosmic order and renewal, fertility and water, and were worshipped as avatars for the potential of the human soul to exist in some sort of dimension beyond the grave.[43] These major Palmyrene deities included the Mesopotamian Bel and Nergal, the Phoenician inspired Baal-Haddad, the Canaanite Baal-Hamon, the more ancient local Palmryene *baals* including Yarhibol, Malikbel, and Aglibol, and their female counterparts, the Hellenisitic Atargatis, and the Arab desert goddesses of war and fertility Allat, Manat, and al-Uzza.[44] Combined with Greco-Roman artistic influences, this religious milieu inspired the development of funerary portraiture within the tombs of Palmyra.

It is the female funerary portraits of Palmyra that present an unprecedented glimpse into the lives of individual ancient women who

---

[40] The most recent works on the religions of Palmyra are L. Dirven, *The Palmyrenes of Dura-Europos: A Study of Religious Interaction in Roman Syria* (Leiden: Brill, 1999); and, T. Kaizer, *The Religious Life of Palmyra* (Stuttgart: Franz Steiner, 2002). See also J. Teixidor, *The Pantheon of Palmyra* (Leiden: Brill, 1979); H. Drijvers, *The Religion of Palmyra* (Leiden: Brill, 1976). For a discussion of the Egyptian and Mesopotamian concept of names in funerary contexts, see E. Lefebvre, *Sphinx I* (Paris: n.p., 1896), 29; G. Contenau, *Everyday Life in Babylon and Assyria* (London: E. Arnold, 1954), 161-72.

[41] Ibid., all sources cited.

[42] M. Colledge, *The Art of Palmyra* (London: Thames and Hudson, 1976), 11.

[43] Kaizer, *The Religious Life of Palmyra*; Teixidor, *The Pantheon of Palmyra*; Drijvers, *The Religion of Palmyra*; H. Drijvers, "Afterlife and Funerary Symbolism in Palmyrene Religion," in *Atti del Colloguio Internazionale su la soteriologia dei culti orientali nell'Impero Romano, Roma 24-28 settembre 1979* (eds. U. Bianchi and M. Vermaseren; Leiden: Brill, 1979), 709-33.

[44] Ibid., all sources cited.

lived within an urban setting that still relied on nomadic skills and customs. Much of this complex system relied upon the military and diplomatic prowess of the major tribal groups of the Tadmor Oasis, the Palmyrenes involved in these endeavors, and the long- or short-term marriage alliances undertaken to enhance these efforts. In the desert environment of Palmyra, resources were carefully allocated and the worth of each individual was great. All these elements made *mut'a* marriages (in their various forms) viable options. Economic, military and health challenges combined to ensure that multiple options for child production and population viability were maintained. Thus, temporary *mut'a* marriage options remained important within Palmryene contexts, alongside the less flexible *nikah* patriarchal marriages. The epigraphic and sculptural evidence from ancient Palmyra indicates that certain classes of women of the oasis were held in high public and private esteem. This does not apply to female slaves and prostitutes whose tax terms are discussed in the famous Palmyrene tariff inscriptions.[45] Remnants of statues dedicated to free women who had contributed to the quality of political, religious or economic life at Tadmor are found alongside those of men in the *Agora* (market) and in other public gathering places.[46] Many of these works of art were dedicated by the governing bodies of the city or by tribal-cultic organizations of the oasis.[47] Additionally, the presentation of women within the tomb, especially in those works that depict brothers and sisters, demonstrates women's position of equality within the nuclear family and hints at the special relationship between male and female siblings that is a heritage of matriarchal organization among some Aramaean and Arab groups during a previous era of nomadic existence.[48] Funerary portraits

---

[45] Matthews, "The Tax Law of Palmyra."

[46] H. Ingholt, "Five Dated Tombs of Palmyra," *Berytus* 2-3, (1935-1936): 57-120; idem, "Inscriptions and Sculptures from Palmyra I," *Berytus* 2-3, (1935-1936): 83-127; idem, "Inscriptions and Sculptures from Palmyra II," *Berytus* 3 (1938): 93-140.

[47] Ibid., all sources cited.

[48] The funerary portrait of Mola (brother) and Bolaya (sister), ca. 190-210 C.E. from the Temple Tomb of Taai in the Southwest Necropolis at Palmyra demonstrates that this relationship was celebrated at Palmyra (see Fig. 6-5). The importance of a woman's brother over and above her husband or her son is reflected in an old Arab saying, "*Al-walad maulood al joz maujood, wa al akh al aziz min wain ya'ood*" ("A child can be born, the husband is there, and the brother, the dear one, from whence shall he come?"). See A. Goodrich-Freer, *Arabs in Tent and Town* (London: Putnam, 1924), 25. For resources on matrilineal descent among the early Arabs, see fns. 4, 6, 8 and 17, and especially Robertson Smith, *Kinship and Marriage in Early Arabia*, 29, 38, 205.

that include a brother and sister often present the woman in a more prominent visual position as she reclines on a symposium *kline* or couch in equal status to her brother (see Fig. 6-5).

Portraits of a husband and wife married in a patriarchal or *nikah* arrangement followed a somewhat different pattern. The man is often depicted as a larger figure reclining on a symposium *kline*, while his wife is almost always seated on a chair in a place of honor to the right her husband (Fig. 6-6). The wife is never shown reclining with her husband. Children and grandchildren usually stand between their parents or a grandparent in an attitude of respect (see Fig. 6-6). In rare cases, other individuals such as stewards or slaves with a special status within the family may also be depicted within the conjugal group.[49] At times, uncles, aunts, and other relatives may be portrayed within the family composition. Married daughters and their husbands sometimes appear in *rondel* portraits beneath the *kline* composition in larger funerary family displays, thus retaining a viable presence within their parents' tomb, but often also with a portrait commissioned for the tomb of their husband's family (see Fig. 6-6).[50] The existence of dual imagery provided for the tomb of a wife's husband's family and also the tomb of her parents underscores the importance of both lineages within Palmyrene contexts.

Numerous other inscriptions demonstrate that Palmyrene women could own sizable amounts of property, which they might donate to worthy causes throughout the city.[51] They could also own or inherit ancestral

---

[49] An excellent example of a slave depicted within an owner's funerary composition is that of a Palmyrene woman and her slave, now at the Ny Carlsberg Glyptotek, Acc. No. 1153. See F. O. Hvidberg-Hansen, *The Palmyrene Inscriptions Ny Carlsberg Glyptotek* (Copenhagen: Ny Carlsberg Glypotek and Statens Humanistiske Forskningsräd, 1998), 75-76.

[50] C. Finlayson, *Veil, Turban, and Headpiece: Funerary Portraits and Female Status at Palmyra* (Ph.D. diss., University of Iowa, 1998), 327-29 for examples of dual portraits for both lineages within the tombs of Palmyra, and discussed with relation to the Hypogeum of Zebida and 'Ogeilu in the Southeastern Necropolis.

[51] Numerous Palmyrene inscriptions attest to this fact and are duplicated by a similar phenomenon at Nabataean Petra. See J. Euting, *Nabatäische Inschriften aus Arabian* (Berlin: G. Reimer, 1885), 79. At Palmyra, even freed female slaves could own tomb property. See, for example, the Hypogeum of Bat-Mitrai and Bat-Elyad in the Southwest Necropolis in Finlayson, *Veil, Turban, and Headpiece*, (1998), 745. Other inscriptions indicate that a "guardian" or "protector" was appointed for both men and women who inherited property at a young age but both of whose parents were dead or unidentified. See Ingholt, *Inscriptions and Sculptures from Palmyra I*, 109-10. Adult Palmyrene women could own and dispose of property without a guardian. By comparison, Roman women through

tombs and dispose of them independently at will, without the governance of an assigned guardian. This contrasts with Roman women who lacked such rights throughout most of the Republic and early Empire.[52] Palmyrene women also played an active role in the various cult rituals of both the Tadmor Oasis and the Palmyrene temple at Dura Europos (see Fig. 6-7). Relief sculptures from the Temple of Bel at Palmyra, the temple shared by the four major tribes of the city, demonstrate that women were part of the protective vanguard chosen to accompany the most important cultic objects of tribal religious veneration during what may have been the original migration of the tribes to the region (see Fig. 6-8).[53] While the well-known Bel Temple relief presents one of the earliest artistic examples

---

most of the Roman Republic and Early Imperial periods were considered incapable of managing economic resources without a legal male guardian or administrator for their property. See Ulpian in *The Book of Rules (The Institutes of Gauis and the Rules of Ulpian)*, (trans. J. Muirhead; Edinburgh: n.p., 1880), 505-6, 544-49, 630-32. Even as a marriage partner, the Roman woman was in a state of *manus* or subjugation to her husband. Women were considered incompetent to perform any of the public duties of male citizens, or to act as witnesses. The Voconian Laws forbade their institution as heirs by a testator worth not less than 100,000 asses, although the prohibition might be avoided by a trust. Women who inherited property had to be appointed a tutor who oversaw their finances and whose permission had to be obtained to accomplish even the simplest of financial transactions or property transfers. See B. Winter, *Roman Wives, Roman Widows* (Grand Rapids, Mich.: Eerdmans, 2003), 17-58, for a discussion of the evolution of the rights of Roman women. By contrast, Palmyrene inscriptions note that once an adult, a Palmyrene woman could govern her own affairs. See H. Ingholt, "Varia Tadmoroea," pp. 101-37 in *Palmyra, Bilan et perspectives*, (ed. E. Frézouls; Strasbourg: AECR, 1976), 109-10. This reference also notes the name of a Palmyrene woman called Thomallokhis (Tumallaku), whose name means, "she shall be made to have the ruling of her affairs."

[52] See Ingholt, "Varia Tadmoroea."

[53] In pre-Islamic eras, the tribal or community *qubbah* (shrine for the tribal deity/deities) was often guarded by women of high rank within the tribe, especially during a tribal migration, or when it was transported in times of war and from an important battle. See H. Lamens, *L'Arabie occidentale avant l'Hégire* (Beirut: Publisher, 1928), 127-28. In the Bel Temple relief, the ritual status of women was indicated by full veiling of the face, which was not utilized in other depictions of Palmyrene women in public sculpture or in tomb contexts. Veiling seems to have been used for special ritual processions. Compare College, *The Art of Palmyra*, pl. 26 (a procession of offering carriers with women) with Fig. 6-9 in this chapter, from the Bel Temple procession. Even into the Christian era, Arab women attempted to retain their rights as priestesses in religious functions. See R. S. Kraemer, *Women's Religions in the Greco-Roman World* (Oxford: Oxford University Press, 2004), 85-86.

of the veiling of women in the pre-Islamic world, Palmyrene women were not veiled in either private tomb or public community portraits. At Palmyra, veiling seems to have been associated with religious functions, a custom that may derive from ancient beliefs concerning status and the protection by women of cultic *baetyls* or tribal cultic objects associated with community identity.[54] Additionally, the ritual and domestic objects held by the women of Palmyra in their earliest surviving funerary portraits, the distaff and the spindle, associate them with the powerful goddesses of resurrection and cosmic renewal venerated in Greater Syria, including the Great Goddess of Syria discussed in Lucian's *de Dea Syria*.[55] It is also significant that in funerary contexts, far more Palmyrene women than men have tomb keys attached to their apparel. They associate the woman as the guardian of admittance or worthiness to the ancestral tomb, and as the holder of the keys of eternity.[56]

---

[54] At Palmyra, women's faces are fully veiled only in ritual processions such as the one depicted on the Bel Temple relief. All other depictions of women, including tomb portraits and public sculptural dedications of important women, did not depict them with veiled faces but rather with a *himation* over the head, or hosting other types of headdresses that covered the hair but not the face. The ritual transport of sacred idols, however, seemingly presented unique ritual circumstances in which the idol or *baetyl*, as well as the women accompanying it as guardians, were veiled. This custom may stem from an ancient belief that events of transition (tribal movement, birth, marriage, death) presented the potential for the presence of progress but also of danger. Veiling functioned as a protection against evil, but also as a sign of high status. Women's roles in important tribal movements are well documented. Even in the early Islamic period, the ancient custom of the Bedouin was to have a woman lead them into battle. See Goodrich-Freer, *Arabs in Tent and Town*, 197. See Kraemer, *Women's Religions in the Greco-Roman World*, 85-86 for a discussion of the attempts by Arab women to retain their ritual roles during the advent of Christianity. See also Lamens, *L'Arabie occidentale avant l'Hégire*, 127-28.

[55] Significantly, Lucian notes that the image of the Goddess of Syria at the holy Temple of Hire (probably the Holy City of Mambij in northern Syria, which was the center of the sacred complex for the Hellenistic Atargatis) held a spindle (Lucian, *de dea Syria* [trans. and ed. J. L. Lightfoot; Oxford: Oxford University Press, 2003], 43). In antiquity, the distaff and spindle were symbolic of goddesses of time, fate, creation, and rejuvenation. The revolutions of the whorls represented revolutions of the universe. Spinning and weaving were symbolic of the goddesses' power to weave the strands of destiny, and of their powers of cosmic creation. See J. Cooper, *An Illustrated Encyclopaedia of Traditional Symbols* (London: Routledge, 1978), 52, 156.

[56] See Drijvers, *Afterlife and Funerary Symbolism in Palmyrene Religion*, 709-33.

Women played an important role in warfare in Palmyra.[57] This helps to explain the personality of Palmyra's last queen, Zenobia/Bat Zabbai who was famous for her skill as a lion hunter, for participating in the military campaigns of her husband, the famous general Odainat, and for leading her own armies against Rome.[58] Indeed, the ancient deity of war and tribal desert raiding among the pre-Islamic Arab tribes at Palmyra was Allat, whose cosmic personality was decidedly female. Roman accounts of wars in the East with the Saracen Arabs, Parthians, Sassanians, and Gauls note the numbers of women found killed on the battlefields dressed in men's armor and attire.[59] The portrayal of women within Palmyrene tomb contexts does not present them as unequal to their priestly husbands, fathers or brothers, but rather as valuable and essential counterparts to men in the Palmyrene political, economic and religious paradigms.

---

[57] Roman writers noted the numbers of women fighting in the Persian forces adjacent to the boundaries of Palmyra. See for example, Zonaras XII, 23 in *CSHB*; Libanius LIX 100 in *Libanius (Orationes: Epistulae)*, (ed. R. Forster; Leipzig: n.p., 1909-1927); and Julian I.27A in *L'Empereur Julien, I, Discours de Julien César* (trans. J. Bidez, J. and F. Cumont; Paris: Les Belles Lettres, 1932). See also S. Lieu, "Captives, Refugees, and Exiles: A Study of Cross-Frontier Civilian Movements and Contacts between Rome and Persia from Valarian to Julian," pp. 475-505 in *The Defense of the Roman and Byzantine East* (BAR S297; eds. P. Freeman and D. Kennedy; Oxford: BAR, 1986), 480. For women fighters within Arab tribal contexts see Robertson Smith, *Kinship and Marriage in Early Arabia*, 295. The custom of women as military leaders among the Aramaean and Arab pre-Islamic tribal regions of Greater Syria, Arabia, and the Sinai are also demonstrated by Queen Iskallatu of the Arabs during the Assyrian Period, Queen Zenobia of Palmyra during the Roman Era, and Queen Mavia of the Sinai during the Byzantine Period. Additionally, at the Battle of Ohod where Islamic forces under Muhammad pushed toward Mecca, women participated in the battle in various ways on both sides. See Robertson Smith, *Kinship and Marriage in Early Arabia*, 295. See also al-Tabari, *Ta'rikh al-Rasul wa 'l-Muluk (History of the Prophets and Kings, or The History of al-Tabari)*, vol. 4, (trans. M. Pearlman and F. Rosenthal; New York: State University of New York Press, 1985-87), 139-50 for an account of pre-Islamic warlike queens in Greater Syria. For the role of Muhammad's wives in the Battle of Ohod, see K. Armstrong, *Muhammad: A Biography of the Prophet* (London: Phoenix Press; 1991), 188.

[58] Maggie, trans., *Scriptores Historiae Augustae, trig. tyr.*, 30, 4-12.

[59] See fn. 57.

Palmyra's Necropoli and Examples of Diverse Marriage Customs

By the first century C.E., Palmyra was divided into four major sectors based on the tribal settlement and geography of the oasis.[60] Each tribe was responsible for the maintenance of its own regional temple, dedicated to a major tribal deity.[61] In addition, each tribe participated in the cults of the Temple of Bel, which by the early Roman period seems to have functioned as a focal point of inter-tribal solidarity. Four major *necropoli* or "cities of the dead" were associated with the families and clans of each tribal region and were located around the perimeters of the urban center. These included what are now known as the Valley of the Tombs, the Southeastern Necropolis, the Southwestern Necropolis and the Northeastern Necropolis, the remains of which may now be covered by portions of the new city of Tadmor. Both the earlier tower tombs and later subterranean tombs of these *necropoli* represent the burials of the aristocratic, upper middle class and middle class populations of the ancient city. The *loculi* or burial receptacles for each of the deceased individuals were sealed with a portrait accompanied by genealogical inscriptions. Almost all inscriptions are in Palmyrene Aramaic (but most utilize Arab names), with only a few inscriptions in Latin or Greek. This indicates the potency of traditional cultural and ethnic constructs within Palmyrene tombs, despite the Greco-Roman influence of the portrait styles. When found intact, these inscriptions allow for the tracing of family organization, marital arrangements and alliances, and progeny.

Two other factors help trace family relationships. First, female headdress styles highlight matriarchal associations, as they were passed down from maternal grandmothers and mothers to daughters, whether or not these women were buried in the same tomb or the tribal necropolis as their parents, or had married into another clan or tribe and were buried in a different necropolis location within the city.[62] Second, the location of the individual's burial with relation to other family members is of significance, for its location often indicates the importance of grandmothers as well as aunts and uncles as protectors and mentors of specific family members. The above factors thus make it possible to begin the process of identifying

---

[60] See D. Schlumberger, "Les Quatre Tribus de Palmyre," *Syria* (1971): 121-33 for a discussion of the inscriptional sources for the divisions of the city and the four major tribes of Palmyra. Debate continues among modern scholars as to the exact number of tribes and clans in classical Tadmor.

[61] Ibid.

[62] Finlayson, "Veil, Turban and Headpiece," (2002-2003), 221-35.

formal patriarchal permanent *nikah* marriages as well as the existence of temporary *mut'a* marriages.

There are just over 430 known female Palmyrene funerary portraits extant in collections scattered all over the world. The largest collections outside of Syria reside in the Vatican Museums, the British Museum, the Louvre, and the Archaeological Museum of Istanbul. Some are held in private collections and have not yet been published or photographed. Of the 430 or so, approximately 218 portraits of women are in Syria, either in the museum or in excavated tombs in Palmyra, or in storage or on display the National Museum in Damascus. Forty-three of these are either too damaged to analyze, or are missing but noted in records or publications. Given the fact that many of the early tower tombs at Palmyra held between 200-300 individuals, extant and known today are portraits equivalent in number to those of only two tower tombs. Many more are either unexcavated or unpublished. Given these numbers, it is significant that of the 218 portraits of women in Palmyra and Damascus, sixteen depict women who are indicated by inscription as being mothers, although there is no father listed as a parent for their children. Additionally, fourteen women are portrayed in association with children, but their portraits have no extant inscription. Thus, it is possible that between 7-14 percent of the known portraits of women indicate women associated with children but not with husbands.

While the limited space allowed for this discussion precludes listing all the female portraits from the Tadmor Oasis that may indicate the potential for *mut'a* marriage at Palmyra, two portrait examples and one literary reference from my extensive study of the tombs and collections of Palmyra and those in the Damascus National Museum (as well as European and American collections) demonstrate the potential for the practice of *mut'a* marriage and particularly for a matriarchal form of *mut'a* marriage during the late Roman period in Syria. These examples include: (1) the portrait of 'Ami, daughter of Hari (son of) Zebida, wet nurse (of) Bariki son of Bara from the Hypogeum of Bariki, son of Zebida (Hypogeum Number 9) in the Southeast Necropolis (Palmyra Museum Acc. Numb. 2006/7163), originally located in the entrance gallery of the tomb between T3 and T4 and dated to ca. 120-150 C.E. (Fig. 6-9); (2) the portrait of Nobai/Nabu, daughter of Asbar with her two sons, Zabgdibol and Asbar, of unknown tomb provenance from Palmyra, Damascus National Museum Acc. Numb. 2654/5318, Palmyra Room No. 5, dated to ca. 100-150 C.E. (Fig. 6-10); as well as, (3) the Roman accounts of Queen Zenobia/Bat Zabbai, which present strong evidence for the importance of a matriarchal form of *mut'a* marriage within Palmyra among the women of the highest status.

The nature of the genealogical inscriptions and the location of at least one of these portraits within its tomb are of special significance. In most Palmyrene inscriptions that indicate a dedication to a deceased woman within a patriarchal marriage situation, the husband's name is given. Thus, for example, the inscription in a dual portrait from the Hypogeum of Sassans reads, "Helas Malku, son of Mattai and Barnim, daughter of Reb'al (his) wife," dated to ca. 90-120 C.E.; or, in a family *klinae* portrait grouping from the Hypogeum of Artaban, son of 'Ogga from the Southeast Necropolis, we find, "Berreta, daughter of Yarhai, son of Barra, wife of 'Ogga, son of Artaban," dated to ca. 120-140 C.E.; or in a single portrait from the Hypogeum of Sassan in the Southeast Necropolis, "Aqmat, daughter of Baruqa, son of Taimsa, wife of Belsuri, son of Mattai Rabba, *helas*," dated to ca. 90-130 C.E.

Typically, in a patriarchal marriage, even if a child's father was deceased, his name would have been noted according to the traditional custom of Palmryene funerary documentation, which was considered critical for the identification of the soul in the afterlife. However, in inscriptions where women are associated singly with children or as heads of families, without the name of the husband being given, the children do not host their father's name, but only their mother's. These women and their children were not simply widows and orphans; their unique inscriptional status indicates that the relationship between the parents was not the common patriarchal style marriage.

The first example of such a woman is 'Ami, daugher of Hari (son of) Zebida, wet nurse (of) Bariki, son of Bara who comes from Tomb 9, the Hypogeum of Bariki son of Zebida in the Southeast Necropolis (Figs. 6-9). This tomb shares a common vestibule with that of Tomb 10, the Hypogeum of Taima'amed son of Moqimu, which was established in 94 C.E., as well as Tomb 11, the Hypogeum of A'ailami son of 'Abnergal, established in 109 C.E. A close relationship between these three families is therefore assumed. Additionally, the foundation text of Tomb 9 gives the name of the clan founder, Bariki, and Sokaibel as the clan name. This tomb is significant since it hosts the first inscriptional name of a Palmyrene clan in the Southeastern Necropolis. Other inscriptional evidence states that the clan was divided into two main branches, that of the family of Bariki son of Zebida, and that of his brother Lisams.[63] From

---

[63] See D. Hillers and E. Cussini, *Palmyrene Aramaic Texts* (PAT) (Baltimore: Johns Hopkins University Press, 1996), 312-14, which lists all the major

Tomb 9 comes the portrait of 'Ami, daughter of Hari, son of Zebida, "wet nurse" of Bariki, son of Bara.[64] Given her genealogy, 'Ami was thus not a woman of low status. Her designation as a "wet nurse" is significant in its Near Eastern context. Contrary to Roman practices in the West, many peoples of the Near East valued the position of wet nurse since they believed that emotional and physical characteristics were passed through the breast milk to the nursed child. A wet nurse was carefully chosen, with first priority given to female relatives within the clan since the link of shared milk established a familial obligation that would be neither politically expedient, nor economically wise to extend to outsiders. Indeed, the wet nurse and nursed child, though unrelated by birth, were thought to become one flesh and one blood.[65] In this way, the act of nursing established a relationship that was even stronger in some respects than that of formal adoption, a relationship that extended to other children nursed by the same woman. The wet nurse and her nursed children were obligated "by the milk" to recognize familial obligations to one another that existed throughout their lives, and, as evidenced by 'Ami's portrait location within the Hypogeum of Bariki, remained strong even in death. In this way, 'Ami, the paternal cousin of Bariki the Priest, was doubly tied to Bariki's family by becoming the wet nurse of his grandson and namesake.

Her portrait is also important in that it represents a woman who is described as the mother of a son, Abnergal, whose portrait, dated to 150-180 C.E., depicts him as a caravan leader. Abnergal's father's name is not stated in either the portrait of his mother, or in his own.[66] This is unusual for Palmyrene male children, given the common genealogical naming pattern in Palmyrene epitaphs, which most often list the patriarch and then the wife and mother. By contrast, 'Ami is a woman who is accorded her

---

Palmyrene inscriptions for Hypogeum 9, including PAT 2702, with the family name of "*skbl.*"

[64] Ibid., 312, PAT 2695, "*'my brt hry zbd' mrbyt bryky br.*"

[65] Of interest is the widespread acceptance of this custom throughout the Eastern Mediterranean Basin and as far east as Muslim Mughal India. A Greek vase depicting Hera offering a breast to the adult Herakles is thus symbolic of his adoption by her in his quest for immortality on Mt. Olympus. The composition has precedents in ancient Egypt where a deceased pharaoh was often depicted nursing from the breast of Hathor. The immortal characteristics of the goddess were thus passed on to the pharaoh, her adopted son. References to "milk brothers" are also found in Mughal India. For references to the Arab custom, see H. Granqvist, *Birth and Childhood among the Arabs: Studies in a Muhammadan Village in Palestine* (Helsinki: Ams Pr Inc., 1947), 107-8, 112-15, 170-71.

[66] Hillers and Cussini, *Palmyrene Aramaic Texts*, 312, PAT 2694, "*bnrgl br 'my hbl.*"

own matriarchal descent line. Additionally, her name, 'Ami, and that of her son, Abnergal, do not seem to be common within the Bariki branch of the Bariki Sokaibel clan. Her portrait, and that of her son, both rest within the first vestibule of the main corridor on the north side of the tomb. Thus, while included with her son in the Bariki tomb as relatives ("mother by the milk" and "brother by the milk"), 'Ami and her son were allotted their own space for subsequent family burials in a place of honor on the right side of the main corridor. At the same time, this is not the highest place of honor, which was at the end of the exedra close to the family *kline* of Bariki, son of Zebida, son of Bariki Sokaibel. It is also possible that the portraits, but not the interments of actual burials of 'Ami and Abnergal, were included in the Bariki tomb due to the breast milk relationship. They may have been buried in a tomb owned by 'Ami herself, as matriarch of a separate family branch. Given her high status as a paternal cousin to the founder of the tomb and the prominent location of her portrait within the tomb, it is unlikely that 'Ami was a prostitute or a woman of lower status. Thus, 'Ami and her son are examples of a Palmyrene *mut'a* marriage arrangement.

A second female portrait, that of Nobai or Nabu, is representative of a number of other female funerary portraits at Palmyra that indicate the family status of a woman, i.e., she produced offspring but there is no mention of a husband or a father (Fig. 6-10). Nobai/Nabu was the daughter of Asbar, and she had two sons, Zabdibol and Asbar (*'hbl nby brt 'sbr wzbdbwl w'sbr bnyh*).[67] The sons are portrayed over her shoulders. The pattern of the central headdress shows a palm frond with dates, wall, or well (the circles at the base of the palm fronds), thus associating her with the powerful clans of the Southeastern Necropolis who often intermarried with the Salamallat Clan of the north side of the city. Like 'Ami, she was not a woman of questionable social or sexual status, even though she had two sons whose father's name is never mentioned. Nobai, too, is an example of a *mut'a* marriage arrangement at Palmyra.

These women and their children are representative of a number of funerary portraits from Palmyrene tombs that seem to indicate the practice of some type of *mut'a* marriage by members of the aristocratic and upper middle classes. These were women from the highest social levels of the ancient city. Accounts of the life of Zenobia, Palmyra's warrior queen, are valuable when considering the exact type of temporary marriage practiced by these women.

---

[67] Direct transcription for this portrait now in the Damascus National Museum, Acc. 2654/5318.

The best primary literary evidence for the existence of *mut'a* marriage as practiced by Palmyrene women comes from Roman accounts of Tadmor's most famous citizen, Queen Zenobia/Bat Zabbai, whose father may have been a Palmyrene senator (Fig. 6-3). This intrepid woman, who challenged Roman might in the East, may have engaged in a matriarchal form of *mut'a* marriage with the famous Palmyrene general and senator, Odainat/Odenathus. While the Roman authors of the *Scriptores Historiae Augustae* did not understand the principles of *mut'a* marriage in the Near East, it was due to the very nature of the Roman patriarchal paradigm that the Latin writer of the sections on Zenobia noted the strange customs of the Palmyrene queen described below. This description of her relationship with Odainat is an accurate account of a matriarchal type of *mut'a* marriage, in which the conditions of sexual access are established by the woman for the production of her child. The offspring of such a match belongs to the mother and mother's clan rather than to the father and his clan:

> For this proud woman performed the functions of a monarch, both while Gallienus ruled and afterwards when Claudius was busied with the war against the Goths, and in the end could scarcely be conquered by Aurelian himself, under whom she was led in triumph and submitted to the sway of Rome…. Such was her continence, it is said, that she would not know even her own husband, save for the purpose of conception. For once she had lain with him, she would refrain until the time of menstruation to see if she were pregnant; if not, she would again grant him an opportunity of begetting children.[68]

The sexual relationship between Zenobia and Odainat was not one primarily established for pleasure, as it was limited in frequency and availability. Additionally, sexual access was controlled by Zenobia, and was timed for the production of a child. While some may see this story as an example of Roman calumny, other primary evidence supports the conclusion that Zenobia was involved in a matriarchal *mut'a* relationship rather than a patriarchal *nikah* arrangement. Significantly, Odainat already had male children from a previous marriage and thus had established heirs within his own family and clan.[69] When Odainat was assassinated by an estranged relative, Zenobia's young son Wahballath (Gift of Allat), fathered by Odainat, assumed all of Odainat's titles including "King of

---

[68] Maggie, trans., *Scriptores Historiae Augustae, trig. tyr.*, 30, 103 and 12-22.
[69] Ibid., 15, 1-5 for a listing of the other sons of Odainat. See also M. Gawlikowski, "Les princes de Palmyre," *Syria* 62 (1985): 251-61.

Kings" and ruled Palmyra under the regency of his mother.[70] This occurred despite the existence of older sons from Odainat's previous marriage.[71] The political and military power of the Zabbai family or clan, coupled with Zenobia's allegations of descent from the Seleucids through Antiochus Sidetes or Antiochus IV Epiphanes, and the Ptolemies through Cleopatra Thea, may have given Zenobia and her young son by Odainat a strong claim to this position of authority in the minds of the Palmyrenes.[72] Although Zenobia's son also assumed the Roman titles given to his deceased birth father as a matter of political expediency, his mother's genealogical claims to the Aramaean/Arab tribes of Tadmor and the Hellenistic glories of both the Ptolemies and Seleucids allowed Zenobia to thrust her son forward as a viable Near Eastern alternative to the inept Roman government in the East during this critical period of invasions by Gauls from the north and Sassanians from the East. This suggests that the institution of *mut'a* marriage in its matriarchal form may have provided a political vehicle for Zenobia's attempt to give her son imperial power in the East based not only on Roman and Hellenistic foundations, but also more importantly on Aramaean/Arab tribal precedents. The acceptance by the Palmyrenes and others in the region of Zenobia's authority, and Wahballat's position even though he was a child, is demonstrated by her initial success against Roman forces in Greater Syria, the Levant, and Egypt.

Conclusions

These examples facilitate a new examination of the possibility of a matriarchal form of *mut'a* marriage at Palmyra during the late Roman Period. The women who seem to have practiced some type of *mut'a* marriage did not originate from the lower classes, or from circumstances in which no other types of marriage alliances were available to them. This

---

[70] Maggie, trans., *Scriptores Historiae Augustae, trig. tyr*, 30, 1-3 and 112-22. Also *CIS* II , 3971, trans. infra. 4.5.5. This inscription refers to Zenobia as both Septimia bath Zabbai and bath Antiochus (*bath/bat*=daughter of). Zenobia claimed descent from Cleopatra Thea and possibly from Antiochus IV Epiphanes or Antiochus Sidetes, who was the third husband of Cleopatra Thea. See also Ingholt, "Varia Tadmoroea," 137. See *CIS* II, 3971 for the titles assumed by Zenobia's son Wahballat, including "King of Kings," "Corrector of the Entire Orient" and "son of Septimus."

[71] See fn. 69 for the older sons of Odainat who were passed over at his death in favor of Wahballat, son of Zenobia.

[72] See particularly *CIS* II, 3946 and 3947.

is especially true for Queen Zenobia/Bat Zabbai and for the two women from the tombs of Palmyra's aristocratic and upper class families. This fact must cause a reevaluation of the many portraits of women at Palmyra whose epitaphs do not mention a husband but for whom there is no doubt that they were mothers of children. Many Palmyrene women must have had some degree of independence in choosing the men with whom they wished to produce children. In addition, they would have had discretion in deciding whether to enter into a matriarchal *mut'a* arrangement, a *nikah al-mut'a* situation in which the man contracted a temporary marriage, another form of *mut'a* relationship, or a formal patriarchal marriage. Women might even have chosen to produce children through various types of marriages at different times in their lives. Their options may have been formally controlled by social conventions within the community for which there is yet no literary evidence. However, contrary to what scholars like Robertson Smith and Peters have assumed, the archaeological evidence from Palmyra indicates that *mut'a* marriages had the potential to act as powerful engines of political power. This suggests that the clan or *hayy* had some influence over the decisions of individual women to enter into marriage arrangements, since the woman's clan bore the responsibility of nurturing and protecting her offspring in an environment of limited resources. Peters stated that *mut'a* marriages were "…instituted without the intervention or consultation of the *hayy*… and the *hayy* was not consulted."[73] However, his discussion demonstrates that he did not understand that there may have been multiple forms of *mut'a* arrangements in ancient Near Eastern societies, including forms that were initiated by women wishing to produce offspring, and not only by men (or women) for temporary sexual gratification, or for obligations of hospitality. Peters, Robertson Smith, and others postulated that the women who practiced a *mut'a* relationship were harlots or ineligible for "regular" marriages, or from inferior classes or less influential tribes, or that their sexual relationships were beyond the interest or control of the clan or *hayy*.[74] These assumptions are not supported by the archaeological and epigraphic evidence at Palmyra, where women of high status engaged in either matriarchal or another form of *mut'a* marriage as a way to bring added offspring to their individual families and clans. Such arrangements would have bolstered the population, in response to the high demands made on the Palmyrene population by military responsibilities, caravan ventures and other health hazards, while also enhancing economic opportunities for

---

[73] See Peters, "Preface," ix.
[74] Robertson Smith, *Kinship and Marriage in Early Arabia*, 167.

families, clans and tribes through temporary connections with outside tribes, clans or families along extended trade routes. Additionally, such arrangements had the potential to bring unprecedented power and influence to the women involved. This helps explain the phenomenon of the many women's names that were later associated with the foundation names of Arab tribes into the Islamic era.[75] It also helps explain some of the possible latent matriarchal characteristics of ancient Aramaen/Arab societies associated with the rise of great female political and military leaders during the ancient, classical, and Byzantine eras. Women such as the ancient Aramaean/Arab Queen Iskallatu who defied the power of the Assyrians, Queen Zenobia of Palmyra who challenged the Romans, and Queen Mavia of the Sinai who broke from Byzantine control, are better understood by reference to the evidence for tribal matriarchal customs.[76] A child produced in a matriarchal *mut'a* marriage or in some form of *nikah al-mut'a* marriage (in which the resultant child was not claimed by the father) would have been protected by the mother's brother and father. A girl was under the special protection of an uncle, and also linked to her mother's sisters and mother. Such links are evident in family relationships as defined by the location of child burials in the ancient tombs of Palmyra. At Tadmor, a child was buried just as frequently next to a grandparent, uncle or aunt, as to parent or parents.[77]

---

[75] Ibid., 29, 38, 202-3.

[76] In his campaigns against the Aramaeans and Arabs, Sennacherib, king of Assyria notes having captured a woman known as Iskallatu, queen of the Arabs, from the stronghold of Adumatu. See *ANET*, 291. For other examples of Arab women warriors and queens, see al-Tabari, *History of the Prophets and Kings*, 139-50. For Queen Mavia of the Sinai, see I. Shahid, *Byzantium and the Arabs in the Fourth Century* (Washington, D.C.: Dumbarton Oaks Press, 1984), 184-85, 308-11, 388.

[77] Salmat, daughter of Salme is an excellent example of a child being buried next to an uncle, aunt or grandparents rather than parents. Her portrait is dated to ca. 180-210 C.E. and is located in the Hypogeum of Zebida (Hypogeum No. 8) of the Southeast Necropolis, main exedra, Travée 3, Loculus 2. Salmat was the granddaughter of Zebida, the founder of the tomb. She was named after her father's sister, Salmat, whose portrait is also extant. Naming children after an aunt or uncle was a custom practiced quite often at Palmyra. Salmat the younger was buried in the same *travée* crypt as her uncle, Maltu, and Ahita, daughter of 'Atetan, a woman from outside the Zebida clan who may have been her aunt. Other examples of burials of nephews and nieces with aunts and uncles or grandparents are found throughout the cemeteries of ancient Palmyra, indicating a role of protection and stewardship among these relatives.

In conclusion, this study substantiates the importance that William Robertson Smith placed on the *mut'a* marriage arrangement in the pre-Islamic Near East, but corrects his assumption that only women of low social status who were beyond the concern of the *hayy* or clan participated in this practice. The archaeological and epigraphic evidence from ancient Palmyra refutes his assumption and indicates that there were multiple forms of *mut'a* arrangements, including the matriarchal form initiated by a women to produce children for her own lineage. Interestingly, this matriarchal form of *mut'a* marriage is more easily substantiated by the archaeological and epigraphic records than are the more patriarchal *nikah al-mut'a* types, although both forms and others probably existed side by side with patriarchal marriages. By the time of Muhammad, the new social and religious paradigms introduced by Islam and eventually Sharia Law created a period of flux and transition from the earlier pre-Islamic practices. The existence of multiple types of *mut'a* arrangements in pre-Islamic and even early Islamic eras may have contributed to the confusion and to the on-going debate among Islamic scholars over the role and acceptability of *mut'a* arrangements.[78] The importance of ancient matriarchal customs as viable options for dealing with political, military and environmental stresses helps explain these optional forms of conjugal relationships. The female funerary portraits of Palmyra, Syria provide links in the evolution of *mut'a* marriage and highlight its importance in understanding the socio-political roles of women in the ancient Near East. The Palmyrene portraits and the individuals they portray provide an invaluable glimpse into the diverse positions that women held in a tribally based community in ancient Greater Syria and Arabia.

---

[78] See Appendix 6-I.

Images

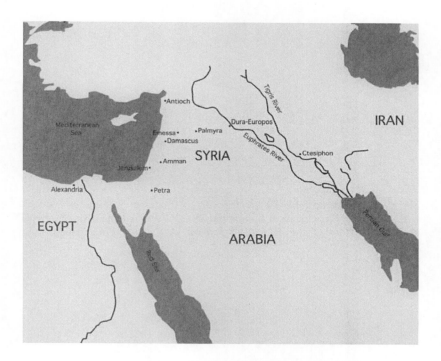

Fig. 6-1. Map. Location of Palmyra with relation to other major urban centers during the 3rd century C.E. (Author).

Fig. 6-2. Palmyrene funerary portrait of an unknown woman, ca. 200-230 C.E., from the Hypogeum of Salamallat in the Valley of the Tombs, central exedra. Courtesy of the Palmyra Museum, Acc. No. B1762/6586. (Photo: Author).

Fig. 6-3. Portrait image of Queen Zenobia of Palmyra (Bat Zabbai) on a billiontetradrachm minted in Alexandria, Egypt, 270 C.E. (Courtesy of I. Browning, *Palmyra* [London: Chatto & Windus, 1979] fig. 17)

Fig. 6-4. Reconstructed exhibit of the Yarhai Hypogeum from the S.E. Necropolis of Palmyra at the Damascus National Museum, ca. 150-200 C.E. Funerary portraits seal the *loculi* of the tomb as well as adorn the *triclinia* at the end of the main corridors. (Photo: Author).

Fig. 6-5. Funerary images of Bolaya, daughter of 'Ogga, son of Borrepha with her brother Mola. From the Tomb Temple of Taa'a in the Southwest Necropolis of Palmyra, ca. 190-210 C.E. Courtesy of the Damascus National Museum, Acc. No. 18802. (Photo: Author).

Fig. 6-6. Funerary banquet *kline* grouping from the Hypogeum of Malku at Palmyra, Southwest Necropolis, ca. 200-230 C.E., now in the Damascus National Museum, Acc. No. 4947. A family grouping originally from the west alcove of the north wall of the tomb. Husband is on the viewer's far right, followed by his father, then two children, and finally the wife and mother of the family, seated in honor on the far right side of her reclining husband. Other children and their spouses are shown below, in *rondel* portraits. Courtesy the Damascus National Museum. (Photo: Author).

Fig. 6-7. Fresco from the south wall of the Temple of Bel/Temple of the
Palmyrene gods at Dura Europos, ca. 180 C.E., now at the Damascus National
Museum. Women participate in a status equal to men in the rituals of the
temple. Syrian priests in their conical hats are also shown. Courtesy the
Damascus National Museum. (Photo: Author).

Fig. 6-8. Bel Temple stone relief with veiled women in a ritual procession behind a camel carrying a *qubbah* with the cult objects of the tribal group, ca. 32 C.E., Palmyra, Syria. (Photo: Author).

Fig. 6-9. 'Ami, daughter of Hari, (son of) Zebida, wet nurse (of) Bariki, son of Bara. Hypogeum of Bariki, son of Zebida (No. 9), Southeast Necropolis, Palmyra, Syria, ca. 120-150 C.E.   Palmyra Museum Acc. No. 2006/7163. Courtesy of the Palmyra Museum. (Photo: Author).

Fig. 6-10. Nobai or Nabu, daughter of Asbar, with two male children, Zabdibol and Asbar, her sons. No known tomb provenance, but from Palmyra. Now in the Damascus National Museum, Acc. No. 2654/5318. Courtesy the Damascus National Museum. (Photo: Author).

APPENDIX 6-I:

CLASSICAL AND ISLAMIC RESOURCES FOR DISCUSSIONS OF *MUT'A* MARRIAGE

Primary Sources

Ammianus Marcellinus, Vol. I, Book XIV, 3.
Herodotus, Book III.
The Holy Qur'an
    Surah 2 al-Baqarah, 235-41.
    Surah 4 al-Nisa, 24.
Scriptores Historiae Augustae, trig. tyr. 30.
Strabo, *Geography*, Book VII, 364-65.

Medieval Islamic Resources

Abd al-Rahman, b. Hujayra. (Egyptian judge, 69-83 A.H.). See al-Kindi below.

Abu Tammam. *Kitab al-Hamasa.* Calcutta: Laysay fi D'ar al-Amrarah, 1856.

Al-Kindi, Abu 'Umar (d. 961 C.E.). *Kitab al-Wulāh wa-Kitab al-Qudah.* Beirut: n .p., 1908.

Al-Qabisi. (Qayrawani jurist, ca. 1012 C.E.). In Al-Wansharisi, *al-Miyar al-Mu'rib wa'l-Jami' al-Mughrib 'an Fatawa Ahl Ifriqia wa'l-Andalus wa'l-Maghrib.* Ed. M. Hajji. Rabat: Wizarat al-Awqaf wa'l-Shu'un al-Islamiyya, 1981-1983.

Al-Tabari. *Jami' al-Bayan 'an Ta'wil ay al-Qur'an.* Ed. Mahmud Shakir. Cairo: Dar al-Ma'arif, n. d.

—. *Ta'rikh al-Rusul wa' l-Muluk (History of the Prophets and the Kings).* Trans. M. Pearlman and F. Rosenthal. New York: State University of New York Press, 1985-1987.

Al-Tahawi, Abu Jafar (d. 933 C.E.). *Kitab al-Shurut al-Saghir.* Ed. R. Awzjan. Baghdad: Matba'at al-'Ani, 1972.

Shaikh-i Baha'I Amili, Baha al-Muhammad Ibn Husayn. *Jami'i 'Abbasi (The Abbasid Compendium).* Tehran: Mirza 'Ali Asghar, n. d.

Modern Islamic Resources

Abdul-Rauf, Muhammad. *Marriage in Islam: A Manual.* New York: Exposition Press, 1972.

Ahmed, Leila. "Women and the Advent of Islam." *Signs* 11 (1986): 665-91.

Al-Fukaikî, Taufiq. *Kitab al-mut'a*, Nagaf: n.p. 1937.

Al-Mut'a fi Islam. n.a. Beirut: n. p., 1961.

Al-Qasimi, 'Abdallah Ali. *as-sirâ baina l-Islâm wa-l-wataniya: fi fiqh as-sî'a.* Cairo: n. p., n. d.

Amini, Ayatollah Ahmad A. *Al-Ghadir.* Tehran: Haydari Press, 1952.

Aminuddin, B. "Women's Status in Islam: A Muslim View." *Muslim World* 28/2 (1938): 153-63.

An-Nahhas, 'Abu Ga'far. *Kitab an-nasih wa-l-mansuh.* Cairo: Matb. As-Sa'ada, n. d.

Ardistani, Sadiq. *Islam va Masa'il Jinsi va Zanashu'I (Islam and Sexual and Marital Problems).* Tehran: Khizir Press, n. d.

Badawi, Gamal A. "Polygamy in Islam." *Al-Ittihad* 9/1 (1972): 19-23.

Daudpota, U. M. and A. A. A. Fyzee, "Notes on Mut'ah or Temporary Marriage." *Journal of the Bombay Branch of the Royal Asiatic Society,* N. S. 8 (1932): 78-92.

Elwan, Shwikar. *The Status of Women in the Arab World.* New York: League of Arab States, 1974.

Fyzee, Asaf A. ed. *Da'a'im al-Islam (The Pillars of Islam),* 2 vols. Cairo: Maaref Press, 1963/1969 and 1961/1967.

—. "Aspects of Fatimid Law." *Studia Islamica* 31 (1970): 81-91.

Hakim, M. T. *Izdivaj-I Muvaqqat va Naqsh-I an dar Hall-I Mushkilat-I Jinsi (Temporary Marriage and Its Role in Solving Sexual Problems).* Tehran: Burhan Press, 1971.

Hamã, O. J. "Nikãh al-mut'a harãm fi l-Islãm," in 'Abd al-Hamîd Tahmâz, *al-'allãma al-mugâhid as-saih Muhammad Hâmid,* Beirut: n. p., 1971.

Hijazi, Qudsiyyih. *Izdivaj dar Islam (Marriage and Islam).* Tehran: Haydari Press, 1966.

Hilli, Muhaqqiq Najm al-Din Abu al-Qasim Ja'far. *Sharay' al-Islam (Islamic Law),* 2 vols. Tehran: University of Tehran Press.

Khomeini, Ayatollah Ruhallah. *Tauzih al-Masa'il (Book of Exegesis)*. Mashahd (?): Kanun-I Nashr-I Kitan (?), 1977.

—. "Non-Permanent Marriage." *Mahjubih* 2/5: 38-40, 1982.

—. *Zan (Woman-Lectures and Slogans, Collected from 1341-1361*. Tehran: Amir Kabir Press, 1982.

Kitab wurûd as-sir'a bi-ibâhat al-muta. Naqaf: n. p., 1928.

Makarim Shirazi, Nasir. "Izdivaj-I Muvaqqat Yik Zarurat-I Ijtinab Napazir-i Ijtima'I Ast (Temporary Marriage Is an Inevitable Necessity in Society)." Pp. 372-90 in Kashif al-Ghita, *A'in-i Ma*. Qom: Hadaf Press, 1968.

Manuchihrian, Mihrangiz. *Nabarabariha-yi Huquqi-I Zan va Mard dar Iran va Rah-I Islah-I An (Legal Inequalities between Men and Women in Iran)*. Tehran: Penguin Press, 1978.

Mirza, Mohammad Wahid. *Kitab al-Iqtisar*, 2 vols. Damascus: Institut Français de Damascus, 1957.

Muhajir, A. "Ta'addud-I Zujat va Mut'a (Polygamy and Mut'a)." *Majalih-I Kanun-I Sar Daftaran* 10/5, 6 (1966): 18-40.

Muhammad, Hasan. "Izdivaj-i Muvaqqat va Savab-I an (Temporary Marriage and Its Reward)." Pp. 144-47 in Allamih Sayyid Muhammad Husayn Tabataba'i, *Izdivaj-i Muvaqqat dar Islam*. Qom: Imam Sadiq Press, 1985.

Murata, Sachico. "Izdivaj-I Muvaqqat va Asar-I Ijtima'i-I An (Temporary Marriage and Its Social Effects)." M.A. Thesis, University of Tehran Divinity School, 1974.

Musallam, B. F. *Sex and Society in Islam*. Cambridge: Cambridge University Press, 1986.

Muslehuddin, Muhammad. *Mut'a (Temporary Marriage)*, 1st ed. Lahore: Islamic Publications, 1974.

—. "Mut'a." *Encyclopedia of Islam*, vol. 3: 773-76. Leiden: E. J. Brill and Luzac, 1927.

Mutahhari, Ayatollah Murtiza. *Nizam-I Huquq-I Zan dar Islam (Legal Rights of Women in Islam)*. Qom: Sadra Press, 1974.

—. *Huquq-I Zan, Ta'addud-I Zujat, Izdivaj-i Muvaqqat (Women's Rights, Polygamy, Temporary Marriage)*. Qom: Ahliyat Press, 1975.

—. "The Rights of Women in Islam: Fixed-Term Marriage," pt. 3. *Mahjubih* (Oct.-Nov. 1981): 52-56.

Nagar, Richa. "Religion, Race, and the Debate over *Mut'a* in Dar es Salaam. *Feminist Studies* 26/3 (2000): 661-90.

Nasir, Jamal J. *The Status of Women Under Islamic Law and Under Modern Islamic Legislation*. Boston and London: Graham & Trotman, 1990.

Nasr, Seyyed Hossain. "Preface," and "Appendix II." Pp. 3-28 in Allameh Sayyid Muhammad Husayn Tabataba'i, *Shi'ite Islam*. Albany: State University of New York Press.

"Nikah." *Encyclopaedia of Islam*, vol. 3: 912-14. Leiden: E. J. Brill and Luzac, 1927.

Qa'imi, 'Ali. *Tashkil-i Khanivadih dar Islam (History of the Family in Islam)*. Qom: Dar al-Tabliqat-I Islami Press, 1974.

Rafsanjani, 'Ali Akbar. "Pishguftar (Introduction)." In *Izdivaj Muvaqqat dar Islam (Temporary Marriage in Islam)*. Qom: Salih Press, 1985.

Shafa'i, Muhsin. *Mut'a va Asar-i Huquqi va Ijtima'i-I An (Mut'a and Its Legal and Social Effects*. Tehran: Haydari Press, 1973.

Shirazi, S. R. Bunbastha-yi Ijtima'i: *Guftari Kutah dar Izdivaj-I Muvaqqat (Social Dead Ends: A Short Essay on Temporary Marriage)*. Qom: Shafa Press, n.d.

Tabataba'i,Allamih Sayyid Muhammad Husayn. "Mut'a ya Izdivaj-i Muvaqqat (Mut'a or Temporary Marriage. *Maktab-i Tashayyau 6* (May 1964): 10-20.

—. *Izdivaj-I Muvaqqat dar Islam (Temporary Marriage in Islam)*. Qom: Imam Sadiq Press, 1985.

Tusi, Shaikh Abu Ja'far Muhammad. *An-Nahayih*. Tehran: University of Tehran Press, 1964.

Wadud, Amina. *Quran and Woman: Reading the Sacred Text from a Woman's Perspective*, 2nd ed. New York: Oxford University Press, 1999.

Yusif Makki, Sayyid Husayn. *Mut'a dar Islam (Mut'a in Islam)*. Damascus: n. p., 1963.

Zanjani, Husayn Haqqani. "Izdivaj-i Muvaqqat az Fahsha Jilugiri Mikunad (Temporary Marriage Prevents Prostitution)." *Maktab-i Islam* 10/7 (1969): 31-33.

Web Sites

http://www.answering-ansar.org/answers/mutah/en/index.php
http://www.islamicweb.com
http://en.wikipedia.org/wiki/Mut'ah
http://www.balagh.net/english/shia/shia/13.htm
http://sisters.islamway.com
http://www.understanding-Islam.com/rs/s-021.htm
http://www.al-islam.org

For the official Sistani view

http://www.alulbayt.com/rulings/11.htm

CHAPTER SEVEN

A RESTLESS SILENCE:
WOMEN IN THE BYZANTINE
ARCHAEOLOGICAL RECORD[1]

MARICA C. CASSIS

Vos tantum, dominae, lumen meum, memores mei esse dignamini,
sive in corpore, sive iam extra corpus fuero.

In any case, ladies, light of my heart, whether I am "in the body" or
"out of the body," please do not forget me.[2]

In the late fourth century C.E., a nun made the pilgrimage from Europe
to the Holy Land, sending extensive letters back to her sisters detailing her
trip. While Egeria expresses little concern for her own safety, often urging
her sisters not to worry if she does not make it back, the one thing she does
ask of them is that they remember her, whether she lives or dies on her
trip. Egeria's plea for remembrance foreshadows the continuing problem
of locating and situating women in the Byzantine period.[3] Although
prominent and unusual women like Egeria, visible in traditional sources,
are more likely to be "remembered" in scholarly literature, ordinary

---

[1] This paper is a revised version of a paper given at the 2004 Annual Meeting of
the American Schools of Oriental Research.
[2] Text from *Itinerarium Egeriae*: 23.10. *Pellegrinaggio in Terra Santa* (ed. and
trans. N. Natalucci; Bologne: Edizioni Dehoniane Bologna, 1999), 154-55;
translation from J. Wilkinson, *Egeria's Travels*, 3rd ed. (Warminster: Aris &
Phillips, 2002), 142.
[3] The term Byzantine is used here to designate the period from the conversion of
the Roman Empire to Christianity following the rise of Constantine in A.D. 313
until the fall of Constantinople in 1453. Although the period between the early 4th
century and the arrival of Islam is more often referred to as Late Antiquity, I have
chosen to use the term Byzantine, for the sake of simplicity.

women (almost never the focus of male writers) have seemingly vanished
from our view of the past. This has begun to change, as historians look for
the voices of these women in lesser-known documents and in passing
references in traditional historical sources.[4] Yet, for the most part, the
study of Byzantine women has remained focused on specific elite or
religious women or groups of women, a result of the limited information
available in traditional historical and ecclesiastical sources. These women,
destined by their unusual roles, continue to be seen as the "other," separate
from society as a whole.

Through the use of archaeology, however, it is possible to more clearly
situate Byzantine women within the context of their society. To date,
archaeological material has been notably absent from discussions of
Byzantine women.[5] In large part, this almost certainly relates to the
inability of archaeology to provide snapshots of individual women or to
provide information that can be closely related to written sources. Yet,
excavation within the framework of gender theory and archaeology allows
us to include women in the discussion, not as a liminal segregated group,
but as part of Byzantine society as a whole. According to R. Gilchrist,
"gender archaeology aims at a more comprehensive, humanistic, and
sensitive study of the lives of men and women in the past" through the
application of a different set of questions to archaeological data.[6] Such
questioning allows for more varied interpretations of archaeological sites,
ones which move us beyond the traditional views of Byzantine
archaeology.[7]

---

[4] See, for example, S. Brock and S. A. Harvey, *Holy Women of the Syrian Orient*
(Berkeley: University of California Press, 1987); C. Connor, *Women of Byzantium*
(New Haven: Yale University Press, 2004).
[5] A. P. Kazhdan addresses the question of women in the Byzantine household,
proving that women were neither segregated in the Byzantine house, nor subject to
a generalized "patriarchy" ("Women at Home," *DOP* 52 [1998], 1-17). He
indicates that the written sources discussing segregation are often religious in
nature, and that the lack of archaeological evidence for segregation in the home
suggests a more significant role for women than what is seen in the literary
sources. However, like earlier scholars, Kazhdan still views the role of women as
polarized between repressed or equal. He focuses on denying that women were
repressed and thus does not address the more complex realities suggested by his
conclusions. The application of gender theory has the potential to enlighten studies
such as this one.
[6] R. Gilchrist, *Gender and Material Culture: The Archaeology of Religious Women*
(London: Routledge, 1994), 2.
[7] Archaeologists working on the prehistoric period initiated this line of investigation
by encouraging a more inclusive questioning of both artifacts and processes. See

A gendered archaeology can be applied to Byzantine studies in three ways. The first involves a reassessment of the privileging of written evidence over archaeological evidence, a problem endemic to historical archaeology. Traditional written sources come primarily from the male elite and, in the case of Byzantine studies, often from ecclesiastical writers. Consequently, they are not always appropriate for understanding other communities, including rural and poor populations, and women. Rather, by giving both types of sources equal weight, we can construct a more inclusive history. The second application involves a more theoretical framework of questioning in order to attempt to define what, if anything, constitutes female space. This may involve extrapolation from written sources or from artifacts and is particularly useful in dealing with female monastic communities. Finally, in the absence of either written sources or clearly gendered and/or identifiable artifacts and spaces (such as weapons or monasteries), gendered archaeology can be used to include women within particular archaeological contexts. This third use provides wide-ranging possibilities for Byzantine archaeology, since by asking gendered questions, we also move away from traditional views of what constitutes Byzantine culture.

Framework

Any discussion of women and gender in Byzantine archaeology draws on frameworks and methodologies established in three separate disciplines. To begin with, the application of gender analysis to archaeology is relatively recent. Following the appearance of the seminal work on gender theory and prehistoric archaeology by M. Conkey and J. Spector in the early 1980s,[8] gender analysis has been applied successfully

---

M. W. Conkey and J. M. Gero, "Tensions, Pluralities, and Engendering Archaeology: An Introduction to Women and Prehistory," in *Engendering Archaeology* (eds. J. M. Gero and M. W. Conkey; Oxford: Blackwell, 1991), 3-30; especially pp. 11-14. The movement towards gender archaeology among prehistorians has heavily influenced medieval archaeology (see Gilchrist, *Gender and Material Culture*, 5-6), which in turn provides the most workable model for incorporating a gendered archaeology into Byzantine archaeology.
[8] M. W. Conkey and J. Spector, "Archaeology and the Study of Gender," in *Advances in Archaeological Method and Theory* 7 (ed. M. B. Schiffer; New York: Academic Press, 1984), 1-38. For an account of the subsequent development of scholarship, see M. Conkey, "The Archaeology of Gender Today: New Vistas, New Challenges" in *Gender in Cross-Cultural Perspective*, 4th ed. (eds. C. B.

Chapter Seven

in many archaeological sub-disciplines, including historical archaeology.[9] This framework allows for the presence of women, as well as the reanalysis of site formation and usage in light of the recognition of female activity.[10] The work of Gilchrist on English medieval archaeology is arguably the most significant for Byzantine archaeology, since there are many parallels between the two sub-disciplines. She has investigated gendered spaces in the medieval world, not to feminize them but to include women within what have previously been perceived as male bastions. For example, her discussion of the gendered living quarters of women within the male enclave of the medieval castle starts with the idea that the internal areas of these castles were domestic spaces, meaning that women were present and can be traced.[11] More importantly, Gilchrist uses gender analysis to approach this inner enclave and to illustrate that the protected area that women inhabited was not about subjugation and complete seclusion, but about protection and status.[12] Thus, women had their own lives and held their own power within this space. Gilchrist's successful reconsideration of gendered space provides a model for a new approach to space and gender in the Byzantine period, particularly as we trace the so-called "invisible" women of the lower classes.

Discussions of gender have been slow to penetrate Byzantine studies, and, in places where gender studies have been applied, they have tended to follow the same pattern evident in Byzantine studies as a whole: they

---

Brettell and C. F. Sargent; Upper Saddle River, N.J.: Pearson/Prentice Hall, 2005), 53-66.

[9] Some of the most important applications relate to medieval archaeology. See particularly R. Gilchrist, *Gender and Material Culture*; and idem, *Gender and Archaeology: Contesting the Past* (London: Routledge, 1999).

[10] As M. Conkey pointed out, the reassessment of the role of women in prehistoric society has led to a reassessment of the man-as-hunter (superior)/woman-as-gatherer (weaker) dichotomy ("The Archaeology of Gender Today," 58 ff.). There are numerous collections of papers that address the reappraisal of site use and formation in light of the inclusion of women. Two of the most useful are *Invisible People and Processes: Writing Gender and Childhood into European Archaeology* (eds. J. Moore and E. Scott; London: Leicester University Press, 1997); and *Handbook of Gender in Archaeology* (ed. S. M. Nelson; Lanham, Md.: AltaMira Press, 2006). See, particularly, S. M. S. Wood, "Feminist Theory and Gender Research in Historical Archaeology," in *Handbook of Gender in Archaeology* (ed. S. M. Nelson, Lanham, Md.: AltaMira Press, 2006), 59-104.

[11] R. Gilchrist, "The Contested Garden: Gender, Space and Metaphor in the Medieval English Castle" in *Gender and Archaeology: Contesting the Past* (London: Routledge, 1999), 109-45.

[12] Ibid., 144-45.

focus on the religious and the elite. This has started to change with research like that of S. Gerstel and A.-M. Talbot, whose article on rural ascetic women uses both written and physical evidence to identify rural female monastic communities.[13] C. Connor's book on Byzantine women attempts to trace the presence of women such as mothers and sisters of saints, who are visible only in the background of sources.[14] Most importantly, a move towards a methodological change was presented in J. Herrin's 1993 article, "In Search of Byzantine Women: Three Avenues of Approach."[15] In it, she indicates that it is possible to tease out further information about Byzantine women by asking different questions of the evidence that does exist. Herrin claims that a more thorough understanding of Byzantine women can be found through a new process of questioning references to women in three different types of sources: standard historical sources, legal texts, and works dedicated to ascetic women. [16]

While gender theory is slowly penetrating text-based Byzantine studies, it has not yet heavily influenced archaeological studies. However, some fundamental shifts within Byzantine archaeology now allow for the use of varied theoretical frameworks. While Byzantine archaeology is still heavily influenced by an overdependence on the archaeology of elite and ecclesiastical structures, such as churches, palaces, monasteries, and fortresses,[17] this legacy from Classical archaeology is beginning to change. Increasingly Byzantine archaeologists are calling for a change in the methodology of excavating Byzantine sites and are shifting their focus away from urban sites to more isolated rural and/or secular ones.[18] Since

---

[13] S. E. J. Gerstel and A.-M. Talbot, "Nuns in the Byzantine Countryside," *Deltion tes Christianikes Archaiologikes Hetaireias* 27 (2006): 481-90.
[14] Connor, *Women of Byzantium*, 146-57.
[15] J. Herrin, "In Search of Byzantine Women: Three Avenues of Approach" in *Images of Women in Antiquity*, rev. ed. (eds. A. Cameron and A. Kuhrt; London: Routledge, 1993), 167-89.
[16] Ibid., 167-68.
[17] For an important discussion of this tendency, see K. Kourelis, "The Rural House in the Medieval Peloponnese: An Archaeological Reassessment of Byzantine Domestic Architecture," in *Archaeology in Architecture: Studies in Honor of Cecil L. Striker* (eds. J. J. Emerick and D. M. Deliyannis; Mainz: Philipp von Zabern, 2005), 119-28. Kourelis argues that through survey work, it is possible to demonstrate that villages in the Peloponnese were not organized along the long-assumed western feudal model; this assumption was the result of the bias towards the large-scale and the elite in the study of Byzantine architectural history.
[18] Two articles began this transformation with their call for more careful excavation of Byzantine strata, which are often characterized by reuse and rebuilding rather than by the monumental architecture of the Classical period. See

the majority of these types of sites are not described in literary or historical texts, their excavation is informed by recent theoretical models. This important change in Byzantine archaeology is beginning to alter the old biases towards the elite and the ecclesiastical that have characterized the discipline.

Text and Archaeology: Parallel Evidence

As noted earlier, the tendency in Byzantine studies has traditionally been to privilege the written word over material culture. However, historical texts tell the stories of the wealthy and the elite and they reflect the history of things deemed important enough to be written down. We know from such texts that wealthy Byzantine women often controlled many of their own legal and financial rights.[19] They also had the right to dispose of their wealth in any manner they saw fit, and many wealthy women did so by establishing monasteries and convents and by providing funds for the upkeep of ecclesiastical life.[20] Examples range from Helena, the mother of Constantine, who endowed a number of important holy sites, to nuns who bequeathed their wealth to a variety of rural and urban monasteries.[21]

Archaeology provides a more complete picture of how often and to what extent this endowment was undertaken by women. Much evidence for this lies in dedicatory inscriptions from ecclesiastical structures throughout the Near East. For example, there are numerous dedicatory inscriptions from churches in Jordan and Syria, which indicate that ecclesiastical benefactors were often women. In the fifth century church of

---

M. Rautman, "Archaeology and Byzantine Studies," *ByzF* 15 (1990): 137-65; and J. Russell, "Transformations in Early Byzantine Urban Life: The Contribution and Limitations of Archaeological Evidence" in *17th International Byzantine Congress, Major Papers* (New Rochelle, N.Y.: 1986), 137-54. A new movement concentrating on the archaeology of secular and rural life in Late Antiquity and Byzantium has also been initiated. Among the discussions are *Recent Research on the Late Antique Countryside* (eds. W. Bowden, L. Lavan, and C. Machado; Leiden: Brill, 2003); and K. Dark, *Secular Buildings and the Archaeology of Everyday Life in the Byzantine Empire* (Oxford: Oxbow Books, 2004).

[19] Herrin, "In Search of Byzantine Women,"168, 175 ff. See also P. Brown, *The Cult of the Saints* (Chicago: University of Chicago Press, 1981), 46ff.

[20] Herrin, "In Search of Byzantine Women," 168, 175 ff.

[21] For Helena's dedications, see Eusebius, *Vita Constantini*, books XLII-XLIII. For dedications by women, see Gerstel and Talbot, "Nuns in the Byzantine Countryside," 482 ff., which offers many examples relating to nuns in the Middle Byzantine period.

the Holy Martyrs in Hama, Syria, there is an inscription in a *tabula ansata* that reads:

'Αλεξάνδρα εὐξαμένη ἅμα Θεοδοσίου καὶ Προμώτω καὶ Καρτηρίης καὶ παντὸς τοῦ οἴκου αὐ τῆς ἐψήφωσεν τὸ προτησκόνχης

Alexandra with Theodose and Promotos and Kartiria and all her household (whole house), in vow, paved with mosaic (the area) in front of the apse.[22]

Another example occurs in Gerasa, in the early Byzantine Chapel of Elias, Maria and Soreg, which contains not only a dedicatory inscription but also an image of the donor Maria.[23] Such endowments by women were not restricted to Christians. A study of synagogues in Asia Minor reveals that four were completely funded by female benefactors. In addition, "...of the fifty-three donor inscriptions from Asia Minor no fewer than nineteen, or 36 percent, identify the donors as women."[24] Epigraphical evidence from synagogues also suggests that women played leadership roles within the Jewish community, including being named *archisynagogai*.[25]

Although nothing further is known about these individual women, the placement of these and similar inscriptions within these public structures provides a spatial location for the inclusion of women in the activities of both religious communities and allows for the restoration of women as active participants within their communities.[26] Rather than focusing on only elite dedication (such as imperial benefaction) or on benefaction that segregates women (such as convent dedication), women are seen as active

---

[22] A. Zaqzuq and M. Piccirillo, "The Mosaic Floor of the Church of the Holy Martyrs at Tayibat al-Imam–Hamah, in Central Syria," *LASBF* 49 (1999): 451.
[23] A. Michel, *Les églises d'époque byzantine et umayyade de Jordanie (provinces d'Arabie et de Palestine) Ve-VIIIe siècle: typologie architecturale et aménagements liturgiques* (Turnhout: Brepols, 2001), 272-74.
[24] L. Feldman, "Diaspora Synagogues: New Light from Inscriptions and Papyri" in *Sacred Realm* (ed. S. Fine; Oxford: Oxford University Press, 1996), 51.
[25] B. J. Brooten, *Women Leaders in the Ancient Synagogue* (Atlanta: Scholars Press, 1982), 149-51.
[26] A gendered approach to such evidence is not about locating or identifying specific women in time and space. Gilchrist argues that when we look for individual women, this creates a view of women as "the other" (*Gender and Material Culture*, 6-7). E. Scott uses the word "tokenism" to refer to the inclusion of women in most archaeological discourses that fixate on finding individual women ("Introduction: On the Incompleteness of Archaeological Narratives," in *Invisible People and Processes: Writing Gender and Childhood into European Archaeology* [eds. J. Moore and E. Scott; London: Leicester University Press, 1997], 3).

members within their own religious and cultural contexts. Although some of these women were wealthy and elite, these inscriptions illustrate that such dedications were the desire of both urban elites and the rural upper classes. Information of this type is neither more nor less significant than the traditional written record; it is part of the entire record.

Archaeology and Text: New Questions

The second application of a gendered archaeology focuses on a questioning process that provides a framework for the archaeological investigation of female space. Although the main focus of a gendered archaeology is to place women within the context of their societies, in some instances it is possible to state unequivocally that a particular site was inhabited or utilized primarily by women. For the Byzantine period, such sites are usually monastic in nature, and can be isolated as female through written texts, specific assemblages of gendered artifacts, or skeletal remains.[27] Since such sites offer a female parallel to known and well-attested male enclaves, they provide the opportunity to ask comparative questions in order to determine which monastic sites can be identified as female through the identification of particular characteristics. Such a framework has important ramifications for our analysis of monastic sites, the majority of which have, until now, been assumed to be male.

One particular location that has a great deal of potential is the site of Aya Thecla, which is located on the outskirts of the modern Turkish city of Silifke (ancient Seleucia) on the southern coast of Isauria.[28] The site was dedicated to Saint Thecla, a female saint from Asia Minor (possibly from Iconium) who, upon hearing the voice of Paul, left her secular life and impending marriage to follow and learn from him.[29] After surviving

---

[27] Tracking women in domestic space is impossible, given the current state of Byzantine archaeology. A. E. Laiou discusses the significance of the domestic sphere for women in the Byzantine period, particularly in relation to the family, but her work is drawn entirely from textual sources. See "Women in Byzantine Society," in *Women in Medieval Western European Culture* (ed. L. E. Mitchell; New York: Garland, 1999), 84 ff. See Kazhdan, "Women at Home," for an attempt to utilize the archaeological evidence.

[28] The site has historically been known as Meryemlık.

[29] The life of Saint Thecla is known from two literary sources, the late 2nd century *Acts of Paul and Thecla*, and the 5th century *Life and Miracles of Saint Thecla*. For an in-depth discussion of the textual traditions associated with these works, see S. Davis, *The Cult of Saint Thecla: A Tradition of Women's Piety in Late Antiquity* (Oxford: Oxford University Press, 2001), 6 ff. See also S. Johnson, *The Life and*

two attempts on her life, Thecla wandered throughout southern Asia Minor, teaching in the manner of her own teacher, Paul. She ended her days outside of the ancient city of Seleucia where, according to the fifth century account, Thecla simply disappeared into the earth.[30] S. Davis characterized the literary accounts of Thecla as particularly female-oriented and suggested that her story appealed primarily to a female audience.[31] The fact that the shrine of Saint Thecla became known for its miraculous cures, led Davis to suggest that such cures may have been sought more often by women than by men.[32]

The shrine of Saint Thecla is known from written sources and from archaeological exploration. Most significantly, the original church is discussed in the *Itinerarium Egeriae*, in which the fourth century nun Egeria leaves this account of her visit to the site:

> (2) Ibi autem ad sanctam ecclesiam nichil aliud est nisi monasteria sine numero virorum ac mulierum. (3) Nam inveni ibi aliquam amicissimam michi, …. sancta diaconissa nomine Marthana, quam ego aput Ierusolimam noveram, ubi illa gratia orationis ascenderat; haec autem monasteria aputactitum seu virginum regebat…. (6)Ac sic ergo facto ibi biduo, visis etiam sanctis monachis vel aputactites, tam viris quam feminis, qui ibi erant, …

> Round the holy church there is a tremendous number of cells for men and women. And that was where I found one of my dearest friends, a holy deaconess called Marthana. I had come to know her in Jerusalem when she was up there on pilgrimage. She was the superior of some cells of apotactites or virgins… For two days I stayed there, visiting all the holy monks and apotactites, the men as well as the women….[33]

During the fifth century, imperial benefaction increased the size and prestige of the site, moving the focus of the shrine to a small cave church, above which the Emperor Zeno established an enormous basilica.[34] The

---

Miracles of Thecla: A Literary Study (Cambridge: Harvard University Press, 2006).

[30] Davis, *The Cult of Saint Thecla*, 41-42.

[31] Ibid., 48 ff.

[32] Ibid., 10-11, 48-51.

[33] Text from *Itinerarium Egeriae*: 23.2-6. *Pellegrinaggio in Terra Santa,* 154-55. For translation, see Wilkinson, *Egeria's Travels,* 141. For discussion, see Davis, *The Cult of Saint Thecla*, 55-56.

[34] S. Davis argues that the archaeological evidence for both the cave church and the large basilica does not predate the 5th century. Thus, it probably indicates the move of the martyr shrine to a space different from the large church seen by Egeria

site continued to grow in importance, becoming an important pilgrimage
destination. Excavated in part by E. Herzfeld and S. Guyer at the turn of
the twentieth century, Aya Thecla has subsequently been surveyed by F.
Hild and H. Hellenkemper, as well as by S. Hill.[35] The site today stands in
desperate need of excavation, since the modern city of Silifke is
encroaching on it. All that remains visible are the apse of the fifth century
basilica built over the cave church (with the latter as its crypt), and some
of the cisterns excavated by Herzfeld and Guyer. Yet, evident through the
weeds are the remnants of other structures that have yet to be explored.

The lack of attention that this site has received is surprising, given that
it is one of the few monastic and/or pilgrimage sites that can be clearly
associated with a female presence. As Egeria's statement shows, this is not
a location that was solely dedicated to women, since there were both male
and female devotees at the site. Nevertheless, the prevalence of women at
the site, as well as their interaction with a contemporary male community,
provides great potential for engaging in a gendered discussion of Aya
Thecla. There are many questions that can be posed. For example, does the
site have noticeably different areas for men and for women? Is there
visible segregation? Is it possible to trace the existence of the two groups
of ascetics by gender within an archaeological context? Are there artifacts
or pottery assemblages that support such observations? These questions
are unanswerable without more excavation, and indeed the responses to all
may simply be "no." Nevertheless, asking such questions raises the
potential of establishing a more inclusive sense of the religious life of this
community.[36]

Although this kind of work remains to be done at Aya Thecla, similar
work has been started at the Samarian site of Hurvat Hanni in Israel. U.
Dahari and Y. Zelinger excavated a monastic site used by, and holy to,

---

(*The Cult of Saint Thecla*, 37). For a longer discussion of the problems
encountered when identifying the structures at this site, see S. Hill, *The Early
Byzantine Churches of Cilicia and Isauria* (Aldershot: Variorum, 1996), 208-34.

[35] For the most recent discussion of the site, as well as bibliography, see Hill, *The
Early Byzantine Churches of Cilicia and Isauria*, 208-34. For the original
excavation report, see E. Herzfeld and S. Guyer, *Meriamlik und Korykos: Zwei
christliche Ruinenstätte des Rauhen Kilikiens* (*MAMA* 2; Manchester: Manchester
University Press, 1930), 1-89. See also F. Hild and H. Hellenkemper, *Kilikien und
Isaurien* (Tabula Imperii Byzantini 5; Vienna: Österreichische Akademie der
Wissenschaften, 1990), 441-43. For a complete list of references to this site by
Hild and Hellenkemper, see Hill, *Early Byzantine Churches*, 208.

[36] Davis raises similar questions concerning evidence about the segregation of men
and women in the baptistery at Abu Mina, an Egyptian site that has connections to
Thecla (*The Cult of Saint Thecla*, 125).

women. The monastery was probably built during the fifth century and was abandoned by the early ninth century. It consisted of two buildings, the first of which, Building A, included a church, crypt and other rooms significant to the monastery. Building B housed the kitchen, dining room and hostel. Its identification as a female center is secured by a number of factors, including an eighth century inscription blessing the abbess of the monastery and the skeletons of a number of women in the crypt. Further, burials for girls continued after its abandonment, suggesting that the site retained at least the vestige of its significance as a site of female piety.[37] By starting with an assemblage of artifacts that suggests a strong female presence, the excavators of this site have been able to make a case for a center of female holiness. Hurvat Hanni now provides some extremely important comparative material for examining other monastic compounds in Israel and Jordan dating to the early Byzantine period. Its identification also enhances the possibility of identifying other monastic structures as being intended for female communities.

"Untraceable" Women

In both of the scenarios involving the inclusion of a gendered archaeology discussed above, excavated evidence coexists with traditional historical sources. However, increasing numbers of Byzantine archaeological sites cannot be identified or explained with evidence from written texts. In addition, the extant structures of many newly excavated sites cannot be located within the traditional categories of Byzantine architecture or archaeology, which have historically been restricted to sites representing the monumental and the ecclesiastical. To a large extent, such categories are inherently masculine, since venues such as churches, monasteries, fortresses and palaces are almost always presumed to be populated by men.[38] The tendency toward traditional archaeological

---

[37] At the time this article was written, preliminary information on Hurvat Hanni could be found on the Israel Antiquities Authority website, http://www.antiquities.org.il/, under the heading "khanni." For the most recent discussion, see "Hurvat Hanni," in *NEAEHL* 5, 1764-66; and U. Dahari, "The Excavation of Hurvat Hani," *Qadmoniot* 126 (2003): 102-6 [Hebrew].

[38] See Gilchrist, *Gender and Material Culture*, 2 ff.; idem, "Ambivalent Bodies: Gender and Medieval Archaeology," in *Invisible People and Processes: Writing Gender and Childhood into European Archaeology* (eds. J. Moore and E. Scott; London: Leicester University Press, 1997), 42-58. For a discussion of assumptions about gender made by archaeologists, particularly in relation to the Neolithic, see L. Hurcombe, "A Viable Past in the Pictorial Present?," in *Invisible People and*

categories, as well as over-reliance on the written sources, often results in an attempt to force newly excavated structures into a framework that does not accurately reflect the remains. However, the application of a framework of gendered archaeology allows for a new set of categories that necessarily include the female: villages, manor houses and storerooms.

A case in point is the Byzantine settlement at the site of Çadır Höyük in Central Anatolia.[39] Çadır Höyük is a multi-phase site, with occupation levels ranging from the Chalcolithic through the Byzantine periods. The Byzantine levels, located on the top of the mound and on the terrace surrounding it, are extensive. The extant fortified area on the top of the mound dates to the eleventh century, while the terrace has at least four occupation levels ranging between (approximately) the sixth and the eleventh centuries.[40] The site exhibits many characteristics that are common to multi-period Byzantine sites, including the reuse of earlier structures, non-monumental architecture, and few *in situ* artifacts.[41]

The function of the site is uncertain. The initial conjecture was that Çadır Höyük was either a fortified castle (*kastron*) or a military outpost,[42] although the idea that it might have been a monastic settlement has also been considered. These first ideas were heavily influenced by a number of

---

Processes: Writing Gender and Childhood into European Archaeology (eds. J. Moore and E. Scott; London: Leicester University Press, 1997), 15-24.

[39] Excavation at Çadır Höyük has been ongoing for a decade and the intensive excavation of the Byzantine period began in 2001. In 2003, I joined the team as the Director of Byzantine Excavations. I would like to thank Dr. Ron Gorny, University of Chicago, for allowing me to use this material in preliminary form. For background on the site, see R. L. Gorny, "The 2002-2005 Seasons at Çadır Höyük: The Second Millenium Settlement," *Anatolica* 32 (2006): 29-54; R. L. Gorny, G. McMahon, S. Paley, S. Steadman and B. Verhaaren, "The 2000 and 2001 Seasons at Çadır Höyük in Central Turkey: A Preliminary Report," *Anatolica* 28 (2002): 109-36; and S. M. Paley, "The Excavations at Çadır Höyük," *Kazı Sonuçları Toplantısı* 28 (2006): 519-38.

[40] The surface area of the mound is 240 x 185 m and it rises some 32 m above the valley plain. For a brief account of the top of the mound, see R. Gorny, "Çadır Höyük: Zippalanda Reborn?," *The Oriental Institute News and Notes* (Winter 2005): 9-12, 29-30. A lengthy publication of the Byzantine material is in preparation.

[41] The dating for the site is done primarily based on seal and coin evidence. The latest strata on the top of the mound date to the 11th century. Due to the complete clearance of the mound prior to this last rebuilding, there is no evidence for the early Byzantine period. On the terrace, the earliest levels are dated to the 6th century, based on numismatic and ceramic evidence. The top stratigraphic level on the terrace is contemporary with that on the mound.

[42] Gorny, "Çadır Höyük," 10-11.

factors, none of which had very much to do with the site. In the first place, Central Anatolia was the breadbasket of the Byzantine Empire. The location of Çadır Höyük, as well as the fortification on the mound, suggested a desire to protect the site, either as land for food production or as a strategic military post. Thus, the original research questions reflected an expectation of finding weaponry or extensive evidence for a wealthy household and were influenced by assumptions about common types of Byzantine sites. As excavation continued, however, the expectations and assumptions about the site needed to be adjusted.

Preliminary excavation results proved neither scenario noted above to be correct. In the first place, although the structures on the mound date to the eleventh century, the extant walls sit on earlier, stronger foundations and were rebuilt quickly and poorly during this period. The fortification walls exhibit the same construction. The extant buildings include a large storage room and a stable. The majority of artifacts date to the eleventh century and do not provide evidence for either a large-scale military garrison or a violent end to the site. Neither weaponry nor human remains have been found. There is also no evidence for an extensive household. The archaeological evidence consists exclusively of coarseware storage and cooking pots, animal remains, and a few small artifacts, including coins, minor Christian amulets, glass bracelets, and farm implements. One of the most interesting finds was a large stable area with the undamaged bones of several farm animals; it appears that this livestock was abandoned and simply died when the population fled the impending Turkish invasions of the region.

The Byzantine settlement continues on the terrace below the mound. The structures here exhibit the same characteristics of reuse and rebuilding, and the finds are restricted to coarseware and few artifacts. The extant structure appears to be a farmhouse with at least one large communal oven. The utilitarian nature of the structures, taken in conjunction with the communal elements of the terrace material and the lack of small finds or fineware, have led to the suggestion that this structure served as a monastery, again based on common assumptions about Byzantine sites. However, there is no evidence for a church or other religious structures or features (e.g., a cemetery), and there have not been a large number of religious finds. Rather, a population, as yet unidentified, lived on the terrace and almost certainly used the mound as a storage area. Both parts of the site exhibit a continuous decline in how buildings were constructed, and both areas possess the same domestic characteristics.

The act of applying a gendered framework to this site does not limit the endeavor to a search for individual women or for space devoted

152   Chapter Seven

entirely to women. Rather, it requires a move away from the traditionally
dominant male categories to a consideration of spaces in which women are
integral. Since Çadır Höyük served no clear military, religious, or elite
function, it almost certainly functioned in a domestic context, as a
communal space or large farmhouse. Given the shortage of information
about such locations in Byzantine studies, the evidence for domestic life
provided by this site becomes very important. Even more significant for
this discussion, an ordinary settlement such as this almost certainly
included a female population. While this statement may seem obvious, it
lies at the crux of gendering space. By moving away from traditional
androcentric definitions of space, it becomes necessary to include women
as part of the population–and to reevaluate our former interpretations of
some Byzantine structures.

    While the architectural evidence illustrates that the structures visible at
Çadır Höyük were neither monumental nor elite, the assemblage of
artifacts provides further evidence for the inclusion of both women and
men at the site. Although the number of recovered artifacts is not large,
among the finds are those traditionally associated with women and
women's occupations. These include fragments of glass bracelets, as well
as loom weights, a huge quantity of cooking pots, and a large communal
oven. Some archaeologists who work with gender theory might argue
against such an attribution, concerned that such assessments are more
connected to modern concepts of gender than to our knowledge of ancient
activities.[43] Nevertheless, by accepting the fact that such items are
indicative of a domestic and/or secular context (and see Baadsgaard,
London, Cassuto, and Ebeling and Homan in this volume), we can move
away from the monumental and the elite and towards a space more
inclusive of women.

    It is not possible to identify the community that resided at Çadır Höyük
at present. It is also not yet possible to further isolate elements that can be
related specifically to a female presence. Rather, allowing the evidence to
speak without the filter of assumptions allows us to construct a more
inclusive view of the past. [44] When we see that the evidence does not fit

---

[43] Gilchrist, "Ambivalent Bodies," 47-52, discusses some of the limitations of
assigning elements or artifacts to a particular gender. Such attributions either serve
to segregate the genders or to diminish the significance of particular artifacts
because they are associated with the female gender.
[44] F. Kidner, for example, argues that removing architecture from its
social context (often out of a desire to organize material in a linear
fashion), limits our ability to understand communities as a whole. See "Christianizing
the Syrian Countryside: An Archaeological and Architectural Approach," in *Urban*

into the old categories of church, monastery, palace and fortress, it becomes necessary to look for new categories. By gendering such categories, we move away from the androcentric and from isolating opposites to a more inclusive archaeology, which recognizes that domestic sites necessarily include women. This leads to a much more interesting set of questions for Çadır Höyük concerning subsistence and production patterns and the evolution of a rural secular site. By allowing for the female voice, we allow for a different set of questions.

Conclusions

The final question remains: is a gendered archaeology for the Byzantine period valid? Those who would argue against it misunderstand the focus of such a framework. Gendered archaeology is not about attempting to locate particular women, but rather about attempting to place women into the picture of the past and to understand the creation of sites within the context of a complete society.[45] In order to do so, it is necessary to ask different questions of the excavated material. As Gilchrist argues, "it is not a matter of the spade being mute, but rather that we seldom ask it the right questions, or understand its answers." [46]

Although Byzantine archaeology is still a relatively young discipline, it is rapidly moving away from the legacy of Classical archaeology's focus on the monumental and the religious. Increasingly, Byzantine archaeologists are using gender theory (among other theoretical frameworks) to create a more comprehensive view of the Byzantine period, which takes into account rural populations, secular populations, and society as a whole. To this must be added a gendered archaeology, which can be applied in at least three ways: the comprehensive combination of text and archaeology to create a more inclusive and complete view of the past; the use of gender theory to create new ways of questioning in order to further understanding of spaces that were dedicated primarily to women, and then to compare them to those of men; and finally, through the use of gender theory, to create a more inclusive conceptual framework for sites with no textual

---

Centers and Rural Contexts in Late Antiquity (eds. T. S. Burns and J. W. Easdie; E. Lansing, Mich.: Michigan State University Press, 2001), 365.

[45] "A crucial feature in our reworking is for us to expand the scope of the current debate to write histories which are the results of dialogue between men and women of all genders" (B. Boyd, "The Power of Gender Archaeology," in *Invisible People and Processes: Writing Gender and Childhood into European Archaeology* [eds. J. Moore and E. Scott; London: Leicester University Press, 1997], 28).

[46] Gilchrist, *Gender and Material Culture*, 10.

referents, or which do not fit into the old categories established for Byzantium. In the end, this approach is one of asking different questions of the evidence–questions that allow the material to speak in new ways. And perhaps then the women of the Byzantine period will not be so silent after all.

CHAPTER EIGHT

FE(MALE) POTTERS AS THE PERSONIFICATION OF INDIVIDUALS, PLACES, AND THINGS AS KNOWN FROM ETHNOARCHAEOLOGICAL STUDIES

GLORIA LONDON

Introduction[1]

Over the past century of archaeological research in the Middle East, as every place else in the New and Old Worlds, the challenge to create a relative chronological order for deposits at ancient sites was resolved by establishing ceramic sequences. Scholars began by recognizing large-scale similarities of pottery assemblages at different sites, as they pertained to texture, color, vessel morphology, decoration, and the presence/absence of accessories. The primary goal was to unite contemporaneous artifacts found within and among sites. Success demanded an emphasis on the homogeneity of pottery within a given time period and to a lesser extent, heterogeneity within time periods.[2] The result is excellent regional ceramic typologies, but lacking are links between each period both in terms of technology and with regard to the people who made the pots. An

[1] My thanks to Beth Alpert Nakhai for organizing the American Schools of Oriental Research session, *The World of Women: Gender and Archaeology*, and for her invitation to contribute to this volume. Her editorial help is most appreciated. I also want to express my gratitude to the Fulbright organization and the National Endowment for the Humanities for making field work possible in Cyprus through grants administered by the American Schools of Oriental Research via the Cyprus American Archaeological Research Institute.
[2] G. A. London, *Decoding Designs: The Late Third Millennium B.C. Pottery from Jebel Qaʻaqir* (Ph.D. diss., University of Arizona), 35.

emphasis on homogeneity between sites obscures details relating to individual potters and workshops.

Given that much is now known about temporal changes in pottery, the present task of archaeologists is to acknowledge small-scale differences, rather than similarities, within individual sites and among contemporaneous sites. Instead of peoples or ethnic groups, the objective is the individual or the workshop. From the perspective of ceramic technology, one can begin to define these entities by reference to an underutilized but abundant artifact – ordinary, plain pots. Archaeology can be less elitist than text studies tend to be, especially if the focus is on utilitarian wares rather than the small percentage of decorated pots. There is every reason to imagine that some potters so identified will be women.

Superficial attributes sometimes suffice for characterizing and naming decorated wares, but can fail with regard to undecorated utilitarian wares unless such wares were made in different ways (wheel thrown or coil built, pinch, mold-made, and so forth). Variation within a class of pots, say cookware, can reflect the fact that the artifacts were made by different people in different and distinct (contemporaneous or not) traditions or in distinct and unrelated times. Archaeologists name wares that are easily differentiated from others, usually due to decoration or surface treatment, despite their relative minority in the overall assemblage. W. G. Dever[3] recognizes the need to focus on technology rather than ideology, an issue H. J. Franken[4] has advocated. If, as with the traditional domestic potters and craft specialists of today, some of the ancient potters were women, the analysis of ceramic technology will offer insights into the roles of women in antiquity.

Ceramic Technology

The goals of the study of ceramic technology are to learn how pots were manufactured and used, and to provide evidence about the makers and users. An emphasis on the individual contrasts with the concept of attributing artifacts to a group of people named in the Hebrew Bible or

---

[3] W. G. Dever, "Will the Real Israel Please Stand Up? Archaeology and Israelite Historiography: Part I," *BASOR* 297 (1985): 75, fn.7.

[4] H. J. Franken, *Excavations at Tell Deir 'Alla: The Late Bronze Age Sanctuary* (Louvain: Peeters Press, 1998); H. J. Franken and J. Kalsbeek, *Excavations at Tell Deir 'Alla I* (Leiden: Brill, 1969); idem, *Potters of a Medieval Village in the Jordan Valley: Excavations at Tell Deir `Alla–A Medieval Tell, Abu Gourdan, Jordan* (North Holland Ceramic Studies in Archaeology 3; Amsterdam: North-Holland; New York: American Elsevier, 1975).

other texts. Normally, pottery is designated with reference to decorated wares. Often, painted or burnished pottery represents a small quantity of the total assemblage and may have been used by only a narrow segment of the population. As such, both the wares and their users represent a thin slice of ancient society. Fine wares provide some chronological anchor for the entire assemblage, but plain wares best encode information about the potters and their traditions. While it was appropriate and necessary that early research concentrate on decorated wares, the undecorated common, normal wares that address non-chronological issues related to the identity of local people are central to learning about those people who made and used them. There is a good chance that both the makers and the users were women.

The study of ceramic technology focuses on people, and on the craft of manufacturing containers often used for food, which suggests use (if not manufacture) by women. Once more is known about pot makers, it becomes possible to extrapolate to pot users. Artifacts constructed from flexible raw materials such as fibers, fabrics, hair and clay can preserve tangible references to the individuals who made them. Organic perishable plant and animal products can embody stylistic and manufacture evidence indicative of the group and the individual craftsperson. Both the technical and individual stylistic patterns in baskets, wood, clothes and textiles, displayed in color and design elements, encode important social information such as village affiliation.[5] Unfortunately, perishable organic materials rarely survive in deposits located in the Middle East due to environmental conditions. However, when they do survive, they preserve information on, for example, the direction of the weave. At Timna in Israel's southern Arava, coarse tenting fabrics were characteristic of the Z-twist traditions of the Syrian coast and Bedouin communities rather than of the S-weave of Egypt, and are thus associated with a non-Egyptian element of the desert population.[6]

Stone artifacts, including utilitarian basalt and chert, as well as semi-precious stones used for seals, can reveal the work of an individual or a tradition of gem carving. Clay, however, is the single most abundant and malleable raw material used in antiquity. It was widespread and free for the taking. It could have been used by a cross-section of the population, male and female, young and old. Of all the plastic raw materials, only clay

---

[5] S. Weir and S. Shahid, *Palestinian Embroidery*, 2nd ed. (London: British Museum, 1989), 19-22; E. W. Barber, *Women's Work: The First 20,000 Years* (New York: Norton, 1995).

[6] A. Sheffer, "Comparative Analysis of a 'Negev Ware' Textile Impression from Masos," *TA* 3 (1976): 85, fn.7.

transforms into a virtually indestructible rock. Initially soft to the touch, it fires rock-solid and is the most abundant artifact at many sites. In the stylistic and technical aspects of their manufacture, clay pots, tablets and figurines preserve data about the individuals who made them. Decorative styles on pottery can mimic those found on cloth. For example, embroidery work and lace patterns might be observed in incised or painted pottery. Checkerboard or grid patterns are more easily woven into fabrics of various colors and threads, or into basketry, and could be the origin of comparable patterns incised into pottery. Of all ancient artifacts, ceramics best preserve emblems and design features once found on perishable fabrics.

Learning Framework

Artifacts made from clay and perishable materials result from a set of learned practices. Potters do not reinvent their craft repeatedly. Instead, it is based on knowledge acquired, accumulated, and advanced from one generation of practitioners to the next. Often, learners acquire skills from several people. Assistants and apprentices, who may or may not be related to the skilled worker, help older individuals who thereby transmit their expertise. Alternatively, younger people learn informally through the observation of their elders or another relatives. They also learn by observing as experts instruct others. Mothers, aunts, sisters, grandparents, friends and neighbors can all be involved in teaching girls.[7] Fathers, uncles, grandfathers, brothers and employers might teach boys.

The accumulated knowledge and learned behaviors, including where to dig clay, how to process it, and how to shape and finish and fire pottery, assure continuity of tradition. Essential elements of pottery fabrication can be passed down with little change in primary forming techniques. In contrast, the individual imprint of each potter can be expressed in non-essential features, such as secondary forming and finishing work. For example, when knobs, handles or other plastic features are typical of a particular tradition, their precise shape, location and number can vary from potter to potter. Similarly, surface finish and decoration might vary subtly

---

[7] I recently observed young women at the Kornos Pottery Cooperative, who were learning to make pottery. In June 2008, experienced potters gave verbal instructions and encouragement, as did other "learners," all of whom had relatives who were formerly potters but are no longer alive. As a consequence, the young women learned from the experienced women, who include mothers-in-law, neighbors, and friends. At times, an older potter sat at the turntable of a learner, in order to demonstrate how to fix and save a pot.

from person to person without harming the tradition. All these features relay information about individual potters. Incised combed patterns or painted patterns, including the number of combed bands and their arrangement, are not random. When analyzed quantitatively, surface treatment becomes consequential on its own. It means something, but not to everyone and not the same thing to everyone. Pattern details are meaningful to those who know and recognize them. As E. T. Hall noted, "A pattern is a meaningful arrangement of sets shared by a group." [8] Subtle variations offer opportunities for expressing the identity and individuality of the potter and/or the painter.[9] The number of incised bands, thumb indentations, burnish patterning, or rows of stippling affords individuals a chance to express themselves while remaining true to their traditions.

Archaeologists encounter and record endless variety within each type of surface treatment. In assessing the debate on discerning ethnic identity from material culture, W. G. Dever concluded that artifacts vary sufficiently to permit archaeologists to observe differences, but the question of what those differences imply remains.[10] Especially in times when pottery was not wheel thrown, such differences are the muffled voices of individual potters, many of whom are women.

Potter Gender

For Cyprus, evidence concerning female potters has been examined by relying on ethnoarchaeological studies of domestic and craft specialists worldwide, in conjunction with a small number of artifacts from Mesopotamia, Greece and Egypt.[11] These artifacts depict women performing some aspect of work associated with pottery production, either the primary forming work or the secondary finishing stages. For the past two centuries if not longer, women have made and continue to make pots,

---

[8] E. T. Hall, *The Silent Language*, 2nd ed. (New York: Anchor Books, 1973), 125.

[9] London, "Decoding Designs," 244; idem, "Ethnoarchaeological Evidence of Variation in Cypriot Ceramics and Its Implications for the Taxonomy of Ancient Pottery," in *Cypriot Ceramics: Reading the Prehistoric Record* (eds. J. Barlow, D. Bolger, and B. Kling; Philadelphia: University Museum of Archaeology and Anthropology, 1991), 221-35.

[10] W. G. Dever, "Archaeology, Ideology, and the Quest for an 'Ancient' or 'Biblical' Israel," *NEA* 61 (1998): 46-8.

[11] V. Hankey, "The Ceramic Tradition in Late Bronze Age Cyprus," *RDAC* (1983): 168-71; G. A. London, "Cypriote Potters: Past and Present," *RDAC* (1987): 319-22.

which they later sell. To do this, they mine and process clay, gather fuel, and produce and fire pottery.[12] Although women have the ability to carry out all of the activities required for pottery manufacture, there are numerous case studies, which show that the work is divided among family members. At times, women make the pots and men are more concerned with fuel, firing, and sales. In Cyprus early in the twenty-first century, some traditional rural female potters remain involved with all aspects of the work, including the backbreaking work of beating the clay. Men can be involved with any or all aspects of the work.[13]

Despite the work of potters in antiquity, evidenced by the vast quantities of pots and sherds unearthed, archaeologists find surprisingly few kilns throughout the eastern Mediterranean. Potter gender might contribute to the dearth of pottery production locations, since ethnographic studies show that women in traditional societies tend to work closer to home than do men. At home, women can make objects for sale while they tend to all their other obligations and responsibilities, prime among them being childcare.

In Cyprus as elsewhere in the world, pottery making is part of the work routine woman carry out seasonally, while caring for children and elders, cooking, washing clothes, weeding and more. Female craft specialists making pottery in the Filipino village of Gubat (southeastern Luzon Island) work in spaces around their homes. Some carry the drying pots indoors at night and learn to live around their pots, but some might have a shelf under their house where pots dry, protected from the rain.[14] One of Gubat's most prolific potters enjoyed the luxury of a covered porch. In Cyprus, too, private potters who work in the courtyards of their homes lack storage space for drying pots. Consequently, they bring them inside, to their bedrooms, kitchens, and wherever else the pots can be moderately safe from children and pets. If women in antiquity were responsible for making pottery, and they carried out the work in the confines of their house exteriors or courtyards as they undertook myriad other daily and seasonal chores, it will be difficult for archaeologists to recognize pottery production areas.

The seasonality of the industry, normally limited to the drier summer through autumn months, also contributes to the dearth of easily

---

[12] G. A. London, *Women Potters of Cyprus* (DVD filmed, edited and narrated by G. A. London, 2000).

[13] Ibid.

[14] G. A. London, "Standardization and Variation in the Work of Craft Specialists," pp. 182-201 in *Ceramic Ethnoarchaeology* (ed. W. A. Longacre. Tucson, Ariz.: University of Arizona Press, 1991), fig. 9.6.

identifiable pottery production locations, even as it allows women to use pottery making space, as needed, for other seasonal activities. In Cyprus, the same area used by private potters to make pottery easily converts to space for food preparation, olive sorting, cleaning and processing, dairy processing, fruit preserving, animal sheltering and more. The multi-functionality of the workspace similarly makes it more difficult to determine where ancient pottery production took place, unless the ancient site was destroyed during the dry (pot-making) season. My visits to pottery production locations during the wet winters, early spring and late fall, reveal remarkably little, if any evidence that potters worked there.[15]

If ancient craft specialists were women who worked at home, seasonally and in between all their other chores, there is little chance of finding their clay, tools or pots. In modern Cyprus, everything related to pottery production, even the shallow, wooden container (*skafi*) for mixing clay powder with water, vanishes. (Indeed, instead of a pre-formed box, a *skafi* can be made of pieces of wood held together by clay.) The Kornos Pottery Cooperative has a workspace, including a kiln (*kamini*), in a location separate from the homes of the craft specialists. Close to a stream and to where other potters reside, eight women worked at the Coop during the summer months. In the winter months, the Coop is converted into a place to store unwanted large objects and sacks of potatoes belonging to their neighbors. In springtime, it is used to hatch chicken eggs, under the watchful eye of the women potters. Discarded pots are absent; there were no sherds to be found during the winter months of 1999–2000. The rate of loss in kiln firing is no more than 2 percent at Kornos, and all misfired pieces are reused one way or another, often away from the kiln area.[16]

The multipurpose use of space in ancient households limits our ability to identify ancient pottery-making sites unless they were destroyed in the dry season. At the same time, if the craft was practiced in the confines of courtyards, it is more likely that pot making was the work of women. This conjecture is supported by ethnographic research demonstrating that women are more likely than men to remain close to home.[17] To some extent, the sparse number of separate Bronze and Iron Age industrial settings, where men and/or women might work, can be explained by the prominent role of women potters. Instead of relocating daily to a separate

---

[15] G. A. London, "Continuity and Change in Cypriot Pottery Production," *NEA* 63/2: (2000): 103.

[16] G. A. London, "Past Present: The Village Potters of Cyprus," *BA* 52/4 (1989): 221, 224.

[17] G. P. Murdock and C. Provost, "Factors in the Division of Labor by Sex: A Cross-cultural Analysis," *Ethnology* 12 (1973): 203-25.

workspace, they would have worked within range of the cooking fire as well as the pottery kiln. Instead of assuming that pottery manufacturing sites would have been outside ancient village and urban sites, perhaps the dearth of industrial sites suggests that pottery was made by women (and men) close to home.

Fingerprint Identification: Male/Female or Child/Adult

Despite potters' attempts to eradicate any trace of their hands or fingers from clay vessels, meticulous inspection sometimes reveals a small number of prints. W. F. Badé, the early excavator of Tell en-Nasbeh, pioneered research strategies designed to focus on people rather than pottery. He brought fingerprints from ancient pots to the attention of a police detective, with the aim of determining the gender of potters.[18] More recently, P. Åström and S. A. Eriksson assembled a collection of fingerprints from ancient Cypriot wares.[19]

A recent fingerprint analysis of archaeological material from North America concluded that print dimensions make it easier to discriminate between children and adults than between men and women. The dermatoglyphic patterns of finger ridges are established by the seventh month of fetal development. As an individual grows, ridges on the fingers and palms alter only in size; as hand size increases, so too does the distance between each ridge. Consequently, it is the distance from ridge to ridge that expands, rather than the number of ridges. Larger distances between ridges typify the prints of adults whereas closer ridges are indicative of children. At the same time, for each person, there are differences from finger to finger and hand to hand. Although the ridges of male fingerprints in certain populations are larger than those of females, the distinction can be as small 0.02 mm. Variations in the size of ridge breadth are better evidence of regionalism than of sex difference, due in part to differences in average height. Certain ethnic communities tend to have fewer but wider ridge distances in hands similar in size to hands with more ridges. As a consequence, one can currently segregate prints based on age or height with greater efficacy than on sex.[20]

---

[18] W. F. Badé, *A Manual of Excavation in the Near East* (Berkeley: University of California Press, 1934), 35.
[19] P. Åström and S. A. Eriksson, *Fingerprints and Archaeology* (Studies in Mediterranean Archaeology 28; Goteborg: P. Åströms, 1980).
[20] K. A. Kamp, N. Timmerman, G. Lind, J. Greybill, and I. Natowsky, "Discovering Childhood: Using Fingerprints to Find Children in the Archaeological Record," *American Antiquity* 64 (1991): 309.

A study of fingerprints found on two different classes of clay artifacts from northern Arizona, animal figurines and corrugated pottery, primarily identified the prints of children. On the crudely made figurines, some associated with child burials but more with fill deposits, print ridge distance averaged 0.37 mm. In contrast, the breadth of fingerprint ridges on the pottery measured an average of 0.49 mm, which was indicative of adult-sized hands. Occasionally, a poorly made corrugated pot preserved child-sized prints, suggesting that it represents the work of a learner rather than the more skilled product of a full-fledged (adult) potter. Additional evidence supporting the idea that the figurines were made by children is found in the imprecise representation of the zoomorphic forms onto which the legs and tails were poorly attached. These stylistic and fabrication details, as well as provenance, imply that children made the figurines as toys.[21]

Clay toys made by and for children are more likely to preserve fingerprints than is most pottery, since skilled potters systematically eradicate all evidence of manufacture, whereas children do not. A smooth, even, unblemished surface on the interior and exterior of a pot is one measure of a good pot, according to traditional potters interviewed in ethnoarchaeological studies carried out in the Philippines and in Cyprus.[22] An exception to this is the corrugated ware of the American Southwest, for which the fingertip creates each corrugation in clay dry enough to preserve the finger ridge impressions. Similarly, moderately dry clay tablets of the ancient Near East are more likely to preserve prints than is pottery, and thus can inform if a tablet belonged to a student learner or an adult unaccustomed to writing. Double prints on tablets or pottery represent the work of multiple individuals. For pottery, more than one set of prints hints at assembly line production involving a skilled potter and assistants. Small prints at handle attachment points can represent the work of a younger assistant who was responsible for handle application. If shaping the pot was the responsibility of the experienced potter alone, no other set of prints might be discernible.

Non-skilled laborers, apprentices, family members, or others participate in the pottery industry in various capacities. They might collect raw materials (clay, temper, water and fuel), process clay into a workable material, or move pots between worktables and drying spaces. They might add accessory pieces (spouts, handles and plastic decoration), as do Egyptian potters working in Jordan, or surface treatment (burnishing,

---

[21] Ibid., 313.
[22] London, "Decoding Designs," 189-214; idem, "Cypriote Potters;" idem, "Regionalism;" idem, "Continuity and Change," 102.

painting, scraping and more), as in the Philippines.[23] In Cyprus, Jordan and the Philippines, every hand available helps to unload the kiln. Kiln loading, nerve-racking and risky, remains a task for experienced hands.

Primary Forming and Secondary Finishing Techniques

Essential to the potting tradition is the *primary* forming and shaping of wet clay by a skilled potter. This early stage of the work embodies knowledge passed down from one generation to another, from relative to relative or neighbor to neighbor. It is less subject to chance or the whim of an individual potter than are the *secondary* finishing work and surface treatment. To a great extent, the raw materials dictate the manufacturing technique and limit the degree of experimentation and individuality. Good clay for one potter is bad clay for another. For potters who have a good experience working with and firing a particular clay, there is no reason to explore other manufacturing techniques with the same clay. In a practice which seems to exist worldwide, potters prefer to use a manufacturing technique suitable to the clay readily available rather than try to fix the clay by adding rocks or minerals, other than carbonates added to cooking pot wares.

Differentiating between the primary forming and secondary finishing techniques used to create the pottery helps to determine in what ways a potter or a person of lesser skill is involved in the manufacture. Nearly all pots made using a traditional technique require more than one stage; *i.e.*, a lump of clay will not be given its final form as a bowl, jar, or other vessel during a single pot-making episode. Instead, it will undergo a slow and gradual metamorphosis. Round-bottomed pots might initially have flat bases; jars might start out as bowl-like, and so forth. Pinch pots alone can be shaped all at once in the hand, with or without subsequent surface treatment such as paint or burnish. However, they are limited in size by the length of the potter's fingers.

Shaping a pot requires greater skill and knowledge than that needed for final finishing, smoothing and decorating, or indeed for any task other than vessel forming. Accessory pieces are normally added once the pot has dried enough to support the weight of the handle, spout, knob, plastic

---

[23] G. A. London and M. Sinclair, "An Ethnoarchaeological Survey of Potters in Jordan," pp. 420-28 in *Madaba Plains Project II* (eds. L. G. Herr, L. T. Geraty, Ø. S. LaBianca, and R. W. Younker; Berrien Springs, Mich.: Andrews University, 1991), 422-25; G. A. London, "Standardization and Variation in the Work of Craft Specialists," pp. 182-201 in *Ceramic Ethnoarchaeology* (ed. W. A. Longacre. Tucson, Ariz.: University of Arizona Press, 1991), 192-95, fig. 9.9.

molding or figurines, or to allow holes to be cut into the clay. These tasks are often considered less essential to the integrity of the pot than is shaping or forming a pot to the correct size and proportions.

After a pot is shaped by an experienced traditional potter, it is set aside to dry slightly, before either that potter or someone else resumes work on it. If more coils are need to increase the vessel height, if the base needs trimming, or if any other work essential to the basic form, size and shape is necessary, the potter continues the work. Most potters find it beneficial to work in an interrupted technique of manufacture, regardless of the precise way in which they make pottery, whether thrown or other. Rather than wheel throw a final finished form, many ancient and modern traditional potters build pots incrementally. They might start a pot from a lump of clay to which coils are added, and then set it aside to dry before adding additional coils. According to this technique, the lower body is made first and a few coils are added. Then the pot is set aside to dry for minutes, hours or days, depending on the weather and the other duties for which the potter is responsible, in the field and at home. Coils might be added in one or several stages, depending on the desired height of the pot and the rate of drying. After the neck and rim are fashioned, another drying period follows before the base can be treated to receive its final form.

Traditional craft specialists observed in Jordan, Cyprus and the Philippines vary the number of pots in progress depending on the rate of drying, the weather, the type of additional work required, and the proximity to the appointed firing time. Most maintain a variety of pots requiring different types of reworking and additional work. They benefit from operating in a limited, slow-paced "assembly line production," working on a series of pots and carefully planning how many pots in progress they can maintain. When they begin with the initial stage of production for ten cooking pots, there might be another ten drying and awaiting shaping or surface treatment. Yet another ten might be finished except for the base formation. Considerable skill is required to balance the number of pieces in progress. The weather, unpredictable at times, impacts the drying rate. If pots are drying at a faster than anticipated due to elevated air temperatures, potters might enlist the help of unskilled workers on an *ad hoc* basis. These might be any family member, whether a child, spouse or adult relative. In such an instance, one might find two sets of fingerprints on a single pot, or some other indication of multiple hands.

Incised, indented and rouletted patterns always represent the work of the person who shaped the pot, since such surface treatment must be rendered in the wet clay. Some professional potters regularly plan for the participation of the unskilled to contribute to their work on drying pottery. Children, apprentices, or assistants might be recruited to add handles, and to decorate pottery by painting, burnishing or glazing. As a consequence, pots might have the prints of multiple people, as do those of Indian potters of Rajasthan.[24]

Clay texture determines surface treatment but within a particular pottery tradition, social factors rather than raw materials determine the precise surface treatment and there is room for personal expression. Social norms might require that a pot have a painted metopic decoration on the shoulder alone, but within this parameter the painter is free to choose the precise patterns, brush width and density of the decoration. An oven might require holes in the base into which the ashes fall, but the number of these functional holes varies from potter to potter or assistant to assistant, thereby representing the work of the individual who carved them. In the Filipino community of Paradijon, craft specialists create no fewer than four types of stoves, each associated with a particular type of fuel (one each for sawdust and wood, and two for charcoal burning). Potters and their spouses carve different numbers of holes into the bottom of stoves, thereby making it possible to differentiate the work of the potter and her spouse.[25] The ability to distinguish between the work of two people involved with the manufacture of a single vessel informs on manufacturing techniques and the organization of the pottery industry that involves an assembly line, regardless of how limited it might be.

At Paradijon, another feature indicative of both a learning framework and of diachronic changes in pottery manufacture is the finger indented and raised band of clay on the charcoal burning warming oven (*kalan sa oring*). The band surrounds the midpoint, where two coil built sections join together. In addition, the rim shows carefully and regularly placed finger indentations. These patterns represent the work of the potter rather than anyone else, since they are impressed in the still wet clay, which is handled by the potter alone. Each potter displays her own unique style in the number and pattern of these indentations. The design, arrangement and number of indentations are most similar for mothers and daughters, and for pairs of sisters. In direct contrast are holes cut into the stove floor to enable ashes to fall down to the lower level. The holes are cut into drying clay, either by the potter or by a helper. The precise number of holes is unimportant and their arrangement depends on personal preference. If a

---

[24] C. Kramer, *Pottery in Rajasthan: Ethnoarchaeology in Two Indian Cities* (Washington, D.C.: Smithsonian Institution Press, 1997), 69.
[25] London, "Standardization and Variation," 192-200.

husband cuts the holes into stoves made by his wife, his pattern will differ from that of his wife without altering function or use.[26]

Burnishing is a facet of surface treatment that a non-professional can perform, thereby releasing the practiced potter for the primary, essential forming work that requires specialized skill. Burnishing is work best carried out on clay that is partially dry. Although burnish strokes leave no fingerprints, burnishing has the potential to introduce variability into the work of the individual potter. If a potter burnishes some pots, but someone else burnishes others, pots of the same dimensions and proportion might have entirely different burnishing patterns. Pots made by the Paradijon craft specialists vary in dimension by some six percent whereas those made by domestic potters who occasionally sell or barter pottery show less standardization and vary by about twelve percent.[27] On pottery of the Bronze and Iron Ages in Israel and Jordan, burnish patterns vary in their distribution, arrangement, width length and frequency. A precise study of vessel dimensions and diverse burnish patterns on the large platters of the Early Bronze II holds the key to the organization of the ceramics industry of the Early Bronze Age. It would have been easy for someone other than the potter to burnish these mold-made platters because the work was done while the platter was still supported by a sturdy exterior mold.[28]

Ceramic Technology and Identification of Individuals

With pottery (whether funerary or domestic) dating to a single time period, one can differentiate among the work of contemporaneous potters whose wares were deposited at a site. Studies of ceramic technology and ethnoarchaeological data allow researchers to use the same criteria as traditional potters use today to identify the products of individual potters working within a single traditional of pottery making.

Each clay body has unique requirements and limitations. Potters learn to work the clay in a manner that accommodates both the clay and their clientele. Whereas clay and manufacturing techniques will be shared precisely and reflect the "conservative" nature of potters, nuances in technique and especially in decoration allow each potter to individualize (whether subconsciously or not) his/her pots. These subtle signs can be deciphered by other potters and by interested archaeologists. Braudel

---

[26] Ibid., 203.

[27] W. A. Longacre, "The Pottery of Paradise," *Sarabibon* 4 (2005): 108.

[28] G. A. London, "The Organization of the Early Bronze II and III Ceramics Industry at Tel Yarmuth: A Preliminary Report," pp. 117-24 in *Yarmouth 1* (ed. P. de Miroschedji; Paris: Éditions Recherche sur les Civilisations 1988), 120-22.

described material culture as "the repeated movements, the silent half forgotten story of men [*sic*] and enduring realities, which were immensely important but made so little noise."[29] Ceramic ethnoarchaeology articulates the marks preserved in clay. They are the sounds of potters, female and male, and their assistants.

Archaeologists occasionally identify several ceramic finds representative of a single potter, using objective criteria based on experience with the wares, as well as subjective, intuitive criteria.[30] Such identification is facilitated if the pots bear an elaborate design pattern. Ethnoarchaeological research provides objective methods of differentiating the utilitarian wares of contemporaneous potters. The same criteria that enable traditional potters in diverse cultural settings to recognize the work of their fellow potters should enable archaeologists to separate contemporaneous ancient wares according to potter and/or workshop. Ethnoarchaeological research demonstrates that the wares of potters working without electrical wheels and kilns, producing pottery for local use and not for a tourist market, can be sorted by collecting quantitative data on vessel attributes. Such data primarily relates to overall vessel proportions and decoration and, when considered in conjunction with studies of manufacturing techniques, enable researchers to distinguish the work of different potters whose wares are found at a single site.

The work of individual potters can be discerned among the Kalinga domestic potters in northern Luzon Island, the Paradijon craft specialists in southern Luzon Island and the traditional potters of Cyprus.[31] Potters in these three settings, quite distant from each other, make utilitarian forms for sale to local people. They also use the pots themselves and occasionally carry one away from the province to present as a gift. In the Filipino communities, paddle and anvil, as well as coiling techniques, prevail. In Cyprus, coiling is the norm for potters in lowland and Troodos

---

[29] F. Braudel, *Capitalism and Material Life, 1400-1800* (trans. M. Kochan; New York: Harper Colophon, 1975).

[30] E. Herscher, "Beyond Regionalism: Toward an Island-wide Early and Middle Cypriot Sequence," pp. 45-50 in *Cypriot Ceramics: Reading the Prehistoric Record*, (eds. J. A. Barlow, D. R. Bolger, and B. Kling; Philadelphia: University Museum of Archaeology and Anthropology, 1991), 46.

[31] W. A. Longacre, "Kalinga Pottery: An Ethnoarchaeological Study," pp. 49-66 in *Pattern of the Past: Studies in Honor of David Clarke* (eds. I. Hodder, G. Issac, and N. Hammond; Cambridge: Cambridge University Press, 1981), 62; W. A. Longacre, "Sources of Ceramic Variability among the Kalinga of Northern Luzon," in *Ceramic Ethnoarchaeology*, (ed. W. A. Longacre, Tucson, Ariz.: University of Arizona Press, 1992), 95-111; London, "Decoding Designs," 208-15; idem, "Standardization and Variation;" idem, *Women Potters of Cyprus*.

Mountain villages. In case studies in each of these three geographically distinct areas, potters were successful at identifying the maker of a specific pot. They consistently relied on the same combination of vessel features, which include aspects of manufacture and finish, overall vessel proportions, wall thickness, and, perhaps of least importance, decoration.

Archaeologists can employ these same criteria with confidence to identify the work of ancient potters, as has been demonstrated for Early Bronze IV domestic and funerary wares from Jebel Qa'aqir.[32] Jars found together in tombs proved to be the work of the same potter, and they differed in vessel proportion and decoration from jars found in other tombs. This is true for nondescript jars found by the hundreds in the Jericho tombs of the late third millennium B.C.E. Even for an undecorated container with a flat base and no handles, knobs, decoration or surface treatment, it was possible to determine which were the vessels of the same potter. Tombs containing many jars and the remains of male and female community elders held the work of more than one potter.[33] When assessing these results for their social implications, it is important to ask whether the pots and other funerary offerings were the gifts of many individuals paying homage to male and female elders, or the contribution of a single donor who collected pots from different potters.

Ethnoarchaeological Field Work among Craft Specialists: 1981, 1986, and 1999–2000

My ethnoarchaeological research into traditional potters in Cyprus began in 1986, to follow up on the earlier study of R. Hampe and A. Winter.[34] It was also designed to build on my 1981 fieldwork project among the Filipino potters of Paradijon, done while a student of W. A. Longacre.[35] This fieldwork enabled me to observe and record the criteria that two groups of craft specialists, separated by thousands of miles, used to differentiate among the work of individual potters. At that time, I recorded the work of twenty-five Cypriote potters, a quarter of whom were

---

[32] London, "Decoding Designs," 219-48; idem, "Identification of Individual Potters Past and Present," in *Contributions to the Study of Pottery Technology* (n.ed., Publicatie van het Gallo-Romeins Museum 34; Tongeren, Belgium: Provinciaal Gallo-Romeins Museum, 1987), 58-74.

[33] Ibid.

[34] R. Hampe and A. Winter, *Bei Töpfern und Töpferinnen in Kreta, Messenien und Cypern* (orig. 1962; Mainz: Philipp von Zabern), 1976.

[35] Longacre, "The Pottery of Paradise."

still producing pottery in 1999–2000.[36] They live in three different villages: the lowland villages of Kornos and Ayios Dimitrios (Marathasa, Troodos Mountains), and Kaminaria, also in the Troodos range. Their single manufacturing technique, coiling pottery, practiced in both the lowland and mountain communities, has changed, but almost imperceptibly, over the course of fifteen years; it is in the decorative elements that this change can be seen.

In 1986, I recorded the precise incised patterns of each of the five Ayios Dimitrios potters and those of the nearly twenty in Kornos. In addition, their combed tools were measured for width and number of teeth. Nuances in manufacturing were documented. Despite a fairly uniform manufacturing technique, subtle differences in the details of handle and decoration application helped to differentiate the product of each woman. In Kornos, potters added the handle after the decoration and thus it invariably smudged or erased part of the incised or roulette pattern. This small detail alone allowed me to classify the work of the lowland versus the mountain village potters. Other differences include the shape of cooking pot lids and the overall vessel proportions. Taken as a whole, they make it possible to distinguish pots made by different potters within and among villages. However, the vast majority local people, who might use the containers in Cyprus, do not distinguish between pots made in the different villages. Most non-potters within the pottery-producing villages cannot identify the work of each potter, yet the potters can and do, using the exact same criteria, as had the Filipina potters.

To examine changes over time for Kornos pottery, I recorded pre-1986 pots visible in the courtyards of two Kornos private potters, who are not members of the Cooperative. (At that time, there was no collection of traditional pottery in Cyprus, although there is at the present.) The courtyard collections were among the only accumulations of pottery in the entire village, where the potting tradition can be traced back 200 years.[37] For one senior potter over age sixty, 92 percent of the older decorated pottery displayed a roulette pattern. When considering all the pots (n=25), undecorated and decorated, 70 percent (all but two) had an incised roulette pattern. In 1986, this potter's signature pattern remained the rouletted design. In the courtyard of a second private potter, the twenty-seven pots

[36] London, "Regionalism;" idem, "Potters in Cyprus: Twelve Years Later," *Department of Pottery Technology Newsletter* 16/17 (1998/1999), "Continuity and Change," 105.
[37] G. A. London, F. Egoumenidou, and V. Karageorghis, *Traditional Potters in Cyprus* (Mainz: Philipp von Zabern 1989), 5.

made prior to 1986 included six (22 percent of the total) forms that are never decorated (ovens, beehives and so forth). Of the decorated pieces, 86 percent (n=18) had zigzag patterns identical to pots she fabricated in 1986.[38] In other words, both these private potters remained true to their signature patterns.

In 1986, I bought pots made by other Kornos potters, including many by members of the Kornos Pottery Cooperative. I put them away for a month and then asked people to identify who had made each pot, in a manner similar to that of Longacre in the Philippines. Potters, and normally only potters, could successfully identify the pot-maker by visually assessing overall vessel measurements, proportions and decoration. These attributes are the ones most often recorded by archaeologists, as well.[39] I then measured pots to determine whether I could sort the pots according to potter, using the same criteria the potters themselves use. To identify cooking pots and jugs made in 1986 in Kornos, Kaminaria, and Ayios Dimitrios, I measured overall vessel proportions and individual attributes, such as cooking pot circumference, rim thickness and diameter, height of pot and height at the maximum circumference.

To assess vessel morphology, I measured fifty-eight round-bottomed cooking pots of normal size, made by eight potters in Kornos, four in Ayios Dimitrios and the lone Kaminaria potter (Fig. 8-1). When plotted on a graph, two unrelated measurements, rim thickness and cooking pot circumference, showed a division between pots made in the mountains versus the lowland Kornos village (Fig. 8-2). For all but one potter, the circumference of Kornos cooking pots was substantially larger than that of the cookers from other villages. There was a small degree of overlap for some pots, which was easily clarified by incorporating one other feature unrelated to size but pertaining to work order: handle application. This is a routine stage of primary forming work that never varies (Fig. 8-3). When measured and plotted for vessel height and rim diameter, 44 jugs made in the three villages exposed an unambiguous separation according to the mountain and lowland traditions (Fig. 8-4). Additional information concerning the order of handle and decoration application reinforces our understanding of the division between two traditions operating at the same time, in the same country, under the same political and social conditions.

---

[38] London, "Ethnoarchaeological Evidence," 226.
[39] Ibid.

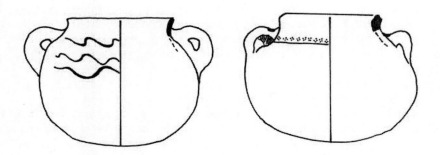

Fig. 8-1. Round-bottomed cooking pots. Illustration by author.

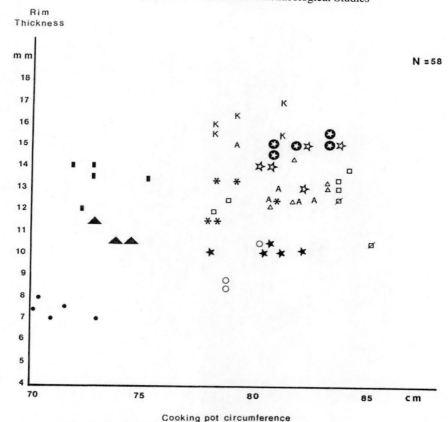

Fig. 8-2. Graph plots rim thickness and cooking pot circumference for 58 cooking pots made by 12 women in three Cypriot villages. These are features archaeologists normally can measure, even from sherds. The five darkened symbols represent two separate mountain villages, Kaminaria and Ayios Dimitrios. The seven open symbols and letters represent Kornos potters who, at the time, included five members of the Kornos Pottery Cooperative and two private potters (K and A). Cooking pots from mountain villages cluster in the lower left area of the graph whereas the same shapes from Kornos, clustered in the upper right, are slightly larger with thicker rims. There is some overlap where the two groups meet, which is corrected by including the order of decoration and handle attachment. One can separate lowland versus mountain village pots by this single detail of the manufacture. If the handle was applied after the incisions, it interferes with the decoration. In Kornos, handles are added in stage two, after the decoration, and consequently they erase part of the incisions. This is a characteristic of all pots represented by open symbols and letters.

Fig. 8-3. In Kornos, all potters finish stage one of manufacture by decorating the shoulder prior to handle application. The order of work in the two mountain communities is opposite, and only after handle attachment is the decoration carefully organized. Here, a Kornos potter rolls a coil in the air for a cooking pot during stage one of manufacture. After shaping the rim, the shoulder is smoothed and decorated. In stage two, the handles smudge part of the incised pattern on cooking pots and jugs (with pinched spouts) that dry in the foreground. At an even later stage, the strings supporting the thick lower body are removed and a rounded bottom is cut from the flat base. Photo by author.

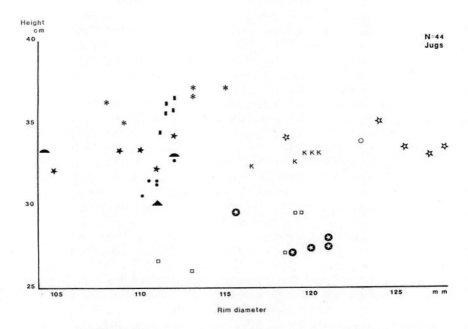

Fig. 8-4. Plot shows vessel height and rim diameter for 44 jugs made by eleven potters. The darkened symbols on the left (below rim diameter of 115 mm) all belong to potters in the mountains while the open marks and letters represent Kornos potters. The mountain and lowland (Kornos Cooperative and private potters) traditions are easily distinguishable. Jugs made in Kornos have larger mouths and are slightly shorter than those made in the mountains. The order of handle application and decoration noted above applies for jugs and all types of pottery.

Change and Continuity

Even as pottery functions as a boundary marker between contemporaneous communities, decoration incised on the vessel shoulders varies from village to village. As with vessel morphology, in 1986 there were minor instances of overlap in the combed decoration but for the most part, specific styles characterized each village. Modest yet clear differences within the combed patterns typified each of the three villages, including the two near each other in the Troodos Mountains. Most easily distinguished, based on the combing patterns, were pots by the last potter to work in Kaminaria. From 1986 until 2000, she stippled the entire upper body and handles of cooking pots and jugs. She alone embellished cooking pot lids with decorative incisions and included her initial "A" on the pot shoulders, where it is clearly visible. She used more than one pattern, but her wares were invariably profusely decorated, in contrast with those of her contemporaries.

In 1986, individual incised wavy lines made with a pointed tool characterized Ayios Dimitrios, the other Troodos village where utilitarian pots constituted the repertoire. Quite distinct and separate were Kornos village incised patterns, which were normally limited to a narrow band encircling the upper shoulder. Rouletted, stamped rosette, stippled and combed designs were still in vogue in 1986 in lowland Kornos, but by the end of 1999, roulettes and rosettes disappeared as the most elderly potters stopped working. A comb was sometimes used to create stippled marks, or less often the comb was dragged along the surface.

A reexamination of traditional Cypriote pottery in 1999 revealed a traditional industry struggling to survive. The Kaminaria potter continued to incise her wares as before, with incisions and her initials virtually covering the upper body. She ceased her work following the death of her husband in June 2000. A single Ayios Dimitrios potter continued to work but had only two kiln firings in 1999, one in 2000, and none since. She devoted time to tending fields, selling fruit in Nicosia, and spending time with family and grandchildren, before her early death.

In Kornos, the four remaining members of the Pottery Cooperative all shared the identical incised pattern, consisting of two bands of horizontal combing with a wavy combed band between them. In addition, they sometimes resorted to their own signature decorations. One woman did not use double horizontal combing, but instead had a single horizontal band below the wavy combed line incised on the cooking pots (n=19) made from September 7–October 26, 1999. She used the same pattern on her jugs (n=13) in September. Another potter, who made cooking pots infrequently, used either one or two horizontals. She also experimented with a roulette pattern using a tool made by a brother visiting from the United Kingdom. The women maintained that without a husband or brother knowledgeable about crafting the rouletting tool (*trokoudi*), the design had almost disappeared. A third potter used either one or two horizontals, with a wavy band above or between them, for the fifty-nine pots recorded during October 8–November 23, 1999. Like the other women, the fourth Coop member used one or two horizontals, but occasionally added an extra wavy band above the uppermost horizontal.

The two remaining private potters, who work independently in the courtyard workspaces of their own homes, never used the decoration described above, preferring a single incised wavy line or one or two straight lines with incised dots above, below or between the straight or wavy horizontals. These two sisters, who work separately, use various combinations of incised dots similar to those they incise on the smaller decorative pieces. The sisters are the only Kornos potters who continue to shape decorative vases, in forms requiring considerable skill. In Fini village, adjacent to Ayios Dimitrios in the Troodos Mountains, where two sisters create primarily tourist artifacts, a single cooking pot observed in 2000 had no combing, but rather individually incised straight or wavy lines. There was no difficulty in distinguishing between the Fini pots and those of Kornos, given that the clay type and color are unique to each village.

Archaeological Implications

One conclusion of the 1999–2000 follow-up study concerns the type of information that pots communicate over time and space concerning potters, male or female, and entire communities. While private potters in all three villages maintained use of the same incised patterns recorded in 1986, the Kornos Coop members did not. As a result, Kornos pottery no longer relayed the same information that it did in 1986, or if it does, it is subtler than ever. Despite the fact that there are fewer potters than in 1986, by the end of the millennium it became more difficult to designate the potter who made each cooking pot, given the sharing of a single decorative incised pattern. The final quantitative analysis remains to be completed, but it is apparent that potters no longer have a signature that is easily and consistently recognized. In Cyprus in 1986, the decoration and overall vessel proportions could facilitate the identification of a specific person in a specific village. By 2000, a glance at the decoration no longer conveyed the identification of the potter who made it. Measurements of overall vessel proportions might enable one to separate the work of each potter. One can still differentiate between cooking pots of the Kornos Pottery Cooperative workshop and those of the Kornos private potters, based on decoration alone. Handle types, overall vessel proportions and size also separate the work of the private potters from the women in the Cooperative. Whereas in the past, the voice of each Kornos Cooperative member was unequivocal, now the four potters seem to share a voice, perhaps in an effort to maximize a dying tradition.

It is also still possible to distinguish between the cooking pots of the private potters and those of the Kornos workshop members. Only while the pot remains in Kornos can an ever-dwindling number of potters and former potters match a potter with her pots. Already in 1986, once it left the village, the pot changed identity and was transformed into a product of Kornos village. If it left through a port (not likely for these heavy friable utilitarian pieces), it changed to represent the entire country of Cyprus or possibly even, simply a Mediterranean island.

The symbolic meaning of the pottery is further exemplified by the Kornos pottery engraved on Cypriot currency. In 2000, the ten-cent coin displayed a small decorated vase and the one-pound note showed a jug and an unfinished jar. As pots move further from their source of manufacture, the information they convey diminishes while their price increases. Outside Cyprus, a utilitarian cooking pot made in Kornos becomes an expression of a traditional handicraft item made by a nameless person in a nameless village. Although it relays less personal information the further it travels from its source, it conversely becomes a prestige item relaying information about wealth of its owner.

In some sense, the Bronze Age Cypriot White Slip (WS) and White Painted (WP) wares found in the Levant and Egypt convey information similar to that conveyed by the Kornos pottery abroad. Relatively coarsely painted pots from Cyprus become prized objects, the further they travel from their source. Simultaneously, they convey less information about the potter, but more about the owner. WP wares found in the Levant and Egypt belong to the southern Cypriot painted tradition. In the Levant, however, they are regarded simply as Cypriot. In Cyprus, the different patterns painted on WS and WP wares can inform about particular potters, workshops or styles, as well as about time periods. When found in the Levant or Egypt, these same pieces relay information about chronology and country of origin, rather than about person or precise place of manufacture. No longer representing a people, they denote place, social standing and wealth. The more carefully painted wares remain in Cyprus. Demand for quality diminishes with distance, or at least quality is beyond the control of the purchaser. A pot that once represented the work of a particular potter and perhaps a painter, as well, comes to personify a place, be it a village or country, or a national or ethnic group. When the imported artifact is found in an ancient tomb, perhaps in association with "prestige" items, it transforms once again. Rather than representing a person or a place, it becomes a thing. It is an important thing to which archaeologists attach great meaning, as it signifies the wealth and power of its owner. It also becomes the cornerstone of dating the entire funerary assemblage.

Initially, pots made by craft specialists can represent a person, village, or workshop tradition. The further they travel from their source, the more they lose this original meaning.

Conclusion

Kiln sites and pottery production locations, two uncommon archaeological finds, are rarely considered as conventional household/courtyard fixtures. In contrast, ethnoarchaeological research records Filipina and Cypriot women potters as craft specialists who work inside and in front of their homes. Women in traditional societies worldwide, of necessity, work close to or inside their homes where child rearing, care giving and seasonal activities occupy much of their time. Pottery manufacture, a seasonal occupation limited to the driest times of the year, can be considered one of the many seasonal chores carried out by women. As they mange the household, children and the elderly, as they cook, clean, visit neighbors, and feed animals year-round, seasonal jobs are equally varied. After planting, weeding, watering, harvesting large or small plots of land, women process, cook, prepare and preserve foodstuffs for domestic use, extended families, neighbors, and for sale or barter. Women conserve and sell foods they grow. Inevitably, they lack certain foods due to the geographical constraints of water, sun and soil. Women obtain foodstuffs from other regions by means of an exchange mechanism.

Pottery manufacture, a seasonal task, overlaps with the space needed for other seasonal and year round activities. The interior rooms and exterior areas function as processing, storage, and living spaces for people and animals throughout the year. Summertime visits to potters find courtyards, porches, and houses full of pottery in different stages of manufacture, along with stone anvils, reused scraps of metal, organic tools and equipment. Off-season, winter visits cause most observers to conclude that no pottery was or would ever be made in those same spaces. The complete absence of pottery, clay, or tools is due to the multi-functional use of space, depending on the season. Despite the domestic setting, pottery and other products made at home can represent critical craft industries, even in the modern world.

In traditional and ancient societies, pottery found close to its source informs about the maker. Ceramic ethnoarchaeological studies of craft specialists in Cyprus and the Philippines, who barter or sell their wares locally and not to tourists, show that these individuals create pottery that they can identify as the work of specific potters, most of whom are women. Pots can be acquired in a number of ways. They break easily and

as they are replaced, slow changes in morphology occur. Changes in rim
form, stance and thickness have been the crux of ceramic typologies for
over a century. Ceramic technology is a skill learned through observation
and practice, oftentimes passed from mother to daughter. It embodies a
wealth of knowledge about a tradition maintained for generations.
Fundamental forming techniques are slow to alter, but vessel surfaces are
available for individual expression and observation. As a ceramic
container moves further from its source, it loses the signature of its maker
and takes on the identity of a village or geographic area. Still, the original
voice remains and can be comprehended and translated by archaeologists
who recognize the silent movements preserved in clay.

CHAPTER NINE

"WORKING EGYPTIANS OF THE WORLD UNITE!": HOW EDITH NESBIT USED NEAR EASTERN ARCHAEOLOGY AND CHILDREN'S LITERATURE TO ARGUE FOR SOCIAL CHANGE[1]

KEVIN M. MCGEOUGH AND ELIZABETH A. GALWAY

In many ways, Edith Nesbit was an unconventional woman by the standards of Victorian and Edwardian British society. As a founding member of the Fabian Society, she helped lay the groundwork for left leaning mainstream politics in England. As an author, Nesbit was equally innovative. She was a successful writer of children's literature, including such classics as *The Railway Children* (1905), one of her works of realistic fiction. Nesbit was also an important writer of children's fantasy, blending adventure, fantasy, and magic with realistic settings that were rooted in a keen awareness of the problems of everyday life.[2] Her fantasy novel *The Story of the Amulet* (1906) is of particular interest to archaeologists of the Near East and Classical world, as it involves children traveling back in time to these locales.[3] One of the things that make this particular novel noteworthy is the care with which Nesbit faithfully recreates ancient Near Eastern and Classical settings. Her depictions of these regions are based on

[1] The authors would like to thank Beth Alpert Nakhai for welcoming their paper in her "World of Women" section at the 2007 American Schools of Oriental Research Annual Meeting and inviting us to submit the paper for this volume. Kevin McGeough would like to thank Patricia Usick of the British Museum for her assistance during his research of E. A. Budge, and would also like to acknowledge funding in the form of a University of Lethbridge Research Fund grant.
[2] E. Nesbit. *The Railway Children* (London: Puffin Books, 1994 [orig. 1905]).
[3] E. Nesbit, *The Story of the Amulet* (London: Puffin Books, 1996 [orig. 1906]).

then-current scholarly understandings, and Nesbit is markedly successful in this enterprise. Nesbit's novel provides a fascinating example of how a woman who was not an archaeologist was able to find out about current up-to-date Near Eastern scholarship and use the insights she gained from this study to argue for social change in Edwardian England (see Fig. 9-1).

Fig. 9-1. Edith Nesbit

In Nesbit's lifetime, children's literature was a medium suited to subversive explorations of such issues as women's rights and economic reform, being deemed a genre of literature that was appropriate for a middle-class woman to write. As C. Nelson observes:

> On the one hand, the nineteenth century saw childrearing as a primarily female duty. Since entertaining children, understanding them, and training them through gentle moral suasion were considered well suited to women's capabilities, few people would complain that a woman who wrote children's books was improper and unfeminine [...]. On the other hand, as today's feminist critics have noted, children's fiction by women often quietly subverts established gender mores.[4]

---

[4] C. Nelson, "Growing Up: Childhood," pp. 69-81 in *A Companion to Victorian Literature and Culture* (ed. H. Tucker; Malden, Mass.: Blackwell, 1999), 76.

Nesbit's *The Story of the Amulet*, with its detailed portrayal of the ancient world, was a safe arena for her to make somewhat controversial arguments about problems she perceived in Edwardian England. Although quite deliberately writing a work of fantasy, Nesbit took careful steps to incorporate the most up-to-date scholarship in her depictions of various ancient civilizations. This interest in realism underscores Nesbit's careful blend of fantasy and reality in the novel. The blend of the purely imaginative with the very realistic enables Nesbit to utilize Near Eastern archaeology to subversively critique what she saw as the social problems of contemporary British society. Critics have noted the evidence of Nesbit's socialist ideologies in her writing (including their apparent inconsistencies), as well as her use of fantasy to help convey some of her views. Scholars such as S. Rahn have noted that Nesbit often uses elements of fantasy to enable her characters to travel to various times and places, in part to offer her own commentary on Edwardian society. Less attention has been paid, however, to the fact that in *The Story of the Amulet*, Nesbit took obvious pains to portray ancient civilizations with accuracy.

This raises an important question: why would a writer of fantasy fiction take such care to ensure the accuracy of her depictions of the ancient world, particularly when the story depends to a large degree on magic and the reader's suspension of disbelief? Nesbit took steps to familiarize herself with the most recent archaeological theories about the ancient world, and this pursuit of accuracy suggests that Nesbit was using these adventures for more than just fanciful entertainment for her young readers. By creating as accurate a picture as possible of various ancient civilizations, Nesbit is able to utilize these as more convincing counterparts to modern British society. In this way, seemingly "scientific" evidence is presented regarding these ancient civilizations, making Nesbit's observations much more convincing. Nesbit uses her objective, archaeological knowledge to highlight Britain's perceived kinship with glorious civilizations of the past, as well as to warn against its perceived decline, represented by the loss of these same ancient societies. Nesbit's novel provides fascinating evidence of the ways in which non-specialists were responding to, and appropriating, recent developments in Near Eastern and Classical archaeology.

As a founding member of the Fabian Society, Nesbit was particularly interested in ideas of social progress. The Fabian Society, founded in 1884, was a socialist society whose members advocated gradual social reform, as opposed to reform through armed revolution. The name Fabian, which Nesbit and her husband Hubert Bland also gave to their son, reflects the couple's antiquarian interests. It refers to the Roman general Quintus Fabius, who briefly led the Roman army against Hannibal, while the Carthaginian army was attacking mainland Italy. Fabius, rather than attack the Carthaginians outright, used "Fabian Tactics" of harassment, hoping to beat the Carthaginians through attrition rather than military force. These tactics were central to the Fabian Society's strategies in Victorian-Edwardian England. H. G. Wells was a fellow Fabian, as were many prominent Edwardian figures with interests in social change. John Meynard Keynes, George Bernard Shaw, and Emmeline Pankhurst all argued for change through the Fabian organization and outside of it. Fabians played diverse roles in Edwardian society and used their own particular skills to push for change: Keynes through economics, Pankhurst through the Suffragette movement, and Nesbit through children's literature.

The Story of the Amulet is the last of three works that deal with the adventures of five middle class English children. In the first novel, Five Children and It, the eponymous children discover an ancient creature called a Psammead, which has the ability to grant wishes, often with disastrous and comical results. In The Phoenix and the Carpet, the same children discover a phoenix and a magic carpet, which takes them to various parts of the globe. In The Story of the Amulet, the children are reunited with the Psammead and discover one half of an ancient, magic Amulet, shaped like an Egyptian Tyet Knot (see Fig. 9-2).[5] They learn from the Psammead that if they can find the other half of the Amulet, it will grant them their heart's desire. The half that they do possess enables them to travel through time, so the children journey to different times and places in the hopes of discovering the missing portion of the Amulet.[6] Their adventures take them to a variety of locales including ancient Egypt, Babylon, Atlantis, and even future London. These adventures are a welcome distraction from their rather dreary summer holiday, which is

---

[5] The tyet knot (or knot of Isis) appears in Spell 156 of the Book of the Dead, where it is stated that it provides protection from anyone wishing to commit a criminal act against the bearer.

[6] Rahn has pointed out more of Budge's influence, regarding the tyet. She observes that Budge claims, in his problematic work Egyptian Magic, that the tyet allowed the bearer to travel through all of the parts of the underworld (S. Rahn, "News from E. Nesbit: The Story of the Amulet and the Socialist Utopia," pp. 185-213 in E. Nesbit's Psammead Trilogy: A Children's Classic at 100 [ed. R. Jones; Lanham, Md.: Scarecrow Press, 2006], 189). While this is not time travel, it is interesting that Budge suggested Nesbit use an actual type of Egyptian amulet that he believed was thought to have allowed some sort of supernatural travel.

spent with their old Nurse "who lived in Fitzroy Street, near the British Museum," while their mother and youngest sibling are in Spain recovering from an illness, and their father is in Manchuria "to telegraph news about the war to the tiresome paper he wrote for."[7] The children's former nurse also rents lodgings in her house, and one of her tenants is known as "the poor learned gentleman" who is a source of information about the ancient world for the children.

Fig. 9-2. The Amulet[8]

Nesbit's description of artifacts and ancient life reflects her familiarity with ancient visual culture. Constant references to the British Museum within the novel suggest that this may have been the source of much of her knowledge of the ancient world. For example, when describing the Babylonian deity Nisroch, Nesbit states that: "you can see it in our own British Museum at this day."[9] Clearly the British Museum was then one of the most powerful mediums through which knowledge about the past was presented to the British public.

Nesbit's ties to the British Museum seem, however, to have been more than those of the typical visitor. *The Story of the Amulet* is dedicated to E. A. Wallis Budge, the reviled director of the Egyptian section. She thanks Budge for his help in ensuring the accuracy of her work, and for his help

---

[7] Nesbit, *The Amulet*, 3.
[8] Ibid., 28.
[9] Ibid., 126.

throughout the process of writing the volume. [10] Nesbit first encountered Budge at a time when one of Budge's responsibilities at the British Museum was to interact with the public, answering letters sent to the Egyptian and Assyrian section by the interested public, or by allowing for a few hours throughout the week when he could answer questions in person. Nesbit visited him to ask about suitable ancient stories that could be adapted as children's literature.[11] While he could not provide her with any appropriate tales, they struck up a relationship and she visited him frequently for his advice on matters regarding the ancient world.

Budge's input is apparent throughout the work. He wrote the hieroglyphs for Nesbit that are engraved on the Amulet and which the children have translated by the learned gentleman (see Fig. 9-3).[12] Budge also suggested some of the names that are used in the story. For example, an Egyptian priest is named Rekh-mara, after a high official whose Theban tomb had been excavated, and the pharaoh is referred to as "great house" (an accurate translation of the word pharaoh).[13] Budge also pointed out the statue of Nisroch in the British Museum and provided Nesbit with a description of an Assyrian banquet.[14]

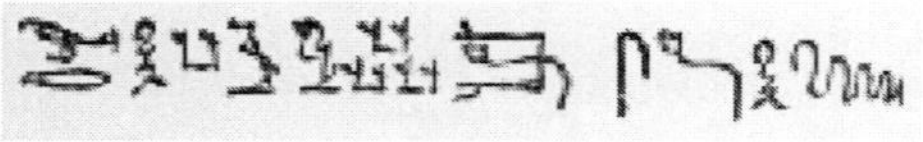

Fig. 9-3. The hieroglyphs on "The Amulet"[15]

It is also likely that Budge told Nesbit about the Amarna letters, which he acquired in Egypt on behalf of the British Museum.[16] Evidence of this can be found in the novel when, at one point in the story, a model of ancient trade is presented that seems based directly on the evidence of the

---

[10] The full dedication reads: "To Dr Wallis Budge of the British Museum as a small token of gratitude for his unfailing kindness and help in the making of it."
[11] J. Briggs, *A Woman of Passion: The Life of E. Nesbit 1858-1924* (New York: Meredith Press, 1987), 245-46.
[12] The hieroglyphs are presented in *The Amulet* (p. 33) using Budge's conventions for transcribing hieroglyphs and are transliterated *ur hekau setcheh* (p. 42).
[13] Briggs, *Woman of Passion*, 247.
[14] Ibid., 247.
[15] Nesbit, *The Amulet*, 33.
[16] For an account of Budge's acquisition of these tablets, see B. Fagan, *Return to Babylon: Travelers, Archaeologists, and Monuments in Mesopotamia* (Boston: Little, Brown and Company, 1979), 185-86.

Amarna letters. In this passage, the Queen of Babylon describes Late
Bronze Age trade patterns to the children:

> "We wanted an Egyptian princess. The King may-he-live-forever has got a
> wife from most of the important nations, and he had set his heart on an
> Egyptian one to complete his collection. Well, of course, to begin with, we
> sent a handsome present of gold. The Egyptian king sent back some horses
> – quite a few; he's fearfully stingy! – and he said he liked the gold very
> much, but what they were really short of was lapis lazuli, so of course we
> sent him some. But by that time he'd begun to use the gold to cover the
> beams of the roof of the Temple of the Sun-God, and he hadn't nearly
> enough to finish the job, so we sent some more. And so it went on, oh, for
> years. You see each journey takes at least six months."[17]

Elements such as this demonstrate what an important source of information
Budge was for Nesbit.

There is some speculation about just how close Nesbit was with
Budge, fuelled in part by the unconventional marriage between Nesbit and
her husband Hubert Bland, both of whom are known to have had extra-
marital relationships. Budge too was married, and it is difficult to know
how intimate his relationship with Nesbit became. Well after his
friendship with the author had ended, Budge discussed her attempts to
become more publicly intimate with him and his concomitant refusals to
visit her at home, go away with her, or be a public presence in her life.[18]
Budge himself was a somewhat interesting figure in *fin de siècle* England,
in part because of his status as an illegitimate child.[19] He demonstrated an
aptitude for ancient languages (although modern Egyptologists generally
do not agree with this assessment). Due to Budge's lack of economic
resources, he was accepted at Oxford only when Gladstone (who later
became prime minister of England and was himself an amateur Homeric
scholar) arranged for a scholarship fund for Budge.[20] Regardless of
whether Budge and Nesbit were romantically linked, her close personal
relationship with him certainly provided one avenue for her discovery of
the ancient world.

Budge is not the only figure from Nesbit's life who is referred to in the
novel. References to fellow Fabians occur throughout, but they are not

---

[17] Nesbit, *The Amulet*, 116.

[18] Briggs, *Woman of Passion*, 249.

[19] For more on Budge's life, see R. Morrell, *Budgie–The Life of Sir E. A. I. Wallis
Budge* (Nottingham: 43 Eugene Gardens, 2002).

[20] Budge's correspondence with Gladstone on this and other issues is archived at
the British Library.

uniformly positive. There is a subtle critique of Nesbit's colleague, Annie Besant. Better known in Edwardian social circles as Mrs. Besant, she was a prominent socialist activist and campaigner for women's rights, and later became an active Theosophist. Mrs. Besant became well known in British society in 1877, when she became a strong supporter of birth control and published an argument that the working class could never be happy until they learned to limit the size of their families. Ten years later she was seen as one of the main figures in a demonstration against unemployment, which culminated in violence. Gradually, she lost contact with her Fabian colleagues, as she became more enamored with a Marxist approach to change through violent revolution. However, after reading *The Secret Doctrine* by Madame Blavatsky, Besant lost interest in social protest, instead taking up the study of theosophy, which sought to study the past through the examination of ancient literature through a spiritualist approach, employing psychics, mediums, and past-life memories to better understand the secrets of the ancient Aryans and citizens of Atlantis. At one point in *The Story of the Amulet,* the Babylonian Queen causes the Babylonian objects to float out of the British Museum. No doubt Nesbit is mocking Besant when she describes a journalist's response to these events and to the figure of the Queen: "'Theosophy, I suppose?' he said. 'Is she Mrs Besant?'"[21] The next edition of the newspaper reports on these events: "Mrs Besant and Theosophy: Impertinent Miracle at the British Museum."[22]

The differences between Besant and Nesbit are such that it is no surprise that they drifted apart. Besant flouted Edwardian conventions regarding gender, religion, and class. She organized strikes and produced political pamphlets. As such she was a notable but marginalized figure in British society and eventually withdrew from London to the Theosophical Society headquarters in Benares. Nesbit, although she did challenge some traditional views, was not nearly as overt in flouting British conventions. Like Besant, she questioned conventional assumptions, particularly those concerning women's roles, frequently serving as the breadwinner in her family and dressing in loose fitting, comfortable clothing that enabled her more physical freedom and mobility than the leading women's fashions of her day. Such actions make it apparent that, like Besant, she may not have upheld many of the middle-class values of Victorian and Edwardian Britain. Unlike Besant, however, Nesbit voiced her protests through what were considered more appropriate channels for a woman. In fact, it seems

---

[21] Nesbit, *The Amulet*, 146.
[22] Ibid., 147.

that Nesbit did not even support women's suffrage. Most of her concerns were geared more towards issues of economic equality.[23]

Children's literature was a safer arena for these protests than Besant's public strikes, but Nesbit's work as a children's author reveals both her challenge and adherence to the framework of established gender roles. For instance, while children's literature was generally viewed as an acceptable form of writing for a respectable middle-class woman to engage in, she wrote under the name E. Nesbit, as opposed to Edith, masking her female identity. This was perhaps so that she might be taken more seriously as an author but perhaps also to increase the market for her books. Reading material for children is often categorized as either "books for girls" or "books for boys," but typically girls will read stories about both boys and girls, whereas boys tend to favor books written by men, or about boys or men. Nesbit's decision to publish as "E. Nesbit" may have helped her appeal to a broader readership, and can perhaps be seen as her caving into, rather than protesting, the difficulties faced by female authors. Even so, it is apparent that Nesbit did not lead a life typical of a woman from the English middle class, and was greatly concerned with social justice, even if her form of protest was less overt than Besant's.

Nesbit uses her knowledge of the ancient world to help argue for the cause of social justice. Throughout the story, the children find out about the Near East through their conversations with the ancient Psammead, and through their discussions with the learned gentleman, who is also described as the "learned scholar." This character is never said to hold a university or museum position. Rather, it must be supposed that he has a pre-existing source of income that allows him to collect artifacts and study the past from his home (see Fig. 9-4). This character well represents the Victorian "man of letters" who studied without formal training or a formal position, before archaeology became professionalized within academia. Children's author and critic N. Streatfeild suggests that this character was what Nesbit "believed Doctor Wallis Budge must have been like at the beginning of his career."[24] Whether or not the character of the learned gentleman was modeled after Budge, certainly the circumstances of his life and work were similar to Budge's before he received his appointment at the British Museum.

---

[23] Briggs, *Woman of Passion*, 333-35.

[24] N. Streatfeild, *Magic and the Magician: E. Nesbit and Her Children's Books* (London: Ernest Benn, 1958), 108. Briggs disputes a direct connection between Budge and the learned gentleman, but suggests that an unnamed Budge does appear in the book, as the "nice man" who works for the British Museum (*Woman of Passion,* 247-48).

Fig. 9-4. In the house of the learned gentleman[25]

Throughout the novel, Nesbit makes allusions to ancient cultures that seem directed more at scholars than children. For example, Ritti-Marduk, the assistant of the Queen of Babylon, is described as "the Queen's man with the smooth face."[26] The implication here is that Ritti-Marduk is a eunuch, in keeping with the Victorian era orientalist fantasy that bled into Near Eastern studies, that the Mesopotamian court was filled with eunuchs, just as the Ottoman court was thought to be. The banquet of the king similarly reflects orientalist fantasies of the Near East, where nearly nude girls and snake charmers entertain the Babylonian court (see Fig. 9-5). These images perhaps more reflect Nesbit's familiarity with French orientalist/realist painters than Near Eastern scholarship, but offhand references to the Babylonian New Year festival show how much Nesbit had in fact studied about the past.[27]

---

[25] Nesbit, *The Amulet*, 36.

[26] Ibid., 131.

[27] When the queen is arbitrating disputes between her citizens, one of the disputes involves a woman who had borrowed a cooking-pot "at the last New Year's festival, and had not returned it" (ibid., 110).

Fig. 9-5. The snake charmer in the Babylonian court[28]

What is particularly striking about *The Story of the Amulet* is how clearly it reflects *fin de siècle* understandings of the Near East and Classical world. Nesbit well understood contemporary scholarly theories about Near Eastern civilization, so much so that it is possible to identify these theoretical frameworks in her children's adventure story. For example, when the children travel back to Predynastic Egypt they encounter a girl of whom it is said that: "Her hair was short and fair, and though her skin was tanned by the sun, you could see that it would have been fair too if it had had a chance."[29] The children subsequently flee Egypt when an invading group disrupts the idyllic village. One of the invaders' faces is described as: "a dark force with, a blobby flat nose...very like the face of Mr Jacob Absolom, who had sold them the charm in the shop near Charing Cross."[30] It is not clear if this should be read as an explicitly anti-Semitic description, although it certainly seems problematic by today's standards. What Nesbit is alluding to here is Petrie's theory of Egyptian state formation, likely pointed out to her by Budge.[31] Petrie and others had argued that Semitic invaders had spurred

---

[28] Nesbit, *The Amulet*, 119.

[29] Ibid., 57.

[30] Ibid., 81.

[31] Budge actually argued against a Semitic origin of Egyptian culture, citing numerous Egyptian parallels to "indigenous African traditions" in his work, standing against the then consensus view. See a review of his *Osiris and the Egyptian Resurrection* by I. M. Casanowicz (*American Anthropologist* 13 [1911]: 615-17).

the development of the Egyptian state.[32] While this theory has obviously long been abandoned, it would have been cutting edge when Nesbit was writing.

Nesbit's use of Victorian era racial theory, which was in keeping with scholarly theories of the time, points to her own interest in using the ancient world as a means of discussing the present, something typical of much historical fiction. Implicit in Nesbit's fictional presentation of the ancient world is the creation and perpetuation of a hierarchy of ancient civilizations. Throughout *The Story of the Amulet*, Nesbit identifies certain ancient cultures as being similar to the British and others as being substantially different. Often she uses the children's reactions to their adventures in the past as a means of presenting these arguments of sameness or difference. One example of this can be found in the episode when the children first arrive in Babylon. As the children are walking up to the gates of Babylon, Robert responds to his brother Cyril's demand that they show "courage" by suddenly singing "The British Grenadiers," thereby proclaiming their "Englishness" at the same time.[33] The lines from the song that Robert sings include references to the ancient world:

'Some talk of Alexander,
And some of Hercules,
Of Hector and Lysander,
And such great names as these.
But of all the gallant heroes…'[34]

The song is cut off there, underscoring the emphasis placed on connecting modern Britain with the ancient empires.

The narrator draws other connections between Britain and the ancient world. For example, when the children first see Babylon, the narrator observes that the city wall "was enormously high–more than half the height of St. Paul's."[35] Other elements of the geography of Babylon are also described as being similar to Western Europe. When the children are walking up the road to Babylon (see Fig. 9-6), the hedge is described as "like those you see on the road between Nice and Cannes, or near Littlehampton if you've only been as far as that."[36] It is highly unlikely

---

[32] K. Bard, "The Emergence of the Egyptian State," pp. 57-82 in *The Oxford History of Ancient Egypt* (ed. I. Shaw; Oxford: Oxford University Press, 2000), 61.
[33] Nesbit , *The Amulet*, 98.
[34] Ibid., 98.
[35] Ibid., 96.
[36] Ibid., 95-96.

that Babylonian roads were lined with hedgerows–this fanciful description (and deviation from the archaeological reality) heightens the reader's expectation that the children will share a "sameness" with the Babylonians. It is interesting to note instances like this when Nesbit deviates from her attempts at accurate descriptions based on scholarly data. These moments of departure are in situations when she is interested in drawing explicit connections between the ancient world and the present.

Fig. 9-6. The children approach the Gates of Babylon[37]

This is in keeping with much of the discourse on race and culture of imperial Britain, where certain parts of the empire (such as Canada and Australia) were deemed "more British" or civilized than other parts (such as India or Africa). Presenting and exploring ethnic or perceived racial difference in an imperial context often played the role of erasing or trivializing difference between disparate groups, and forcing marginal groups to define themselves in terms created by the core or by only allowing these peripheral groups to present their differences in a manner deemed safe for the majority. By presenting otherness in a safe context, this otherness can then only be understood as a curiosity, rather than as a legitimate alternative. The superiority of the established culture, in this

---

[37] Ibid., 134.

case Victorian and Edwardian Britain, is established even though this superiority does not have to have been explicitly articulated.

While Nesbit frequently uses depictions of ancient societies to highlight the perceived superiority of Britain, she nevertheless does provide something of a critique of London, by describing these ancient cities as clean and orderly (in a way that Edwardian London was not), which is in keeping with her work as a social reformer. When the children first visit the city of Babylon, the city is explicitly depicted as different from London:

> And it [Babylon] was very different from London. For one thing, everything in London seems to be patched up out of odds and ends, but these houses seemed to have been built by people who liked the same kinds of things.[38]

Here is a mild critique of the urban planning (or lack thereof) of London, in keeping with Nesbit's reformist tendencies.[39] Throughout the story, differences between ancient Babylon and modern London are differences of aesthetics and quality and the two locales are in many ways mutually understandable. For example, in the following description of Babylon and its environs, Babylonian and English homes and clothes are compared:

> It was all so wonderfully different from anything that you have ever seen. For one thing, all the houses were dazzlingly bright, and many of them covered with pictures. Some had great creatures carved in stone at each side of the door. Then the people – there were no black frock-coats and tall hats; no dingy coats and skirts of good, useful, ugly stuffs warranted to wear. Everyone's clothes were bright and beautiful with blue and scarlet and green and gold.[40]

Here, Nesbit is criticizing the conservative nature of London society, indicating that a great society does not need to have drab architecture and dreary clothes. There is a sense here that she is mocking the sensibilities that lay beneath London fashions. Likewise, the markets of Babylon are

---

[38] Ibid., 101.

[39] The seeming lack of order in the layout of London inspired reformists to argue for dramatic changes in London's approach to urban planning. While the containment of disease and reduction of pollution were of the utmost importance, planners such as Ebenezer Howard argued that an orderly use of urban space based on controlled zoning would lead to better living conditions. See, for example, his *Garden Cities of To-Morrow* (London: Faber & Faber, 1946 [orig. 1902]).

[40] Nesbit, *The Amulet*, 101-2.

described as "brighter than you would think anything could be," and it is stated that "[t]he children had never seen half so many beautiful things together, even at Liberty's."[41] These are critiques of London subtly conveyed through its comparison to another civilized society. The critiques are not particularly substantive social critiques but rather mild critiques of issues of aesthetics. These descriptions are also further evidence of what M. Flegel notes as a Fabian tendency to offer "a model of English gentility as *the* model for the standard of living that should be shared by everyone in society".[42] Rahn may be overstating the case when she suggests that the narrator's emphasis on the greater beauty of Babylon is a clear "denunciation of Edwardian London."[43] She observes:

> London, the ugly city, represents our cruel and corrupt capitalist civilization; the beautiful city represents civilization as it should be. This pattern is designed to be a kind of education process, encouraging the young reader to realize that our civilization is loathsome and that alternative and better civilizations can exist.[44]

Rather than being an outright denunciation of a "corrupt capitalist civilization," Nesbit's emphasis on the aesthetic superiority of ancient Babylon seems to support Flegel's contention that even though the Fabians sprang from the middle classes, they also valorized aspects of upper-class culture.[45]

In actuality, Nesbit both criticizes her own civilization, and frequently draws the readers' attention to the superiority of British culture. In fact, Nesbit is demonstrating alternative possibilities for British society through the exploration of other centers of civilization, which reifies the imperialist centrality of Edwardian London at the same time that it critiques some of its less desirable attributes. Such an approach is further evidence of what Nelson refers to as the "dualities" of Nesbit's fiction.[46] It appears that in Nesbit's view, there were centers of civilization and centers of savagery. As many nineteenth and early twentieth century historians argued, Britain

---

[41] Ibid., 102.
[42] M. Flegel, "A Momentary Hunger," pp. 17-38 in *E. Nesbit's Psammead Trilogy: A Children's Classic at 100* (ed. R. Jones; Lanham, Md.: Scarecrow Press, 2006), 20.
[43] Rahn, "News from E. Nesbit," 190.
[44] Ibid.
[45] Flegel, "Momentary Hunger," 20.
[46] C. Nelson, "The 'It' Girl (and Boy): Ideologies of Gender in the Psammead Trilogy," pp. 1-15 in *E. Nesbit's Psammead Trilogy: A Children's Classic at 100* (ed. R. Jones; Lanham, Md.: Scarecrow Press, 2006), 2.

was fulfilling the role that Egypt, Babylon, and Rome had once played. Thus, much of the interest in studying these particular cultures was to identify root causes of their collapse. The learned scholar from whom the children learn much about the ancient cultures that they visit describes Babylon:

> "Babylon has fallen," he answered with a sigh. "You know it was once a great and beautiful city, and the centre of learning and Art, and now it is only in ruins, and so covered up with earth that people are not even agreed as to where it once stood."[47]

After being frightened by some of their previous adventures in ancient Egypt, one of the children asks the scholar: "Were the Babylonians savages, were they always fighting and throwing things about?"[48] He answers them:

> "The Babylonians were certainly more gentle than the Assyrians," said the learned gentleman. "And they were not savages by any means. A very high level of culture," he looked doubtfully at his audience and went on, "I mean that they made beautiful statues and jewelry, and built splendid palaces. And they were very learned; they had glorious libraries and high towers for the purpose of astrological and astronomical observation."[49]

Babylon, then, is described as a centre of arts and learning, much as London and Paris are, but this civilization had fallen into ruins. Just as George Smith argued in his address to the Society of Biblical Archaeology in 1873 (when he formally announced the discovery of the flood tablet), Nesbit suggests that it is the fact that Babylon was once a centre of learning and is now vanished that necessitates its exploration.[50]

The Queen of Babylon is a figure that Nesbit portrays as particularly empathetic to the values of the British children (see Fig. 9-7). The queen asserts that she feels like she knows the children, pointing to her very "British-ness," stating: "Somehow I feel as though I'd known you quite a long time already."[51] The children first interact with the queen while she is hearing court cases for her subjects. Throughout the cases, the queen demonstrates characteristics associated with the British in her interest in

---

[47] Nesbit, *The Amulet*, 91-92.
[48] Ibid., 92.
[49] Ibid., 92-93.
[50] G. Smith, "The Chaldean Account of the Deluge," *Transactions of the Society of Biblical Archaeology* 2 (1873): 213-34, 234.
[51] Nesbit, *The Amulet*, 109.

careful jurisprudence. However, the rampantly illogical decisions that she makes explicitly demonstrate the progress that the British have made in jurisprudence. Rahn contends that the Queen of Babylon's critique of Edwardian London later in the novel is evidence that Nesbit "shows how specious the modern claims of progress are," and that she "is pointing out that political forms mean less than economic realities".[52] However, there is other evidence in the novel that suggests Nesbit is in fact writing in a scholarly tradition that envisions a hierarchy of civilizations. In spite of its flaws, British society, as demonstrated by its superiority over ancient Babylon in matters of jurisprudence, is seen to have progressed beyond the ancient world.

Indeed, the Babylonian queen is portrayed in many ways as an almost childlike figure. Through her childlike behavior, the reader sees that even though these ancient civilizations are intellectually connected to England, England is still developmentally ahead of these ancient cultures – the adult to their child. This portrayal is very much in keeping with imperial attitudes that saw Britain as the "motherland" and its colonies as her offspring. It is also a familiar conflation of the feminine with the figure of the child. While Nesbit at times clearly challenges some commonly held assumptions about women, she is simultaneously writing within a tradition that both relegated middle-class women to the domestic realm (which they shared with children), and "denied women property and legal rights [and] implied that all women, even those who had legally come of age, were 'minors.'"[53] The figure of the Queen of Babylon is, in fact, a good example of what Nelson notes as the complicated approach to gender in Nesbit's fiction.[54] While in many ways a strong and vocal female character, the Queen is also very childlike in nature, serving as a means by which Nesbit can position British society as the more "advanced" version of the ancient world's most glorious civilizations. Adopting a rhetoric that figures women as the embodiment of both innocence and motherhood, Nesbit's ancient Babylon, through the figure of the Queen, serves to represent both an early civilization that can be seen as the "mother" of British civilization, and a more primitive, infantile state that is clearly less advanced than Edwardian England.

---

[52] Rahn, "News from E. Nesbit," 193, 194.
[53] C. R. Vanden Bossche, "Moving Out: Adolescence," pp. 82-96 in *A Companion to Victorian Literature and Culture* (ed. H. Tucker; Malden, Mass.: Blackwell, 1999), 92.
[54] Nelson, "The 'It' Girl (and Boy)," 2.

Fig. 9-7. The children meet the Queen of Babylon[55]

Indeed, a model of progress and decline is embedded into Nesbit's fictional account, which bears considerable similarity to the model of progress and decline later presented in H. G. Wells' *The Outline of History* (1919).[56] Wells likely based his conceptions of historical progress on then current anthropological notions of unilineal cultural evolution, which posits that all cultures evolve through distinct and consistent stages. Perhaps most noteworthy was the work of Lewis Henry Morgan, who in his 1877 monograph, *Ancient Societies*, argued that societies progressed from savagery to barbarism to civilization.[57] Wells, in his conceptualizations of history, interacts with Morgan and other evolutionary thinkers in articulating his historical schema rooted in this type of progressivism. Given that Wells was a friend of Nesbit's, the fact that similarities in their understanding of historical causality are apparent is not surprising. Children's literature, however, was a more appropriate forum for a woman like Nesbit to make arguments regarding the nature of human progress and decline.

---

[55] Nesbit, *The Amulet*, 106.
[56] H. G. Wells, *The Outline of History: Being A Plain History of Life and Mankind* (New York: Doubleday, 1971 [orig. 1919]).
[57] L. H. Morgan, *Ancient Society* (New York: Transaction Publishers, 2000 [orig. 1877]).

Her interactions with Wells are more explicit in the chapter of *The Story of the Amulet* when the children visit the future. In 1905, Wells' work, *A Modern Utopia*, which criticized Edwardian London, was published.[58] Letters between Nesbit and Wells indicate that Nesbit was not entirely satisfied by Wells' book, but she clearly borrows his ideas and utilizes them in *The Story of the Amulet*. As Nesbit's biographer J. Briggs observes, "[i]n this chapter, Edith rewrites *A Modern Utopia* from the child's point of view, focusing upon the nature of schools and nurseries in this brave new world."[59] One of the children that the protagonists encounter in the London of the future is named Wells, "after the great reformer."[60] It has also been claimed that *The Story of the Amulet* bears a more than passing resemblance to H. G. Wells' *The Time Machine* (1895), in which the protagonist's travels through time serve as the author's means of criticizing capitalism and the class system.[61] Whether or not one sees Nesbit's work as derivative of or inspired by Wells' writing, it is noteworthy that an Edwardian woman would choose to address the same themes through children's literature as opposed to adult fiction or political tracts.

Perhaps the most overt demonstration of British society's progress in *The Story of the Amulet* is in the children's adventures in ancient Britain, ca. 55 B.C.E. The children are transported back in time to a village situated where London is now. Notions of unilinear cultural evolution are explicit when one of the children comments that, "It's like the old Egyptian town."[62] With this, Nesbit suggests that both of these great societies, Egypt and Britain, started out in a similar fashion. The progress that Britain has gone through is even more evident when the children meet Julius Caesar. Caesar is taken aback by them, feeling that they seem to be more like Romans than the barbarians he expects to meet on British soil. Nesbit writes:

"Are you from Britain?" the General asked. "Your clothes are uncouth, but well woven, and your hair is short as the hair of Roman citizens, not long like the hair of the barbarians, yet such I deem you to be."[63]

---

[58] H. G. Wells, *A Modern Utopia* (New York: Penguin Books, 2005 [orig. 1905]).
[59] Briggs, *A Woman of Passion*, 252.
[60] Nesbit, *The Amulet*, 239.
[61] Rahn, "News from E. Nesbit," 188, 189; see also H. G. Wells, *The Time Machine* (New York: Simon & Schuster, Inc., 2004 [orig. 1895]).
[62] Nesbit, *The Amulet*, 189.
[63] Nesbit, *The Amulet*, 193.

The children go on to describe to Caesar what the modern British Empire is like. Caesar is impressed, and although he thinks that the conversation with the children is a dream, he chooses to set out to conquer Britain. Here again, mixed with the comic account of the children influencing Caesar's campaign, a progress narrative is developed where the Roman leader feels a kinship with the children from this modern empire. The children have little in common with the residents of England in 55 B.C.E, but much in common with Caesar and Rome in this period. This portrayal of a common ground, given the temporal and cultural distance between ancient Rome and Edwardian Britain, is further demonstration of Nesbit's acknowledgment of the sense of kinship that exists between these various world empires.

Nesbit uses this sense of kinship to argue for changes that need to be made if Britain's empire is going to succeed and avoid the collapse faced by all those that came before. As we have seen, Nesbit's strong interest in the economic concerns of the Fabians is well reflected in *The Story of the Amulet*. Class and class struggle are common themes of the work. When the children visit ancient Egypt, they find themselves at a meeting much like the union agitation meetings of Victorian and Edwardian times. Nesbit describes the event:

> "Comrades and fellow workers," it said, and it was the voice of a tall, coppery-coloured man who had climbed into a chariot that had been stopped by the crowd. Its owner had bolted, muttering something about calling the Guards, and now the man spoke from it. "Comrades and fellow workers, how long are we to endure the tyranny of our masters, who live in idleness and luxury on the fruit of our toil? They only give us a bare subsistence wage, and they live on the fat of the land. We labor our lives to keep them in wanton luxury. Let us make an end of it!"[64]

One of the children responds to this, saying, "'I've heard almost every single word of that…in Hyde Park last Sunday.'"[65] The similarities with labor unrest in Britain are further implied in the next part of the rally:

> "Let us strike for more bread and onions and beer, and a longer mid-day rest," the speaker went on. "You are tired, you are hungry, you are thirsty. You are poor, your wives and children are pining for food. The barns of the rich are full to bursting with the corn we want, the corn our labour has grown. To the granaries!"[66]

---

[64] Ibid., 205.
[65] Ibid., 206.
[66] Ibid.

With that, the angry laborers move off to protest their poor economic treatment and in so doing wander through the more well-to-do parts of the Egyptian town, where Nesbit describes the residents as: "the kind of people who, nowadays, would have lived at Brixton or Brockley."[67] In Edwardian times, these were recently developed neighborhoods near London popular with the wealthy middle classes. One of the children comments that the reactions of the Egyptian upper middle classes to the striking workers is also reminiscent of what he has heard back home in England. A well-off Egyptian merchant states:

> "Oh, the working-men–discontented as usual," the man answered. "Listen to them. Anyone would think it mattered whether they had a little more or less to eat. Dregs of society!" said the date seller. [68]

In this episode, Nesbit is using the setting of ancient Egypt to not so subtly comment on economic agitation within England. Partially this involves the assumption that these same issues of class conflict were played out in antiquity. She can satirize modern times without actually agitating for change, as Besant did through pamphleteering and striking.

The most direct commentary on the British class system comes from the Queen of Babylon who is accidentally brought to Edwardian era London. The queen is depicted as a somewhat enlightened figure. After the children explain the English wage system to her, she equates the working classes to slaves and predicts that a slave revolt is imminent. The queen, using the magic of the Psammead, wishes that all of the poor people could wear clothes like the ancient Babylonians, to be less dreary. While this reflects a comedic sensibility, the queen's wish that all of the poor should have food can be read more seriously. When food magically appears, Mile End Road is said to have brightened up, a clear argument that a more equitable distribution of wealth will make London a more pleasant place.

Yet in many ways the overall critique of English economic and social structures is shockingly naïve. It does not actually criticize the existence of the class system, and in many ways reifies it by its portrayal of these divisions as "essential" divisions in a society – they are part of what makes a society civilized. Nesbit does not substantially challenge these notions. Instead, her concern for economic reform is more for a better distribution of wealth – to give the poor more goods to make their lives more livable. In her vision of a utopian future London, she portrays a London without

---

[67] Ibid.
[68] Ibid., 207.

homelessness, where everyone is educated. Future Londoners all work (even the women) and are paid fair wages, so that a carpenter is depicted as receiving a fair wage and living in a comfortable home.[69] It is unclear, however, whether Nesbit's utopian vision actually includes the concept of a truly classless society.

Nesbit scholars disagree on how subversive *The Story of the Amulet* truly is and the degree to which it is influenced by her own socialist values. Rahn argues that the quest for a socialist utopia is in fact the underlying theme of the entire work.[70] What is clear is that Nesbit used the field of archaeology to help promote some of her views on the state of contemporary British society. With *The Story of the Amulet*, Edith Nesbit used up-to-date scholarship regarding the Near East as the basis for a fun adventure tale laced with social commentary. For a socially marginal figure such as Nesbit, ancient Near Eastern studies and children's literature were acceptable and safe media for her to comment on and participate in Edwardian public society. Nesbit's well-informed depictions of ancient civilizations serve as a means of both celebrating Britain's achievements by comparing it favorably with many fascinating earlier cultures, and also as a means of drawing her young readers' attention to some of the problems in Edwardian England and to what she saw as some potential solutions. By exploring the ancient Near East in her novel, Nesbit establishes a clear vision of what she hopes British society of the future will look like.

---

[69] Ibid., 238-39.
[70] Rahn, "News from E. Nesbit," 187.

CONTRIBUTORS

Aubrey Baadsgaard earned her Ph.D. in Anthropology from the University of Pennsylvania. Her research interests include gender and the body, domestic activities and relationships, dress and adornment practices, mortuary archaeology, and the cultural heritage of the Middle East. Her dissertation examined fashions and fashion trends in Early Dynastic Mesopotamia. She is a research associate at the University of Pennsylvania Museum, Philadelphia, and an assistant curator in the Department of Ancient Near Eastern Art at the New York Metropolitan Museum.

Marica Cassis is Assistant Professor of History at Memorial University of Newfoundland. She completed her Ph.D. at the University of Toronto; her dissertation won the 2007 Leonard E. Boyle Dissertation Prize of the Canadian Society of Medievalists. She has published articles in *Hugoye* and the *Journal of the Canadian Society of Syriac Studies*. Dr. Cassis is the Director of Byzantine Excavations at the site of Çadır Höyük in central Anatolia, Turkey.

Deborah Cassuto received her Masters Degree from the Department of Land of Israel Studies and Archaeology at Bar Ilan University. Her thesis is entitled *The Social Context of Weaving in the Land of Israel in Iron Age II*. She is a Research Fellow at the William F. Institute of Archaeological Research in Jerusalem and is currently affiliated with the Tell es-Safi/Gath excavations. Ms. Cassuto recently completed reports on the weaving implements from Tell es-Safi/Gath and the loom weights and spindle whorls from Gamla.

Mary Ann Eaverly, Associate Professor of Classics at the University of Florida, is the author of *Archaic Greek Equestrian Sculpture*. Her articles on gender in ancient painting appear in *From the Ground Up: Beyond Gender Theory in Archaeology; Colour in the Ancient Mediterranean World;* and *Common Ground: Archaeology, Art, Science and the Humanities*. Her work with Marsha Bryant on women poets and the Classical tradition appears in *Mosaic* and *Modernism and Modernity*.

Jennie R. Ebeling is Associate Professor of Archaeology in the Department of Archaeology and Art History at the University of Evansville in Indiana. She is the co-editor of *New Approaches to Old Stones: Recent Studies of Ground Stone Artifacts* (Equinox 2008). Dr. Ebeling is the ground stone specialist for a number of excavations in Israel dating from the Neolithic to Byzantine periods, and the author of articles and technical reports on ground stone from sites in Israel. She is particularly interested in women's contributions to household food production in the Bronze and Iron Ages.

Cynthia Finlayson received her M.A. in Near Eastern Anthropology and Museum Studies from George Washington University and her Ph.D. in Classical and Islamic Art History from the University of Iowa. She is Associate Professor of Anthropology/Archaeology at Brigham Young University in Provo, Utah. In addition, she directs the American Expeditions to Palmyra (Bel Temple-Efqa Spring Corridor Excavations) and to Apamea (The Great Roman Theatre), Syria. She is also co-director for the Azem Palace Project in Damascus. Dr. Finlayson has worked in the Near East since 1977.

Elizabeth A. Galway is an Associate Professor in the Department of English at the University of Lethbridge. She earned her B.A. in English literature from the University of Toronto, where she minored in Classical Civilizations. She holds an M.A. in English from Durham University and a Ph.D. in English from the University of Exeter. She is the author of *From Nursery Rhymes to Nationhood: Children's Literature and the Construction of Canadian National Identity.*

Michael Homan is Associate Professor of Theology at Xavier University of Louisiana. He is the author of *To Your Tents, O Israel* (Brill 2002), and the co-author of *The Bible for Dummies* (Wiley 2002). Dr. Homan is the Vice-President of Programs for the American Schools of Oriental Research, and a supervisor on the Tel Zeitah Excavations.

Gloria London specializes in ancient ceramic technology. Her most recent fieldwork includes Tell al-`Umayri in Jordan, and ceramic ethnoarchaeological work in Cyprus and Jordan. She is the author of numerous articles, as well as a DVD entitled *Women Potters of Cyprus.* Dr. London serves on the editorial board of the *Leiden Journal of Pottery Studies*, and is the director of the National Endowment for the Humanities "Summer Institute for Teachers: Daily Life in Ancient Times."

Kevin M. McGeough is an Assistant Professor of Archaeology in the Department of Geography at the University of Lethbridge. He holds a B.A. in History from the University of Lethbridge, an M.T.S. from Harvard Divinity School, and a Ph.D. in Near Eastern Languages and Civilizations from the University of Pennsylvania. He is the author of *Exchange Relations at Ugarit* and is one of the editors for the ABC-Clio *Encyclopedia of World History*.

Beth Alpert Nakhai is an Associate Professor in the Arizona Center for Judaic Studies at The University of Arizona. She received her M.T.S. from Harvard Divinity School and her M.A. and Ph.D. from The University of Arizona. Dr. Nakhai is the author of *Archaeology and the Religions of Canaan and Israel* (ASOR 2001), as well as numerous articles. In addition to editing this volume, she is the editor of *Near East in the Southwest: Essays in Honor of William G. Dever* (ASOR 2003). She is co-director of the Tell el-Wawiyat (Israel) Excavation, and serves on the Board of Directors of the American Schools of Oriental Research.

Elizabeth Ann Remington Willett is an International Translation Consultant (Old Testament) for SIL International, a faith-based non-governmental organization that assists in developing the world's lesser-known languages through literacy, linguistics, translation, and other academic disciplines. She earned an M.A. in Linguistics from the University of North Dakota and a Ph.D. in Near Eastern Studies from the University of Arizona, majoring in the History and Religion of Ancient Israel. Dr. Willett has published on women in the Bible and archaeology, as well as on the religion and language of the Tepehuan people of Mexico.

INDEX

Afghanistan 76, 109, 110
agriculture 19, 79
Akkadian 67, 82
amulet *see* religion
Amulet, *The Story of the Amulet* xv,
    181, 183–85, 188, 191, 192, fig.
    9–5, 192, fig. 9–2, fig. 9–3, fig.
    9–4, fig. 9–5, fig. 9–6, fig. 9–7,
    199, 200, 202
animal 8, 18, 22, 23, 73–75, 77,90,
    91, 151, 157, 161, 163, 179
antiquity xi, xii, xiv, xv, 50, 52, 53,
    67, 101, 156, 157, 160, 201
Arab *see also* Aramaean/Arab xiii,
    xiv, 97, 100, 101, 103–5, 107,
    109, 111, 112, 116, 117, 123,
    125
Arabia ix, xiii, 100, 103–5, 109,
    126, fig. 6–1
Aramaean xiv, 99–101, 105, 109,
    111, 112, 123, 125
Aramaean/Arab xiv, 99, 100, 123,
    125
Aramaic xiii, 96, 100, 117
artifact xiii, xiv, 6, 14, 31, 53, 60,
    64, 65, 67, 70–73, 75, 76, 88,
    90, 91, 93, 100, 141, 146, 148–
    52, 155–59, 163, 177, 178, 185,
    189
Bedouin 24, 76, 157
"Bible, Canaanite" 87
Bible, Hebrew x, xiii, xvii, 20, 21,
    25, 43, 48, 53, 69, 85, 87, 91,
    98, 107, 156
bodies of water
    Aegean 20, 68
    Euphrates 110, 111, fig. 6–1
    Mediterranean xii, 3, 16, 66,
        67, 79, 98, 109, fig. 6–1,
        160, 178

Persian Gulf 109, fig. 6–1
Red Sea 90, fig. 6–1
Bronze Age
    Early Bronze Age 55, 167, 169
    Late Bronze Age 56, 71, 187
    Middle Bronze Age 56
Byzantine *see also* Ottoman; sites,
    Turkey xi, xiv, 125, 139–46,
    149–54
Canaan *see also* sites, Israel,
    Canaan, Philistia 55
Canaanite *see also* "Bible,
    Canaanite" 52, 79, 87, 90, 111
child *see also* childbirth; family,
    child; death, infant mortality
    xiii, xv, 17–19, 24, 44, 46, 51,
    69, 77, 81, 82, 85, 87, 90, 94,
    96, 97, 105–8, 110, 113, 118–
    26, fig. 6–6, fig. 6–10, 160, 162,
    163, 165, 166, 179, fig. 9–6, fig.
    9–7, 181, 182, 184–87, 189–202
    child protecting 83, 92, 97
    child–stealer 83, 84, 86, 94
    child–stealing xiii, 81, 82, 86,
        93, 97
    childcare 18, 160
    child rearing 14, 64, 76, 93,
        179, 182
    children's literature xv, 181–
        202
childbirth 79, 81, 82
    birth 1, 18, 19, 69, 80, 105,
        106, 120, 123, 188
    breast 5, 83, 93, 94, 97, 120,
        121
    fertility 5, 10, 51, 79, 88, 97,
        111
    labor (birth) *see also* mother
        82

nurse ix, 82, 83, 91, 92, 120,
        118, 185
nursery 199
pregnant 86, 122
pregnancy 79, 81
wet nurse 83, 118–20, fig. 6–9
Classical see also Greco–Roman;
        Greece; Roman x, xi, xiii, xv,
        xvi, 3, 10, 69, 70, 99–102, 111,
        125, 134, 143, 153, 181, 183,
        191
community xiii, xiv, xiv, xv, 17, 19,
        29, 42–45, 54, 66, 89, 97, 98,
        100, 101, 105, 115, 124, 126,
        141, 143, 145, 148, 149, 152,
        157, 162, 166, 168–70, fig. 8–3,
        175, 177
control 2, 8, 17, 42–46, 54, 60–62,
        101, 124, 125, 178, 188
death 2, 18, 43, 47, 80, 82, 97, 120,
        176
    burial 6, 80, 97, 110, 111, 117,
        121, 125, 149, 163
    cemetery 6, 7, 151
    funerary xiii, xv, 1, 3, 5, 6, 8,
        11, 68, 99, 100, 105,
        109, 111–13, 115, 118,
        119, 121, 126, fig. 6–2,
        fig. 6–4, fig. 6–5, fig. 6–
        6, 167, 169, 178
    Hypogeum 118–20, fig. 6–2,
        fig. 6–4, fig. 6–6, fig. 6–
        9
    infant mortality xiii, 79–86, 91,
        97, 106
    loculus 110, 111, 117, fig. 6–4
    mortuary 6
    tomb xii, 1, 6, 7, 10, 11, 48–50,
        fig. 3–1, 55, fig. 3–2,
        68, 97, 109–21, 124,
        125, fig. 6–2, fig. 6–4,
        fig. 6–5, fig. 6–6, fig. 6–
        10, 169, 178, 186
        Ti's Tomb, fig. 3–1, 55, fig.
        3–2

deity see also god, goddess xiii, 7,
        50, 51, 52, 69, 82–86, 88, 92,
        93, 94, 111, 116, 117, 185
domestic ix, x, xii, xiii, xv, 13–20,
        22–26, 28–32, table 2–2, table
        2–3, 35, 38, 40–44, fig. 2–3, 46,
        61, 62, 64, 65, 67, 68, 70, 72–
        74, 76, 77, 84, 92, 93, 96, 115,
        142, 151–53, 156, 159, 167–69,
        179, 197
economy x, xiv, 45, 89
    barter 167, 179
    commercial 63
    economic xiii, 13, 17, 18, 42,
        43, 47, 54, 80, 81, 87,
        95, 105–7, 110, 112,
        116, 120, 124, 182, 184,
        187, 189, 197, 200, 201
    industrial 89, 161, 162
    sell 67, 68, 109, 110, 160, 167,
        176, 179, 191, 201
    socio–economic 54, 87
Egypt see also sites, Egypt xi, xii,
        1–3, 6, 7, 9–11, 20, 45, 46, 48–
        50, 52, 53, 55, 56, 58, 61, 62,
        68, 81, 100, 110, 123, fig. 6–1,
        fig. 6–3, 157, 159, 178, 184,
        186, 191, 196, 199–201
    Dynasty 4, fig. 1–1, 9, 11, 48,
        49, 55, 68
    Dynastic xi, xii, 1, 3, 6–8
    Egyptian xii, xv, 1–5, fig. 1–1,
        8–10, 12, 47, 50, 55, 62,
        68, 81, 87, 97, 111, 157,
        163, 182, 184–87, 191,
        192, 199, 201
    First Intermediate Period 50
    hieroglyph 186, fig. 9–3
    Middle Kingdom 50
    New Kingdom 47, 53, 68
    Old Kingdom fig. 1–1, 9, 50,
        54, 55, 68
    Pre–Dynastic xii, 3, 6, 7
elite x, 2, 7, 9, 99, 140, 141, 143–
        46, 152

England xi, xv, 181–84, 187, 197, 200, 201
Britain 183, 188, 192–95, 197, 199, 200, 202
British xv, 181, 183, 185, 188, 192, 193, 195–97, 199–202
British Museum xv, 118, 185, 186, 188, 189
Edwardian xv, 182, 183, 184, 197, 202
English 142, 184, 189, 194, 195, 201
London xiv, 184, 188, 194–97, 199, 201, 202
Victorian xi, 181, 184, 188–90, 192, 194, 200
epigraphic 112, 124, 126
epigraphical 145
ethnoarchaeology 168
ethnoarchaeological xiv, 60, 66, 76, 155, 159, 163, 167–69, 179
ethnography ix, 53
ethnographic xi, xiii, 14, 17, 19, 20–24, 31, 42–44, 54, 60, 61, 64, 66, 67, 76, 96, 160, 161
Fabian Society 181, 183, 184
family xii, xiii, xv, 14, 16–19, 22, 44, 62, 69, 81, 82–86, 88, 90, 93, 95, 97, 98, 100, 102, 103, 106, 107–13, 117, 119–23, 125, fig. 6–6, 160, 163, 165, 176, 188
beit 'av 13
brother 43, 107, 112, 113, 119, 121, 125, fig. 6–5, 158, 176, 192
child xiii, xv, 17–19, 24, 44, 46, 51, 69, 77, 81, 82, 85, 87, 90, 94, 96, 97, 105–8, 110, 113, 118–26, fig. 6–6, fig. 6–10, 160, 162, 163, 165, 166, 179, fig. 9–6, fig. 9–7, 181, 182, 184–87, 189–202

daughter xvi, 105, 113, 117–21, fig. 6–5, fig. 6–9, fig. 6–10, 166, 180
elder 158, 160, 169
extended 16, 107
father 51, 65, 69, 116, 119–23, fig. 6–6, 158, 185
husband 69, 77, 95, 97, 102, 103, 106, 113, 116, 119, 122, 124, fig. 6–6, 167, 176, 183, 187
infant see death, infant mortality
mother see also labor (birth) xiii, xvi, 47, 64, 69, 81, 82, 85, 87, 94, 96, 97, 108, 119–25, fig. 6–6, 143, 144, 158, 166, 180, 185, 197
nuclear 14, 17, 112
patriarch 120
patriarchal xii, 13, 16, 17, 42, 43, 98, 107, 112, 113, 118, 119, 122, 124, 126
sibling 112, 185
sister 47, 112, 113, 125, 129, 143, 158, 166, 177
son 42, 65, 69, 77, 91, 94, 118, 119–23, fig 6–5, fig. 6–9, fig. 6–10, 183
wife fig. 1–1, 11, 68, 69, 71, 81, 86, 88, 91, 102, 103, 106, 108, 113, 119, 120, fig. 6–6, 167, 187, 200
female xiii, xiv, 2, 3, 5, 6, 8-12, 17, 46-48, 50, 51, 60, 62, 64, 65, 68, 69, 77, 79, 80-82, 84, 90-94, 97, 105, 109, 111, 112, 116-118, 120, 121, 125, 126, 141-143, 145-150, 152, 153, 157, 159, 160, 162, 168, 169, 177, 182, 189, 197
food preparation xiii, 14, 19, 23, 24, 25, 41, 43, 65, 74–77, 90, 93, 161

baking xii, 19–21, 24, 25, 43,
    45, 49, 50, 52–55, 57,
    60–62
beer xii, xiii, 46–48, 50–56, fig.
    3–1, fig. 3–2, fig. 3–3,
    59–62, 200
    beer jug *see also* pottery
        54–56, fig. 3–3
    brew xii, 45–47, 49–53, fig.
        3–1, fig. 3–2
    stopper, fermentation xii,
        54, 57, fig. 3–5,
        59, fig. 3–6, 60,
        62, 74
    straw (drinking) *see also*
        pottery 48, 54,
        56, 57, fig. 3–4,
        60
bread 17, 19–21, 23, 25, 28, 42,
    43, 45–47, 50–55, 60–
    62, 69, 75, 200
cooking xii, 13, 14, 18, 20–26,
    28, 30, table 2–4, table
    2–5, 32, 38, table 2–7,
    39, 41, 42, 44, 45, 53,
    61, 64, 65, 76, 90, 162
cooking pot *see also* pottery
    30, table 2–4,
    65, 74, 75, 93,
    151, 152, 165,
    171, fig. 8–1,
    fig. 8–2, fig. 8–
    3, 176–78
food xiii, 14, 18, 19, 21, 24, 25,
    41–44, 57, 62, 65, 74–
    77, 89, 90, 93, 95, 151,
    157, 161, 179
food processing 18, 21, 25, 89,
    90, 93
grain 19, 20, 23–25, 41, 45–47,
    50, 52–54, 62, 88
grinding 19, 20, 24, 25, 30, 41,
    50, 52–54, 60, 61, 65,
    73, 74
grinding stone 53, 61, 65, 74,
    75

ground stone xii, table 2–4, 53,
    54, 60
mortar 25, 53, 65, 74
oven 20–23, table 2–1, 27–31,
    table 2–2, table 2–3,
    table 2–4, table 2–5, fig.
    2–1, 35, table 2–6, table
    2–7, 38, fig. 2–3, 41, 42,
    57, 74, 75, 92, 93, 151,
    152, 166, 171
    tabun 21, 22, 25, 26, 53
    tannur 21, 22, 25, 26, 28,
        31, 53
pestle 53, 65, 74
utensil xii, 23, 41, 74, 93
wine 46, 48, 51, 56, 74, 95
gender ix–xvi, 1, 3, 9, 15, 16, 24,
    44, 60, 62–66, 68, 70, 72, 74,
    77, 89, 101, 103, 105, 140–43,
    146, 148, 151–53, 159, 160,
    162, 182, 188, 189, 197
god, goddess *see also* deity;
    religion ix, xiii, 2, 5–7, 10, 46–
    48, 50–52, 69, 82–87, fig. 6–7,
    90, 92–94, 111, 115
    Allat 111, 116, 122
    Ashera (Asherah) ix, 69, 85–88,
        90, 93
    asherim 88, 91
    Astarte 52
    Baal 81, 86, 87
    Baal–Haddad 111
    Baal–Hamon 111
    Bel 111, 114, 117, fig.6–7, fig.
        6–8
    El 85–88
    God 97, 187
    Hathor 7, 47, 50, 51, 90
    Inanna 51
    Ishtar 47, 48, 51, 52, 111
    Lilith 82, 86, 97
    Ninkasi 51, 52
    Queen of Heaven 51, 52, 95
    Sun God 11, 187
    Yahweh 48, 52, 86–88, 94

Greco–Roman *see also* Greece;
  Classical; Roman 86, 97, 111,
  117
Greece *see also* Classical; Greco–
  Roman xii, 20, 24, 69, 159
Greek 11, 68, 96, 97, 102, 109,
  117
  Hellenistic 58, 100, 104, 108–
    11, 123
  Mycenaean 55
Hebrew *see also* Bible, Hebrew
  xiii, 20, 21, 25, 48, 53, 84, 88,
  103, 105, 107, 156
heterarchy 17, 98
hierarchy 98, 192, 197
historic(al) x, xiii, 14, 19–21, 43,
  44, 48, 53, 64, 99–101, 105,
  108, 140–44, 149, 192, 198
hospitality 43, 124
house xiii, 2, 3, 13, 14, 16–18, 20–
  24, 27–29, table 2–2, table 2–3,
  table 2–5, fig. 2–1, 31, 35, table
  2–6, fig. 2–2, 38, table 2–7, 38,
  41–44, 47, 60, 61, 65, 66, 69–
  74, 76, 77, 81, 84–86, 88, 90,
  93, 95–97, fig. 5–4, 145, 150,
  160, 179, 185, 186, fig. 9–4, 194
  build 22, 28, 42, 165, 169
  building 31, 35, 38, table 2–7,
    41, 70, 72–75, fig. 4–2,
    fig. 4–3, 149
  courtyard 17–20, 22–25, 28,
    29–32, table 2–2, table
    2–3, table 2–5, 35, table
    2–6, 38, table 2–7, 41,
    42, 54, 60, 61, 71, 84,
    90, 92, 93, 160, 161,
    170, 177, 179
  dwelling 17, 18, 20, 23, 41, 65,
    67, 71, 72, 74, 76, 77,
    92
  house, four–room 14, 35, 61,
    70–72, 81, 93
  installation 14, 21, 27, table 2–
    4, 53, 60, 74

roof 18, 19, 23, 24, 29, 54, 71,
  84, 187
storeroom 23, table 2–2, 58,
  150
household xii, xiii, 13, 15–20, 22–
  25, 28, 35, 42–46, 53, 54, 61–
  63, 65, 68, 76, 77, 81, 84–86,
  88–93, fig. 5–3, 95, 96, 98, 110,
  145, 160, 185, fig. 9–4
household archaeology 15, 98
icon 88, 96
  iconographic(al) xiii, 2, 50, 52,
    53, 57, 61, 62, 67, 82
  iconography 4, 5, 7, 9, 20, 23
Iran 23, 60, 76, 102, fig. 6–1
  Iranian 21, 22
  Persian 58, 86, 109, 110
Iraq 23
  Assyria 84, 86
    Assyrian 67, 82, 85, 86, 97,
      186
  Babylon 184, 187, 190, 192,
    fig. 9–6, 194–97, fig. 9–
    7, 201
    Babylonian 79, 82–84, 86,
      185, 188, 190,
      191, fig. 9–5,
      193, fig. 9–6,
      194, 196, 197,
      fig. 9–7, 201
  Mesopotamia xii, 46–48, 51,
    56, 58, 67, 82, 110, 159
    Mesopotamian 9, 52, 82,
      83, 97, 109, 111,
      190
Iron Age xii, xiii, 13–22, 25–28,
  31, 35, 41–44, table 2–1, 46, 50,
  54, 56, 60–62, 70, 80–82, 88,
  90, 98, 161
  Divided Monarchy 88
  Iron Age I 20, 26–28, table 2–1,
    38, 53
  Iron Age II xiii, 26–38, table 2–
    1, 31, 38, 40, fig. 2–3,
    41, 66, 70, 72, 77
  United Monarchy 88

Israel *see also* sites, Israel, Canaan,
    Philistia xiii, 13, 46, 50, 51, 53–
    56, 61, 62, 69, 77, 80, 81, 84,
    87, 89, 107, 148, 149, 167
    Israelite xii, xiii, 14, 45, 46, 48,
        50, 52, 53, 60–64, 70,
        71, 77, 79, 81, 84, 87,
        88, 90–94, 98, 107
king 1, 2, 7, 94, 95, 122, 187, 190
kline 113, 121, fig. 6–6
knowledge xi, 19, 43, 44, 86, 101,
    152, 158, 164, 180, 183, 185,
    189
labor xii, 13, 16, 19, 41, 42, 44, 64,
    66, 79, 89, 95, 97, 200
Levant 66, 70, 105, 123, 178
    Levantine 70, 87
livestock 19, 151
male xii–xiv, 2, 3, 5–12, 16, 17, 48,
    52, 64–66, 69, 84, 91, 97, 98,
    102, 106–8, 111, 112, 120, 122,
    fig. 6–10, 140–142, 146, 148,
    152, 157, 162, 168, 169, 177
marriage xiii, xiv, 100–8, 110, 112,
    118, 119, 121, 122–26, 146, 187
    marital 11, 19, 108, 117
    mut'a xiii, xiv, 99, 101–12,
        118, 121–26
    nikah 101, 105, 112, 113, 118,
        122, 126
    nikah al–mut'a 108, 124–26
    temporary 100–3, 107, 108,
        121, 124
    patrilineal 16
    patrilocal 16, 17
Middle East 61, 66, 99, 155, 157
    Middle Eastern 19, 24, 61
mold 50, 55, 156, 165, 167
monastery 141, 143, 144, 147, 149,
    151, 153
monastic xiv, 141, 143, 146, 148,
    149, 150
Near East ix–xvi, 13, 45, 46, 50,
    52, 53, 56, 61, 62, 67, 68, 79,
    80, 99, 100–3, 105, 109, 120,

122, 126, 144, 163, 181, 189,
    190, 191, 202
Near Eastern x, xiii, xv, xix, 43,
    62, 85, 86, 89, 91, 93,
    97, 103, 107, 120, 123,
    124, 181, 182, 183, 190,
    191, 202
nomadic 71, 100–2, 105, 109, 110,
    112
Northwest Semitic 87
Ottoman *see also* Byzantine; sites,
    Turkey 61, 190
Palmyrene *see also* sites, Syria,
    Palmyra xiii, 100, 102, 109–22,
    124, 126, fig. 6–2, fig. 6–7
pattern xiii, 6, 14, 22, 25, 28, 35,
    38, 53, 54, 67, 76, 97, 113, 120–
    22, 142, 153, 157–59, 166–68,
    170, fig. 8–3, 171, 175–78, 187,
    195
pharaoh xii, 1–3, 7, 10, 11, 186
portrait xiv, 100, 102, 105, 109,
    111–13, 117–121, fig. 6–2, fig.
    6–3, fig. 6–4, fig. 6–6
pottery xiv, 4, 6, 8, 9, 27, 30, 57,
    65, 92, 93, 148, 155–68, 170,
    171, fig. 8–2, fig. 8–4, 175–79
    beer jug *see also* food
        production, beer 54–56,
        fig. 3–3
    ceramic xiii, 6, 21, 22, 52–55,
        60, 155, 158, 167, 168,
        179, 180
    ceramic technology 156, 157,
        167, 180
    cooking pot 30, table 2–4, 65,
        74, 75, 93, 151, 152,
        165, 171, fig. 8–1, fig.
        8–2, fig. 8–3, 176–78
    craft specialist 156, 159–61,
        165–69, 179
    decorated wares 156, 157
    decoration 2, 155, 156, 158,
        163, 166–71, 174–77,
        fig. 8–2, fig. 8–3, fig. 8–
        4

fingerprint 162, 163, 165, 167
finishing, secondary 158, 159,
   164
forming, primary 158, 159,
   164, 171
forming, secondary 158
Kornos Pottery Cooperative
   161, 171, fig. 8–2, fig
   8–4, 177
morphology 155, 171, 175, 180
potter xiv, 156–71, fig. 8–3,
   175–78, fig. 8–4
potter, female xiv, 159, 160,
   161, 179
straw (drinking) *see also* food
   production, beer 48, 54,
   56, 57, fig. 3–4, 60
surface treatment 156, 159,
   163–67, 169
Pre–Islamic 99–105, 107, 108, 115,
   116, 126
production xii–xiv, 2, 3, 10, 17–19,
   42, 44–46, 48, 50, 53–55, 60–
   62, 65–69, 75, 76, 89, 112, 122,
   151, 153, 159–61, 163, 165, 179
reality 6, 15, 16, 168, 183, 193, 197
religion *see also* deity; god,
   goddess ix, x, xi, xiii, xv, 1, 66,
      79, 81, 83, 85, 87, 90, 92, 93,
      103, 188
   amulet xiii, 11, 83, 97, 151,
      184, 186, fig. 9–2, fig.
      9–3
   Christian xiv, 79, 86, 145, 151
   cult ix, 2, 46, 88, 97, 114, 117,
      fig. 6–8
   cultic xii, xiii, 57, 63, 93, 109,
      111, 112, 114, 115
   figurine ix, xiii, 5, 6, 8, 50, 82,
      84, 85, 90–94, fig. 5–3,
      fig. 5–4, 97, 158, 163,
      165, 200, 201
   Islamic 61, 79, 99, 100–5, 107,
      108, 115, 116, 125, 126
   Jewish xiv, 43, 79, 86, 97, 145

lamashtu (lamaštu) 82, 83, 86,
   fig. 5–1
religious xiii, xiv, 6, 7, 43, 44,
   82, 83, 87, 90, 91, 94,
   95, 97, 98, 101, 109,
   111, 112, 114–16, 126,
   140, 143, 145, 146, 148,
   151, 152, 153
ritual xiii, 6, 43, 44, 46, 48, 62,
   86, 88, 90, 91, 93, 96,
   98, 114, fig. 6–7, fig. 6–
   8
sacred 43, 86, 96, 97
sacrifice 57, 84, 95
   sacrificial 48, 62
spiritual 43, 44, 97, 188
temple x, 2, 11, 48, 62, 84, 90,
   97, 114, 117, fig. 6–5,
   fig. 6–7, fig. 6–8, 187
votive xiii, 88, 90, 92, 93, 94
Roman *see also* Classical; Greco–
   Roman ix, xiii, xiv, 2, 80, 86,
   96, 97, 100, 104, 105, 108–11,
   114, 116–20, 122, 123, 184,
   199, 200
rural xiv, 22, 23, 43, 141, 143, 144,
   146, 153, 160
Saracen 100, 102, 116
sculpture 1, 3, 111, 114
   sculptural 112
sites
   Cyprus xiv, 159–61, 163–65,
      168–70, 177–79
   Ayios Dimitrios xix, 170,
      171, fig. 8–2,
      176, 177
   Kaminaria xix, 170, 171,
      fig. 8–2, 175,
      176
   Kornos xix, 161, 170, 171,
      fig. 8–2, fig. 8–
      3, fig 8–4, 176–
      78
   Nicosia xix, 176
Egypt *see also* Egypt

Alexandria fig. 6–1, fig. 6–
3
Deir el–Balah 54
Deir el–Medina 68
Hierakonpolis xix, 3, 7–9,
fig. 6–1
Kuntillet 'Ajrud xix, 87, 88
Iraq *see also* Iraq
Nineveh 84
Israel, Canaan, Philistia (Bronze
Age–Byzantine) *see also*
Canaan; Israel; Syria–
Palestine
Beer–Sheba xix, 26, table
2–1, table 2–4,
31, 38, table 2–
7, 40, fig. 2–3,
88, 92, fig. 5–3
Gesher xix, 56
Gezer xix, 26, table 2–1,
table 2–4
Hazor xix, table 2–1, table
2–4, 30, 31, 41
Hurvat Hanni xix, 148, 149
Jebel Qa'aqir xix, 169
Jerusalem xix, 43, fig. 6–1,
147
Khirbet el–Kôm 87
Tell Beit Mirsim 70, 87, 93,
table 2–1, fig. 5–
4,
Tell el–Far'ah (N) xix, 26,
table 2–1, 28,
table 2–4, 31,
35, table 2–6,
fig. 2–2, 88, 91,
92
Tell el–Hammah 59, 62
Tell en–Nasbeh table 2–1,
30, table 2–4,
93, 162
Tell es–Safi/Gath xix
Tell Halif xix, 88, 93
Tel 'Ira table 2–1, table 2–4

Tell Masos xix, 26–28,
table 2–1, table
2–4, 41, 88, 90
Tell Qasile xix, table 2–1,
30, table 2–4,
57, 60
Timna/Tel Batash xix, table
2–1, table 2–4,
72, fig. 4–2, fig.
4–3, 76
Jordan 20, 22, 23, 56, 80, 109,
144, 149, 163–65, 167
Amman fig. 6–1
Deir 'Alla xix, 27, table 2–
1, 28, 30
Petra 109, 110, fig. 6–1
Tell es–Sa'idiyeh xix, 26–
28, table 2–1,
table 2–4, 31,
32, table 2–5,
fig. 2–1, 35,
38
Philippines xiv, xix, 163–65,
171, 179
Gubat xix, 160
Kalinga xix, 168
Luzon Island xix, 160, 168
Manila xix
Syria *see also* Syria; Syria–
Palestine
Antioch 102, fig. 6–1
Damascus 118, fig. 6–1
Dura Europos 110, 114, fig.
6–7
Palmyra *see also*
Palmyrene;
sites, Syria,
Tadmor xiii,
xiv, xix, 99, 100,
102, 104, 105,
108–12, 114–19,
121, 123–26,
fig. 6–1, fig. 6–
2, fig. 6–3, fig.
6–4, fig. 6–5,
fig. 6–6, fig. 6–

8, fig. 6–9, fig. 6–10

Tadmor *see also* sites, Syria, Palmyra 99, 100, 109–12, 114, 117, 118, 123, 125

Ugarit *see also* Ugaritic 83, 85–87

Turkey *see also* Byzantine; Ottoman

Aya Thecla xix, 146, 148

Çadır Höyük xiv, xix, 150–53

social xii, xiii, xiv, xv 2, 3, 6, 13–20, 24, 25, 32, 42–44, 46, 51, 54, 61, 62, 70, 77, 99–101, 103–8, 121, 124, 157, 166, 169, 171, 178, 182–84, 188, 189, 194, 195, 201, 202

socialist 183, 188, 202

statue 1, 2, 4, fig. 1–1, 11, 50, 110, 112, 186, 196

straw 21

Syria *see also* sites, Syria; Syria–Palestine xiii 13, 56, 81, 83, 84, 86, 99, 100, 104, 105, 109, 110, 115, 118, 123, 126, fig. 6–1, fig. 6–8, fig. 6–9, 144, 145

Syrian 83, 100, 107, 110, fig. 6–7, 157

Syria–Palestine *see also* sites, Israel, Canaan, Philistia (Bronze Age-Byzantine); sites, Syria; Syria 48, 58

Syro–Palestine xii, 13, 15, 16, 44, 58

Syro–Palestinian 16

technology xii, 11, 17, 22, 42, 43, 45, 53, 54, 61, 62, 155–57, 167, 180

text x, xi, xiii, xiv, 20, 46–48, 52, 69, 119, 143, 144, 146, 149, 153, 156, 157

textual x, 7, 46–48, 50, 52, 54, 61, 62, 67–69, 82, 153

textile xiii, 17, 18, 19, 65, 67–69, 75, 76, 90, 95, 110, 157

cloth, 30, table 2–4, 33, 53, 59, 68, 69, 158

clothes (clothing) 85, 89, 157, 160, 188, 194, 199, 201

loom xiii, 19, 22, 57–59, 65, 66, fig. 4–1, 68, 69, 73, 74, 76

loom weight xiii, 30, table 2–4, 31, 57, 58, 60, 63–67, fig. 4–1, 70, 72–76, 152

spindle xiii, 65, 69, 74, 92, 115, fig. 5–2

spindle whorl, xiii, 65, 69, 74, 92

spinning xiii, 24, 64, 65, 67–69, 74, 76, fig. 5–2

weave 58, 157

weaver 189

weaving xiii, 22, 24, 25, 42, 60, 64–70, 74, 76, 77, 90

Ugaritic *see also* sites, Ugarit 87

urban 17, 100, 112, 117, fig. 6–1, 143, 144, 146, 162, 194

urbanism 101